Initial Teacher Training

DISCARDED

Initial Teacher Training: The Dialogue of Ideology and Culture

Margaret Wilkin

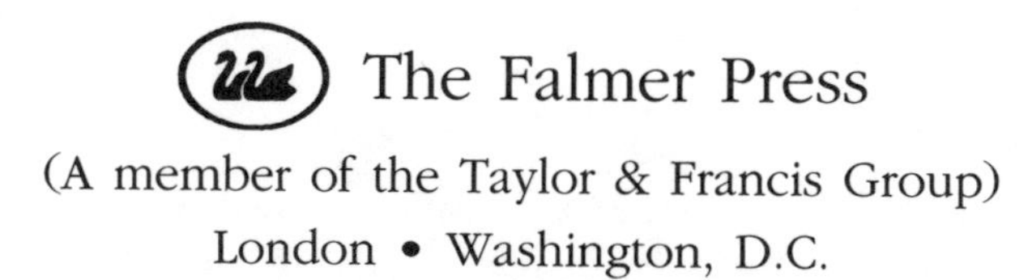

The Falmer Press
(A member of the Taylor & Francis Group)
London • Washington, D.C.

UK The Falmer Press, 1 Gunpowder Square, London, EC4A 3DE
USA The Falmer Press, Taylor & Francis Inc., 1900 Frost Road, Suite 101, Bristol, PA 19007

© M. Wilkin 1996

All rights reserved. No part of this publication may be reproduced, stored in a retrieval system, or transmitted in any form or by any means, electronic, mechanical, photocopying, recording or otherwise, without permission in writing from the Publisher.

First published in 1996

A catalogue record for this book is available from the British Library

Library of Congress Cataloging-in-Publication Data are available on request

ISBN 0 7507 0554 X cased
ISBN 0 7507 0555 8 paper

Jacket design by Caroline Archer

Typeset in 11/13pt Garamond by
Graphicraft Typesetters Ltd., Hong Kong.

Printed in Great Britain by Biddles Ltd., Guildford and King's Lynn on paper which has a specified pH value on final paper manufacture of not less than 7.5 and is therefore 'acid free'.

Contents

Acknowledgments

My grateful thanks to Emeritus Professor Paul Hirst of the Department of Education, University of Cambridge who supervised this, my doctoral study. For their support and encouragement: Professor John Furlong of the School of Education, University of Bristol, Dr John Fletcher of the Queens Medical Centre, University of Nottingham and Dr Lynton Robins of the Department of Public Policy and Managerial Studies, the Leicester Business School, De Montfort University.

Also all the heads and principals of training institutions who in the 1980s gave their permission for me to consult documents in the CNAA archives.

Teacher education is fundamentally a political question. It is concerned with those aspects of society which should be selected for conscious transmission to those and by those who will initiate future generations (Thompson, K. (1974) *Education for Teaching*, 95, p. 13)

Introduction

In recent years, in numerous academic texts and in the media, the term 'ideological' has been applied to the current Conservative Government of the UK. In the areas of education, health, industry and elsewhere, the government is perceived as being ideological in both intention and in practice. What is meant by this is not always clear, however, and the frequent rather loose use of the term raises numerous questions. Why is the term so prevalent today when three or four decades ago it was rarely heard except perhaps in scholarly discussions on the work of Marx? What is the effect on everyday life of having an ideological government? Is such a government more powerful than other forms of government? How does it operate and how does it gain support and legitimation for its policies? What does it *mean* to say that a government is ideological?

The aim of this study is to explore the relationship between the ideology of the government of the UK and the culture of initial teacher training over a period of thirty years. In order to carry out this project a means of representing a government as ideological has to be devised. Any such representation must be sufficiently broadly based and also content free in order to permit investigation of successive governments' ideological engagement with the teacher training system at different historical periods. It must be a descriptive account which will convey the way in which, and the extent to which a particular government is ideological, yet which at the same time can be used as a methodological tool for the investigation of the nature of this relationship. Reference to ideological theory to provide an answer to this dilemma reveals how comprehensive and dense that theory is. Writers in the field take a range of perspectives on the topic, preferring to explore or emphasize one aspect of ideology or one perspective at the expense of others. There seems to be little agreement on the nature of ideological government and it soon becomes clear that ideology is a concept of great complexity which subsumes numerous cross-cutting themes such as the nature of ideological representation, how ideology relates to the individual and *vice versa*, where its origins lie and what is its social function. It is also evident that there is little consensus either on the priority attributed to these themes or on the way in which they are interpreted.

A certain lack of order in the theoretical world is to be expected, but in a practical study theoretical order can be created by the demands of the project itself. Since no one theoretical scheme seemed to meet the substantive and methodological demands (above) of the investigation, it was decided that the approach taken to theory in this study would be that which is recommended for students on initial teacher training courses: start with a practical problem then review theories in the area for those which seem to offer the most relevant and useful insights into that problem; or theoretical eclecticism. Here this process of selection has meant, for example, that reference is made to the work of Gouldner for his insights into the process of ideological change; and to Gramscian theory rather than Habermasian theory because the former's portrayal of ideologies as sequential historical events which can take place within the general framework of capitalism ('we can only escape from one ideology into another' (Goodwin, 1982, p. 27)) seems to reflect recent and current events more closely than a general crisis in the legitimation of capitalism itself; and because the concern of this study lies less with the truth or distortion of an ideology than with ideological practices.

One way of constructing a model or representation of an ideological government is to identify the characteristics which *any* government whether of the Right or of the Left, which is deemed to be 'ideological', exhibits. What qualifies these governments to share this designation? It is suggested that any government regarded as ideological will exhibit three characteristics[1]:

(i) a strongly articulated system of beliefs concerning matters of a fundamental social, political, economic or moral nature. Although the form that these beliefs and principles themselves take may evolve and change over time, their advocacy should be consistent. No necessary internal consistency within the belief system itself is implied however;
(ii) firm or persistent attempts to introduce wide-spread institutional change in accordance with these beliefs;
(iii) the hope and intention that by these means, its values will become first of all accepted by the majority of the populace and will in time attract their complete commitment.

A study of an ideological government will need to include a consideration of the success that that government has in converting the target group (iii) to a belief in its principles (i). By its very nature, an 'ideological' elite will strive to influence the values, motivations and attitudes of individuals in order that they will support it and keep it in power. It is not enough to talk of a government as ideological without also paying attention to ideological effect and this will mean analyzing the degree of congruence between the ideology of the centre and the beliefs held by the mass of the people or the target group. A government is ideologically successful when it has established coincidence between its own ideals and individual preferences. It strives for commitment to its principles and when these principles have been fully internalized, then dominance has been achieved. Thus a study of ideology will have to confront for substantive reasons that long-standing problem of sociological method, the linking of the macro social structures of the state and the views and actions of the individual agent.

How is coincidence of beliefs between centre and periphery to be achieved? The means by which a governing elite gains access to the minds of the people also have to be included in the model. Individuals do not lead context free lives, and it is through the manipulation and control of their social environment (ii) that governments hope to introduce changes of attitude and behaviour. Ideology is not only a system of beliefs but also a process therefore. It is the process of power that links the three dimensions above. Power and dominance are intrinsic to the notion of ideology, it being the power of a governing elite which will enable it to structure the social environment in accordance with its own beliefs and priorities and by these means, and by exhortation, hope to induce the mass of the people to comply. The three-dimensional model above, if used as a basis for the study of ideology in a practical context, would therefore meet the methodological demands of Thompson (1984): that the satisfactory analysis of the operation of an ideology should include consideration of both the macro–micro relationship and the concept of power.

As the quotation by Thompson which opens this study implies, the initial teacher training system might seem to be a suitable target for any government bent on political dominance, since control of this particular social institution might provide access to the hearts and minds of the next generation. If it were possible to persuade tutors engaged in the training of teachers and their students to subscribe to the principles espoused by the governing elite — whatever these might be — then they might in turn influence the views of their pupils accordingly. In this way the teacher training system would act as a vehicle for ideological socialization with far reaching societal effects. Whether the training system has been used in this way recently in the UK and to what effect are the issues to be addressed below. Given that all governments seek to introduce change by intervening in social institutions, to what extent and in what ways has the teacher training system in the UK been used for the purposes of ideological promotion during the last thirty years?

For an exploration of this relationship it would not be enough merely to suggest as above that the social institution of teacher training provides a channel by which the government may hope to influence the behaviour and beliefs of most members of the populace. It is necessary to locate the interface between ideology as a political doctrine and the individual, that is tutors and students, within this particular social institution. Although the government can and does shape the overall system of training, this is of little consequence for the beliefs of the individual trainee teacher. It is the curriculum which is the point of mediation, being both open to influence by the government and the training institution, and the structure of the student's training experience. Using the above three-dimensional representation of an ideological government, confirmation that the initial teacher training system had indeed been used as a channel of successful ideological promotion would require:

- first a demonstration that the government of the day was acknowledged to have been conspicuously advocating a particular system of beliefs;
- second, that government sponsored changes in the curriculum of training would in some way directly reflect those beliefs;
- third, some indication that tutors and students within the teacher training system had not only accommodated but also assimilated these beliefs. Only then would it be possible to say that the government had succeeded in establishing ideological dominance, or hegemony, within this particular social institution, by this particular means.

But the curriculum of training in the UK provides a double challenge to government intervention. The world of teacher training forms an occupational sub-culture with its own technical language, its shared understandings and its common practices, and like all cultures it is resistant to change, evolving slowly and demonstrating continuity over time. In addition, since its inception, teacher training in this country has been characterized by diversity across training institutions (Lynch, 1979). This does not conflict with the notion of a shared culture of training since the differences across institutions are matters of detail rather than principle. But it does offer difficult terrain for the imposition of uniformity of belief. Thus given its stability on the one hand and its variability on the other, the teacher training system, and in particular the curriculum of training may not readily be either diverted from its course nor structured uniformly. We therefore have on the one hand a three-dimensional model which can be used for the analysis of the ideological practices of any government and which provides a framework for each chapter of this study, and on the other the ideologically desirable social institution of initial teacher training which may not be receptive to intervention in the curriculum, this being the point of contact between the two systems, the political and the cultural. This study analyzes this relationship over a thirty-year period from the Robbins Report (1963) to the beginning of the 1990s.

In chapter 1, a theoretical elaboration of the proposed three-dimensional model is undertaken. The views of a range of ideological theorists on each of the three dimensions will be considered. The first section reviews the nature of ideology and its relationship to culture. The focus of the second section is the means by which a governing elite may implement its ideology or strive to gain ideological commitment. Included here is a discussion on ideological strategies. The third section considers the nature of ideological conversion or 'hegemonic' dominance. It has already been noted that the approach taken to theory in this study is eclectic, ideological theory being raided selectively for insights which will aid the investigation of developments in the relationship between the government and the initial teacher training system at the site of the curriculum. On occasion this provides opportunities for critique, but this study is not intended to be a study in ideological theory. Rather it is a study of teacher training from an ideological perspective, and therefore there will be aspects of ideological theory which necessarily must be neglected.

In chapter 2, the model is applied to the period of the Robbins Report, the 1960s. In the first section, a consideration of the state of the post-war social democratic consensus suggests that by the early 1960s, public affirmation of the political process was beginning to wane. It had become important to restore respect for the state, to confirm the support of the government for the principles espoused by the electorate, those of social welfare, and to generate economic growth in order to fund the benefit system. In its report, the Robbins Committee was to meet these requirements. The report can therefore be interpreted as a political and an ideological instrument. In section 2 it is hypothesized that the welfare ideology of the time was reflected in both the structure and the content of the new theoretical curriculum of initial training which was introduced into the colleges in the wake of the report[2].

Since a systematic survey of curricula for this period was not possible, this data having been lost with the demise of the Area Training Organisations (ATOs), these conclusions are reached through the analysis of commentary in contemporary papers and reports. In the third section the reception afforded this ideologically laden curriculum is reviewed and it is concluded that although the new curriculum was well received by some members of the professional community, it was less well received by others. The heads and principals of the colleges welcomed the post-Robbins curriculum for the improved status that it brought as much as for its intrinsic qualities; but many, perhaps even most of those who would have been responsible for the further dissemination of the ideological principles that it embodied, the tutors and students, rejected it. Again this conclusion is reached through documentary analysis.

Chapter 3 reviews the 1970s. In the first section, the lack of a clearly articulated and consistent central ideology during this period is disclosed. There was no direct ideological intervention in the curriculum on the part of the government at this time, and thus the issue to be considered becomes that of what happened in the absence of ideological intervention when development of the post-Robbins curriculum remained in the hands of the profession. In section 2 this is addressed through the analysis of three samples of course submissions to the Council for National Academic Awards (CNAA) and of various research reports which became available at the end of the decade. These sources reveal the continuation of a slow evolutionary trend away from the disciplines of education and back towards a more practical curriculum in the delivery of which teachers are granted partnership status in rhetoric, but in reality have very little power. A review of the possible and respective influences which shaped this trend in the absence of central intervention is then undertaken through the analysis of documentation, and it is concluded that curricular developments, including a lack of rapid development, can be attributed to the action of the teacher training profession itself rather than to the influence of HM Inspectorate, the unions or professional associations or of teachers or students. The decade of the 1970s was characterized by the freedom of the teacher training community to decide for itself on the nature of the curriculum, and the process of its elaboration (Archer, 1988) came about through rational debate and through the operation of the CNAA, which, as a powerful professionally run institution, symbolized the non-ideological character of the decade. Since there was no ideological achievement during this period to review, section 3 in this chapter is a discussion on the relationship between ideology and the culture of teacher training from the perspective of culture rather than that of ideology. Looking backwards, it notes that the training curriculum did absorb some ideological elements in the aftermath of the Robbins Report — those that were considered to be of some professional value — though others were rejected. Looking forwards, this section suggests that the evolution of the curriculum in the two decades following the Robbins Report provided a sympathetic context for the new ideology of Thatcherism. At the end of the 1970s, certain characteristics of the curriculum had come to reflect the principles of Thatcherism and it was thus intrinsically receptive to ideological intervention once more. It is suggested therefore that the relationship between ideology and the curriculum as a cultural practice is dynamic and interactive.

Chapter 4 considers the events of the 1980s. In section 1, the nature of the ideology of Thatcherism is outlined. Section 2 notes the way in which the curriculum of training increasingly reflects this ideology as the introduction of successive measures by the centre including *Circular 3/84*, promote practice at the expense of theory. The birth of the Council for the Accreditation of Teacher Education (CATE), an agency for monitoring the implementation of these measures, suggests recourse by the government, to an alternative form of power: political rather than civil. The reaction of the professional community is considered in section 3 through the analysis of contemporary commentary and of a sample of HM Inspectorate's reports on courses in the middle years of the decade, some discretion in course construction being still possible at this time. Training institutions are found to have responded to the proposals in *Circular 3/84* for closer relationships with schools, but this relationship remains one of high control by the institutions. That the distribution of power does not therefore reflect the ideology of Thatcherism with its privileging of practice over theory, provides a rational reason in ideological terms for the extension of government control in further circulars. Finally there is a short coda on developments in the 1990s. Since there are few developments within the ideology itself to review, this is principally an account of the ideological strategies used by the government during the first years of the decade and the response of the professional community to these measures. This response has been strongly oppositional but latterly it may be possible to detect some slight indications that the post-Robbins pattern is being repeated. Then the professional benefits of the ideologically inspired curriculum were recognized and were absorbed, although the undermining of the theory–practice balance was challenged.

The conclusion suggests that over the period of this study, the curriculum of initial teacher training in England and Wales has reflected government ideologies of diverse types. Initial teacher training therefore appears to offer a home to ideology and so helps to meet the need of governments to restructure social institutions in their own image. The introduction of these ideologies into training seem to create an imbalance between theoretical and practical curricular elements, ideological intervention forcing the curriculum to extremes of either theory or practice. These interventions thus undermine what is proposed as a central cultural value of the teacher training profession: that in training there should be a balance between theory and practice. However, they also bring with them certain professional benefits and these are recognised and retained by the profession itself, and over time become absorbed. In their turn, ideological interventions may be professionally advantageous therefore, and so the relationship between government and profession can be deemed an interactive dialogue. Governments fail in their hegemonic purpose, however, since the object of their ideological strategies, the theory–practice relationship, is of fundamental concern and interest to members of the profession,who will not be readily distracted from their commitment to a balance of the two elements within it. In the past, governmental influence was dissipated, and the curriculum reverted to a loose central balance between theory and practice at the hands of the profession. In this way, the curriculum of training as a cultural domain, has demonstrated continuity.

This study is concerned solely with the efficacy of the curriculum of initial training as a channel of ideological conversion and maintenance. It looks at the potential of the curriculum for this purpose. It is not necessarily assumed that if an ideologically laden curriculum remains in place, then those acting within its boundaries will as a result adopt the ideology that it embodies, though they may do so. But it is assumed that if that curriculum is rejected, either in rhetoric or in practice because for example, it is perceived as contravening the principles of 'what training to be a teacher is all about' then that curriculum will be unable to act as a means of inducing ideological conformity, although members of the profession may subscribe to the beliefs that it embodies for their own private reasons.

Notes

1 That the generation of this three-dimensional model is a circular process is acknowledged, but this is not considered to invalidate it as a methodological tool. Sociological models must be based on common sense perceptions of the world initially since this is the only possible source of their substance. This material can then be selectively refined and reshaped in the process of transformation to the discourse of theory.

2 The term theory in this study, except where otherwise indicated, refers to the disciplines of education and those curricular forms in to which they evolved over time. And the term practice refers to the practical elements of the curriculum: school experience and professional/curriculum/methods courses concerned with the pedagogy of the subject. This is a common use of these terms, but it is recognized that practice as defined here subsumes theory and that practical courses are therefore also theoretical.

1 The Nature of Ideology and of Ideological Practices

Introduction

Although the three-dimensional presentation of ideology outlined above was derived from only a common sense reflection on the characteristics and activities of a range of governments which are generally deemed to be of an ideological nature, it is considered to be an appropriate and adequate framework for the analysis of the qualities and practices of such governments. Before it can be used, however, such a common sense framework needs to be expanded and developed theoretically and that is the purpose of this chapter. It is to explore in turn some of the relevant theoretical assumptions subsumed by each of these three dimensions or themes. Re-presented in a generalized theoretical form, these are:

(i) **Ideological belief**
(above: the conspicuous articulation of a system of fundamental beliefs)

(ii) **Ideological implementation**
(above: intervention in institutions in accordance with those beliefs)

(iii) **Ideological achievement**
(above: acceptance by the target group of those beliefs)

Ideological Belief

Ideology will be defined quite simply initially, and then by the extrapolation and development of themes, this definition will be developed into a comprehensive account of the concept.

Ideology is the set of principles which govern the policies of political parties.

This definition associates ideologies with political parties only on the grounds that to use the term more broadly to encompass any social group which wishes to introduce change in social practices, renders the concept so inclusive as to lose explanatory power (Eagleton, 1991). When the term is used so freely it fails to 'distinguish between the kinds of action or projects which ideology animates' (Thompson, 1984, p. 4). Second this definition attributes equivalence to all parties whether of the Right or the Left. It implies that all parties whether in power or in opposition *must* be ideological in order to function effectively. Ideologies are those images of the desired state of affairs which are held by society's leaders. They are the necessary rationale which provides the basis and justification of political activity. This use of the term covers 'sets of factual and moral propositions which serve to posit, explain and justify ends and means of organized social action, especially political action . . . According to this conception, ideology is as inseparable from politics as politics from ideology' (Seliger, 1977, p. 1). Without principles on which to base legislation and which show continuity over time, a political party will lack direction and force. Where this is the case, political life for the public will be contradictory and cynicism or alienation is more likely than allegiance to be the prevailing mood.

The recognition that all governments are ideologically driven raises the question of how ideology may be interpreted, whether it should be presented as description or as critique (Thompson, 1990; Barrett, 1991). The former position portrays ideology as a *weltanschauung* which is peculiar to a particular social elite in a given historical period. Over time one ideology will succeed another, making way for a new 'conception of the world that is implicitly manifest in art, in law, in economic activity and all manifestations of individual and collective life' (Gramsci, 1971, p. 328). From this point of view the generation, implementation and demise of ideologies is a recurring social event, and ideology is a neutral social fact. The alternative perspective associates ideology with the unilateral maintenance of power through illusion or mystification. As one of the principal exponents of this position, Althusser (1971) holds that the ruling elite manipulates the consciousness of the public through the major social institutions of society: education, the church and the trade unions. It may also exert direct control through the army, the law and the police. For Althusser, ideology is materially represented in education — the school is saturated with the reigning ideology — it being here that the next generation is inducted into the skills and attitudes which will ensure the survival of capitalist society. Althusserian theory thus encourages the analysis of educational practice for the purpose of diagnosing the presence of ideology, not only in overt and obvious locations such as the teaching of selected subjects, but also in less conspicuous symbolic forms. An important weakness of critical theories of ideology, in which ideology is represented as some sort of distortion of thought or false consciousness is their failure to explain a lack of political awareness on the part of the general public. The populace is portrayed as subject to perceptual influence and control and yet remains unaware of this and of the means by which this is achieved. On rational grounds such claims for the power of ideology can be challenged. The diversity of experience, outlook and life style across subordinate groups makes it most unlikely that everyone would be equally receptive to ideological manipulation through the agencies of the state, for the reality and therefore the relevance of any one ideology would vary across individuals. 'Explaining why an individual holds ideological beliefs is a matter of analysing social processes, not of diagnosing intellectual error or individual pathology' (Callinicos, 1987, p. 139).

The approach adopted in this study draws on both the analytic traditions mentioned above. Each has its roots in Marxism and Barrett (1991) regards them as the poles of a continuum. A review of recent political history in the UK suggests that ideologies supersede each other over time. But it is also apparent that they are represented materially and symbolically in our social institutions and patterns of social behaviour and that despite the qualification above, the means by which this is achieved and the extent to which it is the case may not always be recognized by members of the general public. The conclusion of this study will be that the initial teacher training system in England and Wales has been used for the dissemination of alternative ideologies during the 1960s and the 1980s and 1990s. This must be apparent to large sections of this particular population, but one of the sociologist's tasks is to look beyond the more obvious demonstrations of ideological representation and try to disclose those that are less immediately perceptible.

Within the original definition of ideology as the principles which govern the policies of political parties, there is an acknowledgement that ideologies are located only in the major areas of social life. Policies are the expression of a government's intentions for a social group if not for the nation. As manifestations of that government's values and principles, they may cover economic activity, education, defence, morality or domestic affairs that concern large numbers of the population. The minutiae of personal behaviour is of little consequence ideologically unless that behaviour has relevance for national concerns. An elite which is seeking to establish or maintain — without force — its ideology as the governing value system, can operate only through exhortation and through changes to the major institutions in which all participate. By declaration on the one hand and on the other by suffusing institutions with its beliefs and priorities to the extent that the social environment of members of the public is reconstructed in its favour, the party in power will hope to reach the mass of the people and convince them of the value and relevance of its outlook on life and its rules for living.

The notion of 'policy' implies dominance, the enforcement of priorities, of particular modes of behaviour or certain forms of relationship which will reflect the values and beliefs of the governing elite. According to Gramsci (1971):

> The State is the entire complex of practical and theoretical activities with which the ruling class not only justifies and maintains its dominance, but manages to win the active consent of those over whom it rules . . . (p. 244)

Despite the forceful tone of this passage, the State is not unassailably dominant (it 'manages to win' . . .). It has to justify its position and work at gaining the support of the mass of the people. Ideology is thus process as well as substance, and this process is the exercise of political power. The concepts of power and domination are intrinsic to the notion of government, the aim of government being to demonstrate the wisdom of its preferred practices and attitudes and through a variety of means induce as many members of society as possible to adopt them. If, as MacIntyre (1973) says: a 'central feature of any ideology is an account of the relationship between what is the case and how we ought to act, between the nature of the world and that of morals, politics and other guides to conduct' (p. 484), then 'how we ought to act' within the context of active politics is inseparable from attempts to impose one interpretation of social conditions over another. Thus ideology must necessarily be associated with the use of power and with the process of establishing (or trying to establish) and maintaining dominance. The many ways in which dominant elites encourage or facilitate or even enforce commitment to their beliefs is a rich area of study and some of the strategies used for this purpose will be considered below. But the analysis of a society in which those at the top try to persuade those below them to agree the worth and share the values of their particular vision of the world also requires a consideration of the way in which the prevailing ideology relates to the belief systems of the mass, since there can be no assumption that we all share the particular commitments of the elite. The nature of this relationship is an aspect of ideological theory which intrigued Gramsci and which is a major theme of this study. Achieving coincidence between the belief systems of the state and of the individual is unproblematic for Althusser for whom it is an automatic process achieved by means of 'interpellation' — the sudden and unquestioning conversion of the individual to ideological commitment. Here ideology is a structure which is external to individuals and which constitutes them. It is an imaginary representation of something 'out there', and since it is introjected as a totality in an uncritical manner, there is a high degree of coincidence between the external vision of the world or the ideology of the dominant elite and the internal vision of the citizen. Personal ideology represents in imagination the external ideology.

In Gramscian theory on the other hand, this relationship is highly complex. Gramsci's subject is an active human agent and the relationship between the individual and the external world is dialectical. For Gramsci 'concrete experience is the essential raw material of human reflection. But the products of this reflection then proceed to modify the social reality from which they emerge' (Femia, 1981, p. 132). Since the individual responds to reality, the ideology (or 'conception of the world' or 'philosophy' as Gramsci prefers to call it) emanating from the state or the elite, which in all its manifestations is part of the environment of the mass of the people, is not reproduced *in toto* by members of the subordinate class either in thought or action as it is for Althusser, but is acted upon by them and hence modified. MacIntyre (1973) also acknowledges both ideological effect and the independence of the individual. For members of a social group, ideology only 'partially defines for them their social existence . . . Its concepts are embodied in, and its beliefs presupposed by some of these actions and transactions the performance of which is characteristic of the social life of that group' (p. 484). Although ideologies become embodied in the way of life of the group, they do not totally dominate the thoughts and practices of that group, their reception being qualified by the terms 'partially' and 'some'. This qualification allows for the distinction between ideology and the wider belief system or culture of the group. It is also interesting that MacIntyre here identifies the importance of ideological input being 'presupposed' by the social characteristics of the group, a matter which will be considered in the next section.

Gramsci elaborates this distinction between two forms of ideology or 'philosophy'. There is a world view which 'expresses itself in a very elaborate form and at a high level of abstraction . . . or else it is expressed in much simpler forms as the expression of "common sense" which presents itself as the "spontaneous philosophy" of the man in the street but which is a popular expression of higher philosophies' (Mouffe, 1979, p. 186). There is thus both continuity and disjuncture between the philosophy (the ideology) of the ruling group and the so-called 'spontaneous philosophy' of the majority of the people. The ideology of the people or the group is a modified version of that of the ruling elite. For both Gramsci and MacIntyre then, the ideology of the elite or government is only partially absorbed. It does not 'take over' the behaviour, values and patterns of action of the individual or the group, but becomes embedded in the wider, common sense (Gramsci) or culture (MacIntyre) of that group.

Gramsci's theory of knowledge is difficult to interpret. Knowledge consists of layers each of which is associated with a characteristic mode of thinking. Terms are used interchangeably and his definitions are unclear. He equates 'spontaneous philosophy' (i.e. the people's modified version of the dominant ideology) with 'common sense' but elsewhere he suggests that this philosophy is contained *within* common sense (1971, p. 323). This suggests that spontaneous philosophy is a part — but only a part — of a whole internalized corpus of knowledge which he refers to as 'common sense' and which he regards as a 'collective noun' (*ibid*, p. 325). It can be argued that Gramsci's term 'common sense' has affinity with the notion of culture and can be equated with it where culture is defined in the anthropological sense as consisting of the stable patterns of activity within a group or community and the organized system of knowledge and beliefs according to which individuals structure their experience and perceptions. In everyday life this equation is commonplace. We talk of a familiar pattern of behaviour being 'only common sense' or 'what everyone knows'. Yet if further thought were given to the matter, it would become clear that 'common sense' is not always so common. Gramsci would restrict common sense further and limit it to specific groups, for he clearly states that 'every social stratum has its own common sense and its own good sense . . . Common sense is . . . continually transforming itself, enriching itself with scientific ideas and with philosophical opinions which have entered ordinary life. "Common sense" is the folklore of philosophy and is always half way between folklore properly speaking and the philosophy, science and economics of the specialists . . .' (*ibid*, p. 326). Common sense is therefore not widespread common sense. Its social location is restricted thus rendering it akin to a sub-culture. It is structured and unlike folklore lodged in reality and relatively rational. It evolves over time absorbing a range of ideas and so transforms itself. These ideas include political philosophies. Common sense is the repository of philosophy (i.e. ideology). It is also as Mouffe (1979, p. 186) an authority on Gramsci puts it, the expression of the 'communal life of a social bloc'. Elsewhere in discussing the distinction between philosophy and common sense 'in order to indicate more clearly the passage (of the state) from one moment to the other . . .' Gramsci argues: 'It is a matter therefore of starting with a philosophy which already enjoys a certain diffusion, because it is connected to and implicit in practical life, and elaborating it so that it becomes a renewed common sense possessing the coherence and the sinew of individual philosophies. But this can only happen if the demands of *cultural* contact with the "simple" are continually felt' (1971, p. 330, emphasis added). Here Gramsci is making the same point as MacIntyre (above) about the nature of ideological intervention. He notes the need for an ideology to coincide with the perspective of the target group in some way and this can only be achieved if there is a continuous awareness by the elite of the culture of the subordinate group. Culture is therefore the domain of ideological intervention. Yet on other occasions, he suggests that it is common sense which contains residues of previous ideologies and moreover contains 'intuitions of a future philosophy' (Gramsci, 1971, p. 324). This last comment is particularly interesting since it is one conclusion of this study that in the 1970s, the sub-culture of initial training became accessible to the introduction of the ideology of Thatcherism through its own internal developmental processes. It is concluded then that for Gramsci, the terms common sense and culture can be used interchangeably and this seems to be confirmed by Hall (1981).

The representation of ideology as a duality which is found in Gramsci is also supported theoretically by several modern writers, although how each ideological form relates to the other is not always indicated. For example, Giddens (1979) distinguishes between ideology as discourse and ideology as lived experience, and for Therborn (1980) ideology 'includes both every day notions and experiences and elaborate intellectual doctrines; both the consciousness of social actors and the institutionalized thought-systems and discourses of a given society' (p. 2). This duality has also been demonstrated empirically. According to Femia (1981) who reviewed a number of pertinent surveys, 'the average man tends to have two levels of normative reference — the abstract and the situational. On the former plane, he expresses a great deal of agreement with the dominant ideology, on the latter he reveals not outright dissensus, but a limited commitment to the bourgeois ethos, because it is often inapposite to the exigencies of his class position' (p. 223). This is also the view of Lodziak (1988) who suggests that even when the core elements of the central ideology are accepted, 'those ideas which are foregrounded in the consciousness of the subordinated tend to be directly relevant to the demands of the everyday life-world as experienced' (p. 12).

There seems to be no necessary reason why this distinction between the ideology of the centre and the local ideology of the citizen should apply only to social classes. Might it not apply to the relationship between the state and any social group? It is a representation of ideology which suggests that we all entertain at least two sets of principles or perspectives. There are those officially endorsed abstract general guidelines for living which in more politically settled times are embodied in our public institutions and which are enshrined in documents and formal practices and to which we subscribe in varying degrees. But there are also justifications which account for everyday action and which are implicit and shared within particular groups. These localized conceptions of the world will not be a neat mirror reflection of the government's ideology but may well accommodate it in some way.

For Gramsci, ideologies raise awareness for they act as a critique of the *status quo* and this is the first stage of the 'unity of theory and practice' (pp. 333–4), that is the stabilization of a new ideology. Through challenging our common sense interpretations of the world, ideologies reshape our thinking and our practical daily action and bring these into line with the 'theoretical' system of beliefs espoused by the elite. In this way, Gramsci associates hegemony, a concept which usually portrays complete ideological consensus from the perspective of the state, with the cultural identity of the individual. Ideologies highlight and give voice to our dissatisfactions with the social world; they bring into relief feelings of dis-ease and suggest remedies for them. Geertz (1964) also attributes to ideologies the function of reconciliation between the individual and the anomalies of the environment, but his perspective is psychological as well as cultural and social (p. 64). He reviews two theories of ideology, those of 'interest' ('ideology is a mask and a weapon') and of 'strain' ('ideology is a symptom and a remedy'). The latter approach refers to both a condition of societal dislocation and a state of personal tension to which the development of an ideology and adherence to it is a remedial response. When the intrinsic inconsistencies within a cultural environment become so exaggerated that the individual is unable to reconcile them, then this is felt as a personal threat. Geertz lists the sorts of 'insoluble antinomies' within daily social life which if they become oppressive in their presence might open the door to ideological change. These include tensions between liberty and political order, between efficiency and humanity, between an emphasis on profit and on quality in business for example. He also mentions conflicts between the economy and the other major sectors of society such as the polity.

For both Gramsci and Geertz the relationship between central ideology and personal identity (sub-cultural identity in the case of Gramsci, psychopathological identity in the case of Geertz) is uncertain or unreliable from the perspective of the state. In the case of Gramsci, the individual is embedded in his/her cultural environment and may be more or less receptive to the blandishments of a new ideology, for as Eagleton (1991, p. 36) says, groups often have 'their own rich resistant cultures which cannot be incorporated without a struggle into the value-systems of those who govern them'. In the case of Geertz, reaction to the divisions and contradictions in society is individualized and so difficult to either predict or assess. This is in contrast to the presentation of this relationship in Althusserian theory where the subject individual is so well socialized that his/her *weltanschauung* is coincident with that of the ruling elite. For Therborn (1980) as well as for Gramsci and Geertz, ideologies provide order in a disordered world. By mapping social life and telling us 'what exists, what is good and what is possible' (p. 18) they provide social and personal stability. In this view, ideologies are comforting for they structure the social environment. They delineate features, suggest priorities, indicate what is legitimate and what is worthy, and as Geertz points out, their ability to render the incomprehensible meaningful accounts for the intensity with which they are held.

Gramsci's theory of the relationship between ideology and common sense or culture focuses on the two domains of knowledge themselves and the way in which they interrelate, the individual being implicitly active and autonomous. Archer's (1988) concern is with the process of cultural change itself. Culture is conceptualized in terms of parts and people, and the change of a cultural state is represented as the end of a process of:

> cultural conditioning (or context) ------> action by the
> individual agent ------> cultural elaboration

This simple temporal sequence is not always straightforward. First of all there is the state of the initial cultural context and how receptive it is to a new alternative mode of action. Second, there is the actual response of agents to this inherited cultural context. In Archer's model both culture and individual are autonomous and engaged in a dialectical relationship. Agents may choose whether or not to exploit their cultural freedom by taking advantage of inconsistencies or by combining compatible elements, and so arriving at a new cultural form. Cultural stability and cultural change (elaboration) are governed by the dynamics within the interface of existing culture and chosen action.

According to this presentation, the likely success of an elite attempting to introduce a new ideology into a (sub-)culture would depend upon two aspects of the current situation — the distance between the ideology and the cultural context and the perception by individuals of loopholes and flexibilities in the current system, and their willingness to take advantage of them to grant the ideology access.

Returning to our original simple definition once more, it can be argued that it subsumes a relationship between ideology and the economy, for policies cannot be independent of available resources. The exact nature of this relationship has preoccupied theorists since Marx. Both Althusser and Gramsci reject Marx's economic determinism, proposing rather that economic base and ideological superstructure are reciprocally related although the economy is ultimately the more powerful influence. Althusser's model of this relationship is a structural one in which social change follows cumulative and excessive 'contradiction' between elements either within the superstructure or between the superstructure and the base, and takes the form of revolutionary ruptures of a volcanic nature. These contradictions are at the macro level of social structure and do not impinge upon individual consciousness. For Gramsci (1971) political activity is 'born on the permanent and organic terrain of economic life' (p. 140) although the superstructure (the Civil State and the Political State) does not immediately fall into line when economic changes occur. There may be some delay while adjustments take place, for the Political State consisting of the government and the law has to win support for new policies through the institutions of the Civil State.

The view that the economy is the principal determinant of political activity is shared by writers working outside the field of ideology. For example, Klein (1976) analyzing the politics of public expenditure concludes that: although 'there is indeed a slight political or ideological effect . . . this effect tends to be swamped by the responses of governments to economic circumstances' (p. 414). Nevertheless, the economic effect is not total. The state of the economy will set limits on government expenditure but within those limits policy is given direction by ideological intent:

> It may be ruled out that intermediate economic crises of themselves produce fundamental historical events: they can simply create terrain more favourable to the dissemination of certain modes of thought and certain ways of posing and resolving questions involving the entire subsequent development of national life. (Gramsci, 1971, p. 184)

The need for the State to win over the people to its new policies following a shift in economic fortunes will have to be justified within the framework of the current ideology. Ideologies therefore have to be flexible. They cannot be too clearly defined or too 'pure' — that is uncontaminated by apparently irrelevant elements — for this would constrain the possibility of their 'drifting' (Therborn, 1980). Necessarily an ideology is never static but in a state of constant flux. It must be able to respond to changes in the public mood, to events and to challenges from a variety of sources including other incipient ideologies, and it will do this most successfully if it is at least partially inconsistent internally. Yet it must not become so diffuse or contradictory that it lacks direction and fails to attract supporters to its cause. It must appear to be true in its diagnosis of the social condition and rational in its proposed remedies. Ideologies have their own form of rationality (Gouldner, 1976) or as Althusser puts it their 'own logic' for explaining changes in policy and for justifying taking alternative action. According to Manning (quoted in Williams, 1988) ideologies also have their own form of truth: what is relevant to the ideologist is not decided by a formal criterion of truth but rather by what squares with his programme of action. 'Ideologists and academics operate with radically different conceptions of truth. An academic operates with a formal criterion of truth which establishes whether what he says is permissible or not'. Whereas, for the ideologist, 'the interpretation of a past event which is permissible is the one which accords with the end in sight' (p. 48).

If the adherents of an ideology have their own standards of truth, share particular interpretations of what is good, right and desirable, and agree on the contexts in which their principles can most readily and appropriately be introduced, then they constitute a discourse (Eagleton, 1991). Foucault's (1972, pp. 50–3) concept of a discourse is broadly based. It consists of three elements: language, site and procedures. Language subsumes membership and therefore also exclusion. It defines or contains a group, allocates status to its members and makes it clear who is not an adherent; and the sharing within a linguistic group of a common perspective on the world, will continually confirm the truth of that perspective. Site refers to the contexts in which the principles (as expressed in language) are represented. A governing elite will wish to extend its ideological influence or domination and will attempt to do this by restructuring social institutions and relocating power within those institutions in ways which materially represent the new belief system. It will also be its task to facilitate and foster appropriate procedures or practices which will not only reflect the new ideology but will stabilise it at the level of everyday action.

The simple initial definition of an ideology with which this section began has now been expanded to the following comprehensive definition. Ideology is a composite system of beliefs, values and images which indicates how we should look at the world, how we should evaluate what we perceive and what actions we should take. It is shaped by economic circumstances and mediates between the governing and the governed. Politics *is* ideology or ideological struggle. Since ideology performs the function of transmitting the values of the governing elite to subordinate groups, it is inseparable from the notion of domination. It may be a powerful presence in that it is represented in the social institutions which surround us and in our daily practices, but we may not internalize it in its entirety. It is unlikely that we will do so, since the circumstances of our daily lives will probably force a compromise.

Summary

The conclusions reached in this section on the Nature of Ideology are as follows:

- that ideology is a belief system which diagnoses the state of the world and tells us how to remedy what we see. Since it evaluates the current situation and tells us what we ought to do, it is moral;
- that the social manifestations of this belief system constitute a discourse. Use of the language of an ideology defines the membership of that ideology and confirms its truth; proposed changes in practices will reflect its principals; and sites in which these practices may flourish will be selected;
- that ideology is necessary for coherent government whichever political party is in power;
- that ideologies will be represented in the major areas of social life. They are transmitted through our social institutions (including the educational system) which are structured to accord with it. Subordinate groups may not always be aware of the extent to which this is the case;
- that the exercise of power is the means by which this is achieved. Thus ideology is unavoidably associated with power;
- that although ideology will effect the everyday lives of individuals, it will be modified through local practices or the process of sub-cultural elaboration. The form that an ideology

takes at local level thus both reflects and differs from the central ideology. Sub-cultures may be resistant to ideologies;
- that ideology may act as a source of identity for individuals;
- that ideologies need to be flexible in order to allow for 'drift';
- that ideology has its foundations within the economy;
- that ideologies rise and fall and are succeeded by new ideologies. Ideology is a neutral concept.

Ideological Implementation

A governing elite must necessarily strive to bring individuals into the ideological fold since their subsequent support for its principles and practices will legitimate its position. The task for any elite therefore is to convince substantial numbers of the general populace of the value and truth of its diagnosis of the state of social life so that in turn they will assume a similar outlook; they will wish to become members of that ideological discourse. This does not imply the reintroduction of the notion of false consciousness. If subordinates are persuaded, their consciousness is not false for their beliefs are true for them. However, in the previous section the relationship between elite and potential ideological recruit was termed 'unreliable', it having been argued that ideology is mediated through local interpretations of social life. Coincidence between the governing ideology and the common sense belief systems of the general populace is likely to be achieved only with some difficulty therefore and the central ideology may be subject to considerable distortion within sub-cultural groups. As Gramsci concludes it is a struggle not only to obtain ideological domination — by which he means willing commitment to central principles and policies — but also to retain it once it has been achieved.

The need for an ideology to be both flexible and lacking in specificity has already been mentioned and also follows from the above comments. These characteristics will facilitate the perception by subordinate groups of the parallels to their particular life circumstances within an ideology and so enable them to identify with it. Like the good horoscope, a well constructed ideology will be open to rather different interpretations by the many individuals who are confronted by it. Ironically therefore, the most effective ideologies in terms of attracting commitment are those that admit compromise of their ideals and are continually being distanced from their pure form. Despite the best efforts of the elite, however there may remain a significant disjuncture between the central ideology and local belief systems. Callinicos (1987) suggests one reason for this: that an elite may have difficulty in its attempt to provide for the interests of subordinate groups within its ideology because their ideological inclinations may be difficult to assess from the perspective of the central state. Since 'viewing society from a particular class position involves having a certain perspective on the world, which may set limits to what one sees or does not see' (p. 152) the interests of others are by no means easy to ascertain. The State may therefore seriously misjudge the mood of the people and so have difficulty in establishing its interpretation of the world because the vision of its ideological exponents, coloured as it is by a particular 'philosophy' is so circumscribed. Another reason for the failure of an ideology to be adopted by the target group may be epistemological. In his discussion on ideology as a symbol system, Geertz (1964) talks of the need for ideological concepts to be 'meaningful', to provide 'the suasive images by means of which (politics) may be sensibly grasped' (p. 63). This implies that ideologies may fail to take hold because they are meaningless to many people who may be unable to make the necessary translation from image to attitudes and action. Not only the substance of an ideology but also its presentation is therefore of crucial importance if that ideology is to become voluntarily supported and well sedimented.

But challenging though it may be for the government to gain the loyalty of the people, it is also a challenge to retain their commitment. Ideological unity is always under threat, always being undermined, and an elite must struggle continuously to re-establish it. For Kolakowski (1980) as for Geertz (see previous section) obvious disjuncture between the elements of an ideology and the circumstances of ordinary living will weaken its appeal. This he regards as a loss of efficiency in an ideology, since if an ideology is well managed it cannot be wrong. The notion of management is central in the process of ideological domination. An elite must be perceptive of the drift of opinion but also alert to economic trends which will limit how it can respond. It must retain a sense of direction but also be willing to compromise its values when faced with forceful opposition. It must actively *work* to retain the necessary harmony between the economic base and the superstructural elements of politics and ideology. 'Ideologies actually operate in a state of disorder . . . To understand how ideologies operate in a given society requires first of all that we see them not as possessions or texts, but as *on going social processes*' (Therborn, 1980, p. 77).

How then can the governing elite attract adherents and extend its influence? Within what Gramsci terms the Civil State, that is without the use of force, there are two means available: exhortation and the restructuring of social institutions — actions which must be publicly justified in such a way that they will be perceived as normative, perhaps inevitable, but certainly desirable. Successful intervention in the patterns of daily living therefore also relies upon the skilful use of language and on presentational skills.

The principal purpose of ideological talk is not to convey information but to extend recruitment, consolidate commitment, reinforce discourse and legitimate the leadership. The speeches of leaders thus introduce claims which will have wide appeal: they highlight achievement, they identify opponents and exaggerate their evils and they reinforce the appeal of the leadership by indicating the alternatives. Such talk does not predict political developments or contribute to policy decisions. Nor is it easy to falsify for it rarely tells us anything factual. Its purpose is to communicate commitment (Manning, 1980). If ideological talk becomes too specific, then it can be used as a weapon against the committed. It must remain vague therefore. Yet it must not be so vague that it fails to be of relevance to the listener, that it fails to capture understanding and interest. According to Gouldner (1976) ideologies utilize the language of the everyday, but in a particular way. Ideology restructures ordinary language, giving it new meaning and assigning a new significance to familiar terms. The purpose of ideological speech is to frame reality in an alternative way. Its own definition of reality must now become *the* definition of reality. It must engage the interest of subordinate groups and appear realizable. Gouldner suggests that this is achieved through a reciprocal process of translation. The sentiments of an ideology must be translated into those of the localized 'philosophy' of such groups which must in turn be reformulated in ideological terms. Thus 'what the ideologist requires above all is creative imagination to draw upon contemporary themes and exhibit them in a coherent manner' (Rayner, 1980, p. 100). Eagleton (1991) sums up these points:

> (Ideologies) must engage significantly with the wants and desires that people already have, catching up genuine hopes and needs, reinflecting them in their own peculiar idiom, and feeding them back to their subjects in ways which render those ideologies plausible and attractive. They must be 'real' enough to provide the basis on which individuals can fashion a coherent identity . . . In short, successful ideologies must be more than imposed illusions, and . . . must communicate to their subjects a version of social reality which is real and recognizable enough not to be simply rejected out of hand. (p. 15)

If, as is being suggested, ideological talk somehow frees individuals from their social context, then it also frees them from regular normative constraints (Manning, 1980). Fired with the desire to establish the reign of *their* belief system, members of an ideological discourse will acquire opinions and undertake actions which, in the context of the previous ideology, would have attracted inhibiting disapprobation. Standards and rules are overthrown and new enemies identified and brought low. All of this is necessary if the changes in society which the ideology demands are to be achieved. Introducing a new ideology means 'thinking the unthinkable' and moreover, daring to doing it, for ideologies must be translatable into action. A successful ideology must work both theoretically and practically. It must not only describe and diagnose situations but include moral and technical prescriptions for their remedy and rules for the implementation of these prescriptions (Seliger, 1976). All these aspects of the ideology must be present as elements within a coherent system.

So far three ideological strategies have been considered all of them promoted through ideological talk: unification, the reformulation of reality and the provision of a programme of action. This list is extended by Eagleton (1991) to include rationalizing, legitimating, universalizing and naturalizing and by Thompson (1990) to include dissimulation and fragmentation. To rationalize an ideological intervention, say, is to justify it as logically, morally or intellectually desirable. In other words rationalization of ideological practices is to cloak their real meaning and present them in a way that will ensure their acceptance. This view of ideologies presents them as 'more or less systematic attempts to provide plausible explanations and justifications for social behaviour which might otherwise be the object of criticism' (Eagleton, 1991, p. 52). Legitimation 'refers to the process by which a ruling power comes to secure from its subjects an at least tacit consent to its authority' (p. 54). Eagleton interprets legitimation as likely to take the form of 'pragmatic' rather than 'normative' acceptance, because the former is convenient and suffices where there is no real alternative. In this he disagrees with Held (1989) who clarifies the range of ways in which governments can realize support from the governed. Held proposes a continuum from coercion through tradition, apathy, pragmatic acquiescence, instrumental acceptance, normative agreement and finally ideal normative agreement (p. 102). He would reserve the term legitimacy for the latter two categories only, regarding 'a legitimate political order as one that is normatively sanctioned by the population'.

But since power has such negative associations, to achieve this degree of support for its policies an elite will have to be prepared to engage strategically with the subordinate mass over time. Having obtained power by ignoring rules (above), it must now begin the long process of securing its own legitimation by establishing alternative rules which will justify its incumbency and which in time will become normative in their turn (Beetham, 1991). But these rules will exclude the majority from positions of power or influence and so they will have to be rationalized: 'the expanded powers of the dominant have to be seen to serve a general and not merely a particular interest; the limitations of freedom of the subordinate have to be made good by actions expressive of consent' (p. 63). Or the strategy of universalization could be used when the modes of behaviour, values or priorities of the elite are projected as applying to all. By this means a government can disguise or lose its intentions because they become the intentions of all. Ideology has become what we all believe. Finally Eagleton considers the strategy of naturalization. Here the ideology creates 'as tight a fit as possible between itself and social reality, thereby closing the gap into which the leverage of critique could be inserted. Social reality is redefined by the ideology to become co-extensive with itself . . .' (p. 58). Here reality and ideology are mutually self confirming and ideology will become a reification of social life. The beliefs and priorities of the dominant ideology become natural the only possible way of organizing social practices and perceiving the world.

Thompson (1990) classifies rationalization and universalization as two forms of legitimation. A further mode of operation of an ideology is dissimulation which he defines as the concealment or denial of relations of domination. He also identifies fragmentation. 'Relations of domination may be maintained, not by unifying individuals in a collectivity, but by fragmenting those individuals and groups that might be capable of mounting an effective challenge to dominant groups, or by orienting forces of potential opposition towards a target which is projected as evil, harmful or threatening' (p. 65). In his theory of ideology, Thompson takes the critical position rather than the descriptive (see previous section), and his discussion on strategies reflects this. The maintenance of an ideology is a process of manoeuvring and deception in order to maintain groups or individuals in power. This is the case for Eagleton too, but Thompson portrays ideological activity as the relentless pursuit of domination. Like Lukes (1974), whose model of power includes the ability to control the political agenda in its widest sense — for example by keeping potentially threatening issues out of politics — Thompson invites scepticism about the nature of consent where there is an apparent lack of conflict.

Perhaps because they *are* theorists, few theorist seems to distinguish between ideological strategy and ideological tactic. But the study of specific governments and their practices within an ideological framework suggests that there are broadly-based strategies which are relatively few in number and which can be applied across a wide variety of situations; but that there are also tactics which are situation specific and which may be subsumed by or representative of or otherwise linked to strategies. This distinction is not always clear cut, but nevertheless helps to clarify the many layered nature of ideological penetration by the governing group.

The above strategies are all to be exercised without force within the Civil State. Their purpose is to bring about voluntary ideological domination or hegemony. But if general dissatisfaction with the regime in power and a disrespect for its unrealistic policies should begin to grow and if the regime is unable to maintain influence or to attract support through the organizations of the Civil State, then it may have to resort to using the instruments of the Political State in order to retain its position, to rely on laws to secure compliance. This signals a crisis of confidence in both the competence and the policies of a government that introduces not only the possibility but also the necessity of creating a new culture (Gramsci, 1971). The revolutionary overthrow of an ideology is what Gramsci terms 'a general crisis of the state'. How then is the State to retain its position when its legitimacy is under threat? Gramsci suggests this can be done through the strategy of 'passive revolution'. The term refers to the neutralization of opposition interests by the process of absorption or adaption — concepts which illustrate the extent to which Gramsci regards the relationship between State and mass as dialectical. One strategy of passive revolution is to incorporate the leaders of potentially hostile groups into elite networks in order to render their threat ineffectual and restabilize ideological commitment. In this way, passive revolution is more than a mere defence measure. Implicit in it as a strategy is the extension of the influence of the State since new members of the ideological movement have been recruited (Carnoy, 1984). On the other hand, the elite may assess the threat as being too serious to be 'decapitated' in this way. The interests of the challenging groups force a modification of the ideology and so a new consensus is created. There are therefore two ways in which the State or ruling group can defuse the threat of challenging subordinate groups: 'the interests of these groups can either be articulated so as to neutralize them and hence to prevent the development of their own specific demands, or else they can be articulated in such a way as to promote their full development leading to the final resolution of the contradictions which they express' (Mouffe, 1979, p. 183). In this way, consensus can be sought either passively or proactively.

So far, the discussion has focused on ideological strategies exercised by the party in power. Those seeking to bring about political change will use these strategies themselves of course but will also have strategies peculiar to their position. These will have the same underlying purpose: the realignment of the attitudes and actions of the mass of the people. That ideological management is as important for the opposition as it is for the resident political group is suggested by Gramsci's advocacy in the modern politically sophisticated state of a 'war of position' or protracted strategic offensive rather than a 'war of manoeuvre' or sudden confrontation. Since ideology resides in all manner of groups and institutions of the Civil State, it is here that the struggle of collective wills — which is the essence of ideological change — must take place. Ideological revolution is not just an exchange within the offices of formal power of members of alternative social groups or classes. An incoming party must try to introduce a consensus by establishing its own ideological base within and across as many social groups as possible. This redirection of ideological inclinations or convictions is achieved by the process of disarticulation-rearticulation. This refers to the need first of all to accomplish the breakdown of existing ideological commitment and then to reassemble these elements in an alternative juxtaposition with a new system of values. It is difficult to understand Gramsci's meaning here, but reference to other aspects of his theory suggests the need for a new ideology to be continuous with the old at least initially and to some degree. He suggests that an alternative class or party wishing to mount an effective challenge to a resident class or party must have a sound knowledge of its opponents culture. The new should incorporate some elements of the resident common sense (which subsumes aspects of the previous ideology in an elaborated form) perhaps with a different emphasis or rejuxtaposed relationships. Given the dependence of the mass on spontaneous philosophy, this would seem to be a condition of the new general philosophy attracting support. A new ideology must follow on from the old, yet it must be detached from it; it must be novel.

> Undoubtedly the fact of hegemony presupposes that account be taken of the interests and the tendencies of the groups over which hegemony is to be exercised, and that a certain compromise equilibrium should be formed. (Gramsci, 1971, p. 161)

It is the intellectuals who have the task of stabilizing and legitimating ideologies whether they are waxing or waning. They are responsible for the creation, introduction, maintenance and dissolution of an ideology and are thus the impetus for and restraint upon social change. The traditional intellectuals have the task of sustaining the regime that is in office. They are the former organic intellectuals of the ideology *in situ.* The organic intellectuals challenge the existing elite. As organizers of opposition groups, they have a consciousness raising function. They give a social group 'homogeneity and an awareness of its own function not only in the economic, but also in the social and political fields' (p. 5). They do not transmit an alternative philosophy to the group. This alternative philosophy will already be implicit in some form in that groups activity, though what is implicit in practice may not be acknowledged. The task of the organic intellectuals is to articulate and represent latent beliefs and so generate a new group spirit. Gramsci thus defines intellectuals in terms of their function. The intellectuals are the organizers of any social group and hence are not limited to members of academic institutions.

When considering the means by which an ideology can become established, Gouldner (1976) suggests a number of additional strategies by which a new party, class or group may gain ascendancy. For example, it may 'detraditionalize' existing institutions. This is more than just a *post hoc* argument or an alternative presentation of the concept of disarticulation, for it is associated with the already existing waning of tradition. It is this taking advantage of existing situations that typifies Gouldner's approach and it parallels the emphasis in Gramscian theory on the need of the exponents of a new ideology to identify some points of access, usually contradictions, in the old. For example, Gouldner suggests that the bureaucracy 'provides a functional alternative to and substitute for ideological motivations, and thus competes with and deteriorates ideology' (*ibid*, p. 242). They therefore could impede the progress of an ideology, a point recognized by Gramsci who notes the tendency of bureaucracies to ossify and develop caste like qualities. Yet according to Gouldner, bureaucracies are also potential sites of ideological conversion or entry since their concentration on means rather than ends renders their unclarified goals open to ideological critique. Gramsci (1971) interprets bureaucratic growth as a symptom of a crisis in the relationship between the Political and Civil States, it being an indication that the Political State is seeking to impose ever more firmly its ideology on subordinate groups. Bureaucracies cannot be dispensed with by the incoming party since they convey the ideology of the State to the people. Yet neither can they be allowed to take their own course. They must therefore be regenerated and given new direction.

Gouldner's account of ideological change is seen from the

perspective of the individual rather than that of the State. The introduction of an ideology is about flouting tradition and finding new loyalties. 'Modern ideologies distance themselves from prior epistomological positions which had commonly allowed reliance upon authority to justify policy recommendations' (p. 57). He imputes to a new ideology or ideologue a relentless missionary quality. The ideological representative is active and has the 'task of spreading the word, to tell and convince others' (p. 47). Those institutions which are deemed to block the path of innovation can be disregarded. Since 'those whose careers have been involved in normal politics . . . acquire a certain ideological deafness' it may be necessary to 'circumvent existing political institutions and place successful ideologists at the pinnacles of power where they can exert pressure to reshape the conventional patterns of allocation previously reached by normal politics' (p. 248). Ideology is over confident. It acts as if 'all relevant empirical issues have been resolved satisfactorily' (p. 46). The ideologue experiences himself as engaged in a new purified kind of politics. He is also in a hurry for he has 'to produce results within a single lifespan' (p. 79). 'Ideology . . . serves on the one hand to permit ruthlessness to others in the name of high values and on the other to present oneself as having a selfless ambition' (p. 29). According to Gouldner, the old codes of morality are jettisoned in favour of the new at times of ideological change. Adherents to a new ideology absolves its proponents from commitment to existing rules since they are engaged in projects of public reconstruction. 'With the waning of traditionalism, there is now an increased struggle over "ideas". This means a greater struggle over which definitions of social reality (or reports) and which moral rules (or commands) are to be dominant' (p. 34).

This account suggests that ideological change is a complex *organized* process. The language of battle to describe it is appropriate. It entails strategic action on many fronts and taking advantage of situations as they present themselves. It requires watchfulness and careful planning. It also requires some courage in disregarding tradition and so risking the wrath of those in established positions. A new ideology espouses its own codes of conduct.

Summary

The conclusions reached in this section on the Implementation of Ideology are as follows:

- the incorporation of subordinate groups into the ideological discourse of the elite is an arduous process, a continuous struggle;
- the process is facilitated by flexibility within an ideology;
- the failure of an ideology to recruit adherents may be due to misjudgment of the mood of the target group;
- an ideology will be weakened when it is perceived as contradicting the facts of daily life;
- if an ideology is to retain its dominance, it has to be managed;
- this entails the elite engaging in ideological strategies such as rationalization, universalisation, unification or legitimation. It also entails the use of tactics at local level;
- the language of ideology discloses little that is factual. Its functions to redefine ideology, and to persuade the listener that this is the one true reality;
- this redefinition of reality is achieved through the translation of everyday events and everyday language into the new ideological discourse;
- 'intellectuals' who need not be academics, play a leading role in both maintaining an ideology and in introducing a new ideology;
- a new ideology must be legitimated by a new set of rules which justify the power of the elite;
- a new ideology flouts tradition, disregards existing institutions and frees its exponents from normative constraints. It is constrained by bureaucracies yet must rely on them;
- a new ideology is over confident and in a hurry.

Ideological Achievement

When ideology no longer seems to exist, when it is denied that there is an ideology which dominates and shapes social life, then hegemony has been achieved. The power accrued to the controlling group remains unrecognized, it being voluntarily approved by the mass. Now the relationship between the leaders and the led is one of a sense of representation by the former of the latter (Therborn, 1980). This situation, which Gramsci refers to as an 'historic bloc', is an ideal for which all parties or classes in power will strive but which is unobtainable. Were it to be achieved, and were the populace as a whole to subscribe to the ideology of the centre, this would indicate extreme competence on the part of the elite in coordinating the affairs of the economic base and the political and ideological superstructures. It would also suggest a pliable and unreflective public.

The concept of hegemony is central in Gramscian theory. He defines it as:

> The spontaneous consent given by the great masses of the population to the general direction imposed on social life by the dominant fundamental group, consent 'historically' caused by the prestige (and therefore by the trust) accruing to the dominant group because of its position and function in the world of production. (quoted in Femia, 1987, p. 42)

Hegemony then is a form of control that is based on sound and skilful leadership which elicits willing consent to the policies and practices of the State. This consent can only be achieved if the elite mediates its policies through the institutions of the Civil State. It is clearly lost with the use of force through the agencies of the Political State. The greater the reliance on force through the law for example, the further from hegemony will the relationship between leaders and led have become. Buci-Glucksmann (1980) regards Gramsci as the 'theorist of consent by legitimation'. This phrase may suggest that the mass readily gives its support and legitimation to the party in power. But despite his emphasis on consent, Gramsci's position remains Marxist. The use of the term 'imposed' in the above definition, and his appreciation that above all it is efficiency in the management of the economy that attracts support from the mass, reflect his fundamental perspective.

This definition emphasizes the leadership element in hegemony, leadership which must be both political and cultural. The elite must not only obtain a sufficient degree of hegemonic support if it is to continue in power, it must retain it. Hegemony is therefore not only a state in the relationship between political centre and general populace, which varies in degree. It is also a dynamic process. It is the process whereby the dominant class or group tries to establish its own interpretation of reality as universal and ensure that social institutions and practices reflect and support that interpretation. This must be achieved against opposition and indifference, despite unintended distortion and deliberate misinterpretation. '(Hegemony) does not just passively exist as a form of dominance. It has continually to be renewed, recreated, defended and modified. It is also continually resisted, limited, altered, challenged by pressures not at all its own' (Williams, 1977, p. 112).

Williams' definition of hegemony stresses its substance rather than the leadership element:

> It is a whole body of practices and expectations over the whole of living: our senses and assignments of energy, our shaping perceptions of ourselves and our world. It is a lived system of meanings and values — constitutive and constituting — which as they are experienced as practices appear as reciprocally confirming. (*ibid*, p. 110)

This account is so broad that it seems at first to equate hegemony with culture. But the opening phrase — 'It is *a* whole body of practices . . .' suggests that Williams perceives them as distinct. He interprets hegemony as the infusion of power throughout the whole fabric of social life. If hegemony has been achieved, the representation of it surrounds us. It *is* us, for it is more than a conscious system of ideas and beliefs. It is not merely structural. It is a psychological state which mirrors the external world and which may not even be consciously recognized. If ideology is internalized to this degree, to the extent that it governs our perception of reality, it is a facet of identity and for Ricoeur (1986) referring to Geertz and Erikson, this means that it has an integrative function. Ideology provides society with an identity — the 'social cement' theory. In addition, it provides the individual with an identity at which level it is also integrative. By extension of this theme, it holds the individual together in the face of the anxiety generated by the conflicts and tensions in the real world. Once again hegemony features the dissolution of boundaries between the individual self and externality, but the retention of an ideology in this case is a reflection of the need of the individual for personal security rather than a belief in the competence and wisdom of the government.

In the previous section on the implementation of ideology, the perspective taken was that of the State. But how do individuals of their own volition come to support an ideology? Althusser and Gramsci differ fundamentally in their views on this. For the former, ideological recruitment is automatic, a result of the thoroughness with which the ruling group has managed to saturate social institutions. Being surrounded by representations of ideology, the individual becomes convinced of (is 'hailed' by) its 'rightness' for him or her. He or she has become a convert to that ideology, or has been 'interpellated' to use Althusser's term. The individual absorbs the ideology uncritically and so becomes a representative of that ideology.

Although some aspects of this model of ideological socialization can be accepted without difficulty — for example we are more likely to be convinced of the worth and viability of a principle for action if we see it operating successfully in our social surroundings — it gives no credence to the possibility that ideologies in all their manifestations may be opposed. For Gramsci, whose individual is critical, sceptical and sometimes disinclined to be the obedient subject, the state is fallible; and because its authority is challenged, it must continuously renegotiate its relationship with subordinate groups. For Gramsci political life is a struggle between centre and periphery and the truth of an ideology lies not in any intrinsic quality of that ideology, but in its ability to attract followers.

In Gramscian theory, a new ideology emerges as intellectuals take advantage of the weakening legitimacy of the current regime. Before coming to power, they must in turn have acquired a degree of voluntary support within the mass of the people, thereby giving themselves a basis from which to develop a new hegemony. Therborn's (1980) approach is rather more sophisticated. He distinguishes between the failure of an ideology due to a loss of support for the ideas of the ruling groups ('a loss of legitimacy') or due to the breakdown of the social institutions which mediate that ideology (the 'disorganisation of legitimacy'). That is, a contradiction develops between the elite and their means of disseminating their ideology. The apparatuses of hegemony become detached as it were from the central state. This provides a vacuum for a new ideology of the people to become established.

Summary

The conclusions reached in this section on Ideological Achievement are as follows:

- hegemony represents the willing consent of the mass to the ideological rule of an elite;
- total hegemony or legitimacy of a party or group in power is impossible. Hegemony is always a matter of degree;
- hegemonic success depends upon the quality of leadership of the elite. This leadership should be both intellectual and moral. It should also demonstrate competence in the handling of the economy;
- hegemony is a process as well as a state. The elite must continually recreate its authority in the face of changing circumstances and opposition to its policies;
- hegemony has an integrative function for society and for the individual. It provides an identity at both levels;

- the group or class in power may lose legitimacy either because support for its principles falls away or because its instruments of ideological dissemination become detached from central influence and control.

2 The 1960s: The Robbins Report and the Ideology of Progress

Introduction

In 1969 in his comprehensive account of the education of teachers in Britain, Taylor stressed the importance of the teacher training system for the control of society by the state:

> The power elites of a society . . . cannot afford to remain indifferent to the nature of the inter-personal relationships that exist in classroom and school and their impact upon the social attitudes and behaviours of pupils. The principal responsibility for shaping such relationships belongs to teachers. . . . Hence society is necessarily concerned with the way in which teachers are selected, trained and certified: although responsibility for some part of these processes is sometimes delegated to largely independent bodies such as universities and individual colleges, a fairly close oversight is maintained by agencies of political and social control at the national level. It follows that . . . we must pay attention to the procedures that are being used to bring influence of this kind to bear. (p. 26)

Twenty years later, and writing in a harsher more overtly politicised age, Popkewitz (1987) reiterates these sentiments: '. . . the discipline centred curriculum or back-to-basics are not merely pedagogical practices, but contain assumptions and social relations that emerge from and are related to structures of power found in the larger society' (p. 12). Both authors highlight the instrumental importance of the teacher training system for the control of society by the state. For Taylor it is the system as a whole that functions to this end. For Popkewitz, it is the curriculum. These two quotations signal the focus of the following three chapters. Their purpose is to investigate the way in which, and the extent to which, the initial teacher training curriculum has been used as a context for ideological influence over the past three decades.

To acknowledge that the state may seek to exert influence on society through the curriculum of teacher education is not to suggest either that it consistently attempts to do so or that when it does establish a degree of control that it meets with no resistance: nor that all that happens within teacher education contributes to ideological innovation or maintenance. This study suggests that the ideological relationship between central government and the curriculum of training is a complex one in which patterns of power and control evolve over time. It suggests that even if the ideological principles of the government do become established as the sub-text of the training programme that this is not always entirely a direct and outright consequence of state intervention, nor is the long term legitimation or security of tenure of ideological representation guaranteed.

Following the three-stage framework already used in the previous chapter, the aims of this chapter are as follows:

(i) **Ideological belief**
to consider the nature of the ideology of UK governments during the 1950s and 1960s;

(ii) **Ideological implementation**
to indicate that the Robbins Report was ideologically motivated, that setting up the Committee entailed the use of ideological strategy and that the curriculum that was the outcome was itself highly ideological in both structure and content;

(iii) **Ideological achievement**
to suggest that the changes introduced into training by the report failed to become normatively sedimented and hence hegemonic because they challenged the cultural ideal of training held by members of the teacher training profession.

Ideological Belief: The Ideology of UK Governments in the 1950s and 1960s

The previous chapter suggested that politics and ideology are inseparable. It is therefore difficult to dispute that the period in question, the 1950s and 1960s, was 'ideological' in the sense that successive governments formed an assessment of the condition of society and on the basis of this diagnosis formulated policies which subsumed moral priorities, technical prescriptions and so on. That the first twenty years of the post-war period did not appear to be ideological is frequently mentioned. Because Nazism seemed to have been eliminated overseas and because at home there was a considerable degree of agreement between the two political parties across a range of policies (although disagreements within the parties) it seemed that ideologies were a thing of the past. The common external enemy of the emerging Soviet nuclear threat also had a binding effect on all Western governments and further detracted from internal ideological tensions. But ideology had not disappeared; it was merely less salient. The questions to be asked therefore are less to do with its existence than with its substance and its power to dominate.

The ideological message emanating from the centre was very forceful during the first two decades of the post-war period. Although there was some conflict within the Labour and Conservative parties between the exponents of extreme policies of the Right or the Left and their more moderate colleagues, there is generally considered to have been agreement across the parties on the desirable direction of many aspects of both domestic and overseas policy (Beer, 1965; Leys, 1989; Deakin, 1989). It was on matters of implementation rather than on matters of principle that disputes between the parties arose (Ryan, 1990). As Kavanagh and Morris (1989) put it: 'The governmentalists in both political parties were overwhelmingly drawn from the centre of the political spectrum and for all the differences of nuance and rhetoric, it is the continuity of policy which stands out' (p. 14). Even those commentators who are less convinced that the parties were in substantial agreement consider that this was a period of 'relative consensus' (Tivey, 1989). Thus over time, the political message from the centre to the electorate appeared to be uniform, and so constituted a powerful ideological presence. The substance of this ideological message was welfare capitalism or social democracy which Kavanagh and Morris regard as consisting of a commitment to the mixed economy, full employment, conciliation of the trade unions, welfare and a retreat from Empire, of which only welfare and to a limited extent the role of the unions are of direct interest in this account. It was inevitable that the execution of such policies would entail high public spending, high taxation and considerable central intervention.

This sketchy representation of the post-war political scene could be misleading however if it were taken to imply that by introducing legislation and the various welfare agencies, the state had achieved hegemonic dominance. This was not the case since social democracy or the substance of the ideological message was demand led. Leys (1989) states explicitly that it was not hegemonic, but this can also be assumed from the emphasis which many writers place upon the influence of the electorate in determining the general direction of government policy during the mid and late 1940s. One of the most potent reasons for the attraction of social democracy to both parties and for its continuity, was the force of public opinion. The war had disclosed extremes of wealth and poverty and had disrupted traditional expectations. People were tired of austerity and looked towards a better future, a fairer and more just society. It was pressure from the electorate above all that forced the construction and subsequent implementation of the comprehensive welfare package of which the Beveridge plan was a part. As Kavanagh and Morris (p. 73) put it: 'it seemed clear that the public would not be appeased by anything less', and Leys suggests that 'The "Beveridge Plan" gave concrete expression to what most people wanted' . . . and that 'many Conservatives became persuaded of its political necessity' (p. 65). And in discussing the 1950s, Ramsden (1980) goes so far as to suggest that in order to survive as a governing party the Conservatives had to express their commitment to the Welfare State and the Keynesian approach to economics that supported it. Moreover the Right was also able to support the Beveridge Report ideologically since the proposals echoed the paternalism of traditional Toryism although as Sked and Cook (1984) note: 'Its embrace appeared to lack the passion of conviction' (p. 38). Nor could the Labour party be indifferent to the views of the electorate although the Beveridge proposals captured the intrinsic quality of Labour ideology. Both parties therefore, although differentially, can be said to have supported the post-war welfare programme for ideological as well as political reasons. Far from being neatly hegemonic, the post-war situation was what Held (1989, pp. 107–8) describes as an 'instrumental consent'. The ideological relationship between public and government was interactive. Compliance to political and economic institutions was 'linked directly to an expectation of a qualitatively new and more egalitarian life' . . . 'the post-war Labour government and the Conservatives after them, were constantly anxious to emphasize that the state in Britain was the symbol of common values . . . Utilising techniques of . . . public opinion management . . . governments went to extraordinary lengths to try to manage opinion, to reinforce acceptance of the state's authority and to create "consensus"'. Thus the formation of the Welfare State introduced a precedent into British policy making: the power of the popular viewpoint to determine government reaction (Ashford, 1986).

Until the late 1950s, this ideological scenario remained relatively stable, but by the end of the decade the legitimation of the government by the electorate was beginning to fade. The 1950s was the era when 'most of our people have never had it so good' as Macmillan declared in 1957. At home, economic growth was unprecedented. Unemployment was minimal, earnings rose faster than prices, house ownership doubled, consumer goods were purchased on a scale never even envisaged before. The mood became one of optimism. Domestic economic growth enabled successive Conservative governments to sustain the policies of their predecessors. During the thirteen years when they were in office, spending on welfare increased substantially and amendments to the policies of the consensus were limited to token acts such as adjustments to the nationalization programme (Ramsden, 1980). A climate of expectation had been established.

But this happy state of affairs was not due to the monetary skills of the Conservative Chancellors of the Exchequer but rather to a worldwide boom and the absence from the international markets of countries such as Germany and Japan which had been dislocated by the war. Retrospectively, the 1950s were years of illusion when at home the Conservatives did little except maintain the *status quo* and overseas tried to prolong Britain's position as a world power at considerable cost to an economy which relatively was in decline. Sked and Cook regard the end of the 1950s and the beginning of the 1960s as the Conservative anti-climax. Troubles for the government had accumulated. Key industries had remained underfunded, defence had been overfunded. There had been the Suez crisis; there had been troubles in Kenya and Rhodesia and problems over immigration policy. At home there were sterling crises and industrial unrest. There were scandals which rocked the government. There were the wrangling discussions which culminated in the rejection by de Gaulle of the UK's bid to join the Common Market. And in Douglas Home, Macmillan's successor, the country had a Prime Minister whose manner and appearance failed to engage the confidence of the voter. As the public began to realize that the promises of the Macmillan years had been a chimera, support for the Conservatives fell away. By 1961, Labour was leading in the polls, and the Liberal party was attracting support in by-elections. This crisis led to 'a steady deterioration in the authority of governments and the state, and to a progressive weakening of popular support for the dominant ideas of the political order built up over the previous four decades' (Leys, 1989, p. 71). After so many years of stability, the electoral scene had suddenly become more volatile. The turnout at the 1964 election which returned the Labour party to power was lower than at the 1959 election, a result which Childs (1986) regards as 'a harbinger of the unsettled state of opinion, the more questioning, more doubting, more cynical attitude of the 1970s . . .' (p. 156).

Despite the drain on resources that the Welfare State was becoming, the Conservatives (and also the Labour party) remained committed to it and continued to promote it publicly. Privately however, and for their respective reasons, the two parties were beginning to go their different ways. On both sides shifts of ideological ground were becoming apparent. These were internal and did not yet inform policy in any coherent fashion but they reflected the need to reassess and redefine political priorities in response to persistent problems. For the Conservatives, the party in power, the political and economic consequences of continuing to fund universal welfare benefits posed a very real dilemma. Consideration of how this might be done within the context of economic decline and continued public demand seemed to legitimate the release of an alternative ideology which heralded the future emergence of the New Right. Confronted with an economy which failed to respond to attempts to regenerate it and ever increasing public expenditure, the Conservative party was now able to advocate privately at least that people should work hard to provide for themselves, and community provision should replace universal state provision:

> The significant growth of our national income is going to depend, as it always has done, largely on the activities and decisions of exceptional men and women. . . . By rewarding them, by reducing disincentives to work and save, (the nation) can enrich itself . . . Why . . . do we not give maximum and consistent encouragement to people to be self providing . . . It is no part of my argument to say that we should spend less on social provision. My argument on the contrary is that we should aspire to spend more, much more . . . It does however seem to me that there is both a need and an opportunity now and in the years ahead for a major shift in the nature, direction and emphasis of social spending — away from the crude services which working people ought increasingly to be able to provide for themselves, and towards modern services crying out for community effort or finance . . . (Goldman, quoted in Pope *et al*, 1986, pp. 174–6)

It is interesting to compare this quotation with an excerpt from a Conservative Political Centre publication of 1950 in which a consensus view of the relationship between the Welfare State and the economy is clearly indicated. Here there is an awareness of the difficulties of generating sufficient income given other commitments, but no doubt is expressed that welfare benefits must be maintained at all cost:

> After nearly half a century of almost uninterrupted expansion of the social services, we are faced with three choices. We can

> continue with the present policy of apparently uncontrollable expenditure which will imperil not only our defence but our whole way of life. For us this is unthinkable. Secondly we can build up our defences at the cost of our social services. That is undesirable and must be done only in the last resort. Thirdly we can make a supreme effort to meet the needs of Defence and at the same time to maintain the social services. Our task is plain. Our emphasis now must be on finding ways of maintaining the social services. (Conservative Political Centre 1950, quoted in Pope *et al*, 1986, p. 167)

The Labour party being in opposition did not have to confront this intractable problem with such urgency. Their major concern was that they had lost two elections. If the party were ever to regain power it was clearly necessary for it to redefine itself ideologically as distinct and apart from the Conservatives (Callaghan, 1989). The obvious prosperity of the electorate seemed to indicate that the Welfare State might have been successful in its aim of eliminating extreme poverty. Labour was to find new direction and rejuvenation in the proposals of the intellectuals of the Left. For both Crosland and Gaitskell, modern socialism could, and should, cast off its cloth cap image. Its concern was no longer with the nationalization of industry (which generated inefficient bureaucracies), nor only with welfare provision (since there seemed to be less need) but with equality. This did not mean equal rights to receive benefits such as health care since the availability of such benefits demonstrably did not alter the fundamental inequalities of a class based society. In *The Future of Socialism* (1956) Crosland distinguished between a concern with social welfare and the desire for an equal and classless society. Both of these were clearly still relevant but the concept of need had been redefined in terms of opportunity rather than immediate physical needs. Equal educational opportunity above all, was the key to the classless society and to the redistribution of privilege.

By the end of the 1950s the ideologies of both parties were being redefined. In their own ways, and in accordance with their respective analyses of society, they each stressed equality which no longer referred to provision but to opportunity. In order to control the rising costs of universal benefit provision, the lone Conservative voice was beginning to promote selectivity as a means of directing help to those in need, a solution to an economic problem which would have consequences for ideological redefinition. For alternative reasons, the Labour party was also beginning to recognize that the egalitarian welfare programme was due for reassessment, for it was unlikely to have the long-term consequences for societal change that it had seemed to promise. Thus by the time of the Robbins Report, the ideology of welfare egalitarianism was being questionned.

The realities of the economic situation at the turn of the decade — repeated failures to significantly raise output, an adverse balance of payments, falling exports and a large loan from the IMF — forced both parties to confront the issue of modernization. How could Britain elevate itself in the international economic stakes and earn enough to meet the burgeoning cost of public expenditure? As the 1964 election approached, the Labour party under Wilson promoted technical efficiency and particularly 'science' as the key to industrial growth. The Conservatives, still clinging to the vestiges of Empire and with a former Foreign Secretary as Prime Minister, emphasized defence and foreign affairs. It was only reluctantly and belatedly that they acknowledged that Britain's own resources, the ability of the youth of the country, might provide the necessary stimulus for economic regeneration. Thus it was possible for both parties to accept the report of the Robbins Committee which advocated a vast expansion of higher education, particularly in the areas of science, technology and management. But even here, where the recommendations of the report coincided with the emerging views of the two parties, it was public opinion which in the end, forced political compliance. 'Parents were more anxious than ever that their children should be given the chance to develop their potentialities. Politicians were forced to respond to this — which is not to say there were not genuine reformers among the politicians' (Childs, 1986, p. 148).

Summary

The conclusions reached in this section on the Ideology of UK Governments in the 1950s and 1960s are as follows:

- in the post-war period both parties supported social democracy for ideological as well as political reasons. Social democracy was demand led and therefore not hegemonic;
- this consensus between the parties created a strong ideological presence;
- by the early 1960s support for the government was falling away for a number of reasons including scandals and its evident

inability to manage the economy, but there is no evidence to suggest that the electorate was losing faith in social democracy;
- at this time, both parties for their respective ideological reasons were beginning to challenge the principle of egalitarian welfare and to promote instead equality of opportunity;
- in 1963 the Robbins Report emerged as a means of remedying the difficulties of the government. Its recommendations for the extension of higher education were intended to improve the country's economic performance and its emphasis on equality of opportunity was to rally support for the state from a sceptical electorate. Since its recommendations embodied social democracy it was also a highly ideological instrument as the next section will show.

Implications for Ideological Theory

Further:

- That the electorate continued to support the ideology of social democracy although disillusioned by the incompetence of government appears to contradict the assumption of many ideological theorists that support for an ideology and for a government espousing that ideology are necessarily coincident.
- The notion of domination is central in all ideological theories although Gramsci does supplement this with the concept of negotiation. Such a perspective attributes power to the state. What emerges from the above presentation is that the mass can have the power to do more than just accommodate and modify an ideology. Ideologies can be demand led even in non-revolutionary times.
- The events of the 1960s support the hypothesis that failure to manage the economy is a major factor in the decline of ideological power.
- The influence of the economy on the nature of ideology is apparent here. As money flowed less freely and industry began to falter, it was becoming necessary for the party in power, the Conservatives, to consider revising its ideology to accommodate these changes. The Labour party, which was not in power, had the luxury of revising its commitment of social democracy on a matter of principle.

Ideological Implementation: The Robbins Report as an Ideological Strategy

It seems hardly novel to suggest that new structures or practices that are introduced or endorsed by a government embody its ideology since no government is likely to promote policies which do not reflect its fundamental principles. It may appear unremarkable therefore to suggest an ideological link between the government and the new training curriculum which followed the Robbins Report (1963). But the introduction of ideologically infused legislation is never straightforward. First there is the question of access. Will there be a need to modify the ideological content of the measure and so weaken its political message in order to lessen opposition either actual or potential? Will the measure appear reasonable to the intended recipients, or in Gramscian terms, will it be possible for the target group to integrate it into their cultural common sense? Additionally, once an innovation has been introduced into the receiving community the government loses control of it, and the ideological message may be either ignored or manipulated. It cannot therefore be assumed that a strong replication of a central ideology will emerge within the social structures and practices which are the product of government recommendations or legislation. This was the case, however, in the aftermath of the Robbins Report. In initial teacher training the developments that flowed from the report echoed social democracy both substantively and structurally.

It was noted in the last section that by the beginning of the 1960s, the support of the electorate for government had declined, and that disillusion with the parliamentary process had set in. The economy also was less robust. Yet there was no evidence that commitment to social democracy was waning and the demands for welfare provision continued to increase. The government was therefore in a difficult position: beginning to doubt privately the possibility of continuing to fund the Welfare State, yet in too weak a position electorally to attempt to introduce radical measures to counteract this problem. To set up an enquiry into higher education which, given the proclaimed support of the political parties for social democracy and the general political climate, was unlikely to recommend a reduction of provision, but rather the reverse, therefore, appears to have been a shrewd tactic. Such an initiative would increase government support at a time when it was floundering. But to suggest this would seem to attribute to politicians a substantial degree of cynicism and to deny that their motives may be for the best of reasons — here that they wished to see an extension of higher education for the personal and social benefits that this would bring. A political act can subsume both these forms of motivation, but the question is raised of whether action can be termed tactical or strategic if that action is not consciously or intentionally so. This problem will be more fully considered at the end of this section, but throughout the discussion there is an assumption that there may be a distinction between action that is intentionally tactical and that which has tactical significance from the perspective of the observer.

The brief of the Robbins Committee was 'to review the pattern of full-time higher education in Great Britain and in the light of national needs and resources to advise Her Majesty's government . . .'. The setting up of the enquiry therefore reflected concern about the economic situation and the need to modernize in order to meet the challenge of overseas competition. Its proposals for more than doubling the percentage of students in full-time higher education by 1980 were justified on the grounds that 'to meet competitive pressures in the modern world, a much greater effort is necessary if we are to hold our own' (p. 268). Although the cost of funding these recommendations would clearly be substantial, this was considered to provide a good return in terms of improving the efficiency of the economy and so enhancing our trading position. But a more productive economy would also enable the government to meet the welfare demands of the electorate. As yet, no alternative central ideology to that of social democracy had emerged. If the government wished to stay in power it had to be both seen and heard to continue to support it. Thus the economic basis of the enquiry also had political and ideological implications.

Given the brief of the Committee and the pervasive ideology, the assumption must surely have been that an expansion of HE would be proposed and thus the intention in setting up the enquiry was not only instrumental but also political. In the area of teacher training particularly the report was to have extensive and ideologically advantageous consequences. But how could the government ensure that the recommendations of the Committee would be accepted by the educational community? The discussion of the previous chapter suggests that ideologically motivated innovations may be willingly or indifferently received by the target community depending to a considerable degree upon the skill with which they are introduced. In this respect, the setting up of the Robbins enquiry was sound ideological strategy. The selection of the Committee members was judicious. By nominating predominantly educationists the potential problem of competing discourses mentioned in the previous chapter was eliminated. To the author's knowledge, only two members of a committee of twelve were from the world of industry, a fact which may seem at odds with the economic implications of the Committee's brief but which supports the suggestion that setting up the enquiry was not merely an economically motivated event, but was also political in intent. The educationists were all persons of considerable experience, status and prominence. Their nomination appeared rational, but it also helped to ensure that the recommendations of the report were transmitted to their destination with authority. It is suggested therefore that the composition of the Committee contributed significantly to the power and efficacy of the report as an ideological instrument.

The report proposed an unprecedented expansion of higher education and in so doing symbolized and reflected the general climate of opinion that prevailed at the time. It was infused throughout with principles of social justice and equality. For example, parity of esteem between universities was implied, and although 'nobody really believed this was or could be so, the alternative of conceding the possibility of competition or variation was so invidious that it could not be thought of' (Carswell, 1985, p. 41). It was also made clear in the discussion of staffing of higher education that the Committee believed the 'disparity between the incomes and prospects of persons doing similar work in different universities which are all in receipt of public funds to be unjust' (para. 542). Above all, the report is probably most frequently remembered for the axiom that 'courses of higher education should be available for all those who are qualified by ability and attainment to pursue them and who wish to do so' (para. 31). Carswell suggests that this 'call to maintain opportunity . . . was the main social and political appeal of the Report . . . the scale of which caught the public imagination and ensured its immediate success. The press, the public, the political parties were full of enthusiasm for higher education, especially university education. Money flowed in abundance' (pp. 43 and 52). The report therefore emerged as a highly ideological document, confirming in the eyes of the electorate the commitment of the centre to social democracy. 'The real achievement of the Robbins Committee was to make increased public expenditure on higher education politically acceptable . . . It was a notable achievement, inspired by a vision of society in which social improvement was possible and could be engineered by bringing the greatest amount of education to the greatest number' (Williams and Blackstone, 1983, p. 15).

It can also be shown that not only the report itself but the curriculum of initial teacher training that developed in its aftermath and as a consequence of government action on its recommendations, similarly reflected the social democratic tenor of public and political opinion.

That a curriculum can materially represent and hence reinforce structural and normative aspects of the wider society was one of the important insights to emerge from the the 'new sociology' of the 1960s and 1970s. Schooling was shown to be a many layered experience. The surface structures and processes of teaching — its organization, content and methodology — subsumed the 'hidden curriculum', the means by which pupils were socialized into supporting the social and political *status quo*. It also became evident that the content of the curriculum contributes to the legitimation and therefore the retention of existing social structures. The school was thus recognized as a site of social reproduction, and education as a politicizing experience, the curriculum being the form in which this experience was presented and structured. If during the 1970s, it was the links between the educational process and differentiation within the social structure which were emphasized, more recently, as education has become more overtly political, the focus of attention has shifted to the relationship between education and the dominant ideology. Apple (1982) is uncompromising in his portrayal of the school curriculum as a vehicle for potential ideological control: '(ideologies) are embodied by our common-sense meanings and practices. Thus if you want to understand ideology at work in schools, look . . . at the concreta of day to day curricular and pedagogic life . . . the workings of ideology can be seen most impressively at the level of form as well as what the form has in it . . .' (p. 139). Thus it is suggested that the social structures and processes of the school may not only confirm and so reinforce the specific external power hierarchy. They may also mirror ideologies, which are here recognized as economically based, and so as Althusser indicated, socialize pupils into them.

Although these comments focus on the association between the school curriculum and society, and in the case of Apple the state, do we need to assume that this reproductive relationship is limited to that particular context? The case study accounts of schooling in the 1970s imply that any well institutionalized social practice may have a number of dimensions and on analysis be found to be reproducing and hence legitimating elements of the national political or ideological systems. The Robbins Report gave substance to the egalitarian and welfare principles of central government. It recommended that those entering teaching through public sector institutions might now train by one of two routes. A student could continue on the existing two or three-year certificate course or could work towards a four-year professional degree, the new BEd. An obvious consequence of these developments was a reduction in the status differential between the universities and the public sector colleges. While the BEd degree did not place college students on a par with their university counterparts, it nevertheless raised their qualification level, and so challenged the elitism of university trained students. Those who wished to elevate their position or to improve their lot in life had the chance to do so as the choice between certificate or degree became freely available. As with any other welfare benefits the student only had to demonstrate eligibility (ability) to qualify. The benefit was provided by the state. In this way, the report promoted structures which, being supportive of government policies, were ideologically enabling.

In addition, the report noted that there were students in the colleges with sufficient ability to occupy university places, and it seemed appropriate that this should be recognized. The new title of colleges of education which the report proposed is significant for it indicates a shift of emphasis away from training in favour of the personal education of the student. It implies a non-instrumental attitude to higher education, that attending a college just as much as a university in order to improve ones knowledge is an intrinsically valuable activity, an activity which had formerly been regarded as a privilege of the elite. To make higher education (rather than mere training) more freely available in this way was to formally assert and to institutionalize a political commitment to a more open and just society. It structurally represented and consolidated a concern to reduce disparities of status in the interests of greater equality. To the extent that no student could avoid them, these measures were ideologically enforcing. These points were summarized by Elvin (1963) who was a member of the Robbins Committee:

> The Committee itself early adopted the principle that there ought to be equal availability of awards for equal work, irrespective of the institution in which the work was done.
>
> (The conclusion of the Committee was that): the time required for both a degree and a professional qualification should be four years not three. The decisive argument for this is one of equity. It would be unfair . . . that a university graduate following the consecutive pattern should have to take four years for a degree plus a professional qualification, while a college student could get both in three. (pp. 8 and 9)

It is evident then that in the post-Robbins era initial training, if it were to take the form that the report suggested, would echo and so reinforce the proclaimed dominant ideology. However, the power of the training programme as a vehicle for ideological dissemination and confirmation becomes more apparent when the changes in the content and status of one dimension of the curriculum, the courses in educational studies that were ushered in by the report, are reviewed.

The Robbins Committee had proposed that the universities should assume administrative, financial and academic responsibility for the colleges. Only the latter was accepted by the government, and although the report identified the four traditional elements of training, it was left to the institutions to devise their own curricula. No specific recommendations were made concerning either the organization or the content of the revised form of teacher education. However, the structural framework proposed by the report and supported by the government offered little choice. The endorsement of training as a degree worthy course of study exerted a strong pull towards the 'academization' of the curriculum, and there can have been little doubt as to which elements of training were to become the candidates for elevation. It is difficult to see how it could have been anything other than main/personal subject or education studies, since with an injection of theoretical rigour these elements could most readily be revised to a standard or level which would meet the demands of the universities who were to award and monitor the new degree. It was the members of the university departments who were influential in determining the form of the curricular flesh that filled out the academic structural bones indicated by the Committee. For some time, they had been critical of the current form of teacher training in the colleges for its jejune traditionalism. For example, in an early paper of considerable prescience, Holmes (1954) a lecturer at the University of London, criticizes the current form of training for its 'undue emphasis in some training colleges on teaching practice to the neglect of problems of theory, and the difficulties of establishing education as a university discipline . . .' (p. 5). However, it was the philosophers of education who were the principal architects of the form that education studies came to take in the wake of the report. They were critical of current courses of training for two reasons, and so from within the academic community itself, principally from within the universities, there also came a push factor. Their first criticism of the current education courses concerned their lack of rigour:

> The teacher can no longer rely on experience, common-sense and common room conversation . . . the teacher has to learn to think for himself about what he is doing . . . A beginning must therefore be made at the level of initial training to equip him with the rudiments of disciplined philosophical thought and with those parts of psychology and the social sciences which

> are of particular relevance to his complex task. (Peters, 1967, p. 153)

The second criticism concerned the need to recognize that education was not a subject but a form of practical activity to the elucidation of which the disciplines of education each contributed a unique perspective:

> The theory (of education) is not itself an autonomous 'form' of knowledge or an autonomous discipline . . . Educational principles are justified entirely by direct appeal to knowledge from a variety of forms, scientific, philosophical, historical etc.
>
> To discern where and precisely how a given discipline contributes to the theory demands first a highly specialized knowledge of the discipline and the kind of problems with which it deals. It demands too the ability to see beneath the practical problems of education those underlying questions which this discipline alone can hope to answer. (Hirst, 1966, pp. 55–6)

Peters' comments imply a criticism of teaching method, Hirst's a criticism of the content of education courses as a whole. The former is more difficult to substantiate than the latter for which there is considerable evidence.

What was being criticized here? Prior to the Robbins Report, what was variously termed 'Education' in the colleges, or 'Principles of Education' or 'General Education', consisted of a number of topics or subjects which were considered relevant for the trainee teacher, but which seemed to have varied considerably in level of scholarship. Richardson (1968) undertook 'an extensive analysis of college syllabuses, prospectuses, and examination papers' and concluded that Principles of Education fell into ten categories. These included teaching methods (including school organization and school libraries), fundamental problems in education, health education and the history of educational ideas. Writing in 1962, Harrison notes that 'what generally purports to be "philosophy of education" is nothing more or less than reflections on education' . . . Now the difference between philosophy of education and reflections on education is clear. The former is stringently self-critical and logically consistent thinking . . . reflection on education is relatively superficial and inconsistent' (pp. 13–14). There seems to be scope here for Peters' concern with disciplined thought. A telling example of the sort of weakness in education to which he is drawing attention is given by Taylor (1961) who discusses the content and teaching of many of the sociology courses in the colleges at that time. Calling for 'a frank recognition of the primacy of sociological method' (which he defines as objective techniques and empirical investigation), he cites college 'sociological' courses in which 'the topics considered would not be recognized by most sociologists as being within their legitimate province'. These include discussions of citizenship, the role of the United Nations and environmental studies! 'To rely too much on the ability of non-specialist staff to think sociologically serves . . . to encourage the presentation of a somewhat secondhand, unsystematic, and diffuse impression of the nature of sociology . . .' (p. 46). This seems to confirm Peters' evaluation of the quality of some of the courses in the colleges. It appears that sociology of education particularly (but probably other topics also) was frequently taught superficially, and quite possibly inaccurately as well.

Hirst's criticism goes to the heart of the college tradition of teacher training, with its diffuse child centred semi-mystical approach. This is epitomized by a letter from a college principal lecturer in *Education for Teaching*[1] in 1960 (p. 36) 'It takes the fusion of many kinds of knowledge to produce the wisdom we want in teachers. It is where the "ologies" cross and recross with each other and with experience . . . that significant learning may take place. For this reason . . . education tutors ought to venture into many fields to attempt a synthesis . . .'. The language of this paradigm reflects the intangibility of the approach: here the term 'wisdom', elsewhere it is the 'spirit' of the child which must be nurtured, and the teacher has a 'vision' of the person the child will become. The lack of specificity in the education courses which is glimpsed here was compounded by the diverse role of the college tutor. An extract from *Education for Teaching* (1967) describes the role of the Lecturer in Education. It includes practical work in schools, obtaining school places, integrating courses, making apparatus, and of course teaching all the subjects of the education course. The situation in the colleges prior to the report was summarized by Katz (1959): 'The theoretical background knowledge required for success in the teaching profession is at this stage rather ill defined. . . . The inherent dangers of vagueness and wishful thinking should be combated by greater reliance on experimental evidence . . . It does require a change in attitude not only by the students, but often by the staff' (pp. 33–4).

The above comments all refer to pre-Robbins training as it was conducted in the colleges where over three-quarters of initial training took place. As might be expected, the titles of the education studies element of the postgraduate training courses in the university departments of education (UDEs) indicate a more coherent and scholarly approach. A brief review of accounts of these courses between the mid-1950s and the mid-1960s suggests that child development or psychology was common; also philosophy (sometimes called educational ideas), sociology, comparative education and history. Thus what were to become, post-Robbins, the 'four disciplines of education' were already well established in the initial training system by the early 1960s although an understanding of the intrinsic qualities of each subject area and the standard of their teaching varied considerably between institutions, but particularly between the universities and the colleges.

The event which consolidated the Robbins initiative and irrevocably channelled and redirected the course of educational studies in initial training was the 1964 Hull Conference of representatives of the universities and of the Department of Education and Science. The conference was to realize a curriculum which would reflect the recommendations of the report and hence structurally stabilize the ideology which they represented. The problem that the meeting had to address was how, in the light of the Committee's proposals, could teacher training as a whole be made degree worthy? How could academic standards be improved and courses be made more coherent? In the event and perhaps because there were no or very few representatives of the public sector institutions present, agreement on the future development of training was remarkably rapid. Teacher training should now include 'the rigorous study of those disciplines which underlay or contributed to educational knowledge . . . Thus the model known to educationists as "the four disciplines" was born. This model quickly became institutionalized — in a sense, it simply crystallised contemporary developments in the field. It was acceptable to universities since . . . it seemed to lend academic respectability to the study of education' (Simon, 1983, p. 8). It can thus be concluded that the introduction of the post-Robbins theory-oriented curriculum which came to dominate teacher education for the next decade at least, and which was residually present in some courses into the 1980s, was achieved with such ease and rapidity because it was already extant in the system (although in diverse forms), and because it was the strongly held and expressed opinion of authoritative figures in the education world that initial training should take a more rigorous form. The reappraisal of courses therefore seemed to need little explanation or justification. To include the theory of education in the form of the four disciplines, was the natural course of events. In elevating the academic standards of teacher education, the Robbins Report would remedy a situation which had attracted considerable adverse criticism by the leading professionals themselves. The 'ologies' of education could either be retained in the case of the university departments or introduced in their reformulated states in the case of the colleges where meeting the criticisms of the philosophers and the demands of the degree-awarding universities, they were in the future to be more discrete in substance, and more scholarly in presentation. Thus Gramsci's condition for ideological stabilization within social institutions — that innovations should marry to some degree at least already existing practices or structures — was at least partially met. The disciplines already existed in the UDEs and the UDEs were the leaders in the field. They influenced the curriculum in the colleges through the status and publications of their members, and they controlled it through the Area Training Organizations (ATOs). Through this series of events the new form of training which materially represented the principles of social democracy was introduced into the colleges, the main centres of training. The ideology of social democracy had come to constitute the structure of training itself.

Since the universities were to monitor and award the new BEd, they had the power to define both what should be included in the syllabuses of the disciplines and the level of attainment to be achieved. Thus it was the university model of the disciplines that came to be installed in the colleges. This was a model which met the criticisms of Peters (for rigour) and Hirst (for the distinctiveness of the contributions of the disciplines). It remains to consider the extent to which this post-Robbins model of the disciplines of education which came to supplant the diffuse impressionistic theory which had featured in the colleges, reflected the concern of central government with social justice, equality and progress, and the belief that man's environment (which could be improved) was of greater influence than his inheritance in determining what goals he could attain in life. In other words, to what extent did the disciplines of education which came to dominate the training curriculum in the aftermath of the Robbins Report also mirror the ideology of the state? This was most obviously the case in the psychology and sociology of education, the purpose of these courses being to promote a disciplined and reflective understanding of the pupils whom the students were eventually to teach. In the chapter on the psychology of education in what must be regarded as one of the most authoritative and influential texts on the disciplines that was available at the time, Tibble's *The Study of Education* (1966), the reader learns of the 'failure' of the 'psychology of mental measurement . . . (which) developed into a technology concerned with establishing and measuring the more or less fixed intellectual abilities with which it supposed children to be endowed at birth, irrespective of the cultural and educational milieu in which they developed' (p. 156). The kind of psychology recommended is humane and interactive; it 'will be very close indeed to that also required as one of the foundations of education for a wide range of "welfare" professions' (pp. 156–7); in the study of perception, imagination and thinking, students should 'pay close attention to individual differences . . .' (p. 161); texts which have 'played a powerful part in freeing cognitive psychology from the rigid bonds of the doctrine of innate abilities' (*ibid*) are recommended. In this chapter, the individual is presented as an active being ('an agent') who in interaction with the environment (the quality of which is therefore important) actively contributes to his/her own development in relationships with others.

In the same text, the chapter on the sociology of education exemplifies social democracy just as fully. Taylor tell us that '. . . the improving and reforming spirit of the early social surveys is still present, not least in the sociology of education . . .' (p. 181). The scope of the sociology of education is broad, and includes, 'questions about the role that schools fulfil as agents of social mobility, the extent to which children of varying social origins are provided with opportunities to find the place in society for which their abilities and aptitudes fit them, and the degree to which the generally accepted principle of equality of opportunity has meaning within a system that differentiates as well as selects and deals with pupils whose performances are not determined wholly by heredity . . . the sociologist must also concern himself with the factors that make it more or less easy for the pupil or student to profit from education . . . and among (the) social determinants of educability will be the structures and processes of the educational institutions themselves' (in Tibble, 1966, pp. 183–4 and 185). One of the most prominent texts on post-Robbins sociology of education courses was Douglas's *The Home and the School* (1964) which suggests that measured intelligence responds to environmental factors including housing conditions, parental encouragement and the practice of streaming in school. Hypothetically such psychological and sociological knowledge would enable prospective teachers to tailor their teaching of a pupil and also their behaviour towards that pupil according to the pupil's needs; or if this were somewhat ambitious, at least to be sensitive to the pupil as a unique individual. These courses in the educational disciplines were thus other directed, their sub-text being consideration for the well being of the child, commitment to equality of opportunity, and rejection of any notion of the immutability of social structure or processes. It can therefore be said that they structurally represented the value orientation of central policy and implicitly conveyed this to students.

A similar sort of relationship between the history of education and the prevailing ideology of the time can be demonstrated. Seaborne suggests that the curriculum for teacher trainees is likely to include such topics as universal education and what sections of the community benefitted from Education Acts. But students should especially undertake the study of live issues such as progressive education, the raising of the school leaving age, and the need to reduce the size of classes (in Tibble, 1971a). The common underlying theme here is that of the extension of equality. But prior even to this, during the early and mid-1960s, history of education was presented descriptively as a linear progression to a golden age, a succession of Acts and reforms each of which in its turn contributed to the progressive advancement of education and hence of society. It seems less likely that these sorts of connections could be made between the philosophy of education and the dominant ideology of the day because of the second order nature of philosophical enquiry. Philosophy, it might be assumed,would pursue an independent line because of the neutrality and stability over time of its techniques. But approach, perspective or methodology in the disciplines is only one of two relevant dimensions here. The other fundamental dimension is that of the topics that are chosen for analysis, measurement or review, and the philosopher of education is just as likely as the psychologist or sociologist to select a certain topic, the high profile of which will represent the current orthodoxy. In this way, philosophy is as susceptible as the other disciplines to the influence of prevailing perspectives and preoccupations. For example, equality of opportunity features as a topic of interest for the philosopher (Dearden, 1971) as well as for the sociologist (above). In addition, in attempting to clarify say, the nature of the integrated day, or what it means to be educated, the philosopher will arrive at some form of 're-presentation'. These may be reviewed for the extent to which they oppose or coincide with current doctrines. This is clearly illustrated in the discussion on the nature of education by Peters (1966): 'The concept of education . . . is almost indistinguishable from that of "liberal education" . . . the demand for liberal education might not be for a special kind of education but for the removal of certain restrictions or impediments that might hinder education as ordinarily understood' (p. 43). Education can best take place when constraints are removed then, a theme which lies at the heart of the principles on which the Welfare State was founded. Elsewhere, Peters discusses the place of the individual in the educative process in general:

> It is salutary to stress the aim of individual self-realization when an educational system is either geared to the demands of the state such as for more scientists or technicians, or when individuals are being relentlessly moulded in accordance with

> some doctrinaire pattern. There is point under such conditions, in stressing the differences between people and the ethical principle of respect for each individual's unique viewpoint on the world, together with the aspirations, abilities and inclinations that are peculiar to him. (p. 55)

The text from which these quotations are drawn, *Ethics and Education* was widely read. It went into six impressions within three years of publication. This short excerpt gives a flavour of the way in which philosophy, just as much as the other disciplines of education, can and did promote socially predominant values.

The aims of any government will be to persuade the mass of the people to adopt its own vision of the world and to manage this process in such a way that the support generated is voluntary rather than enforced. Even when as here, an ideology is as much determined by the electorate as it is by the state, politicians will strive for coincidence between their own perceptions and those of the populace in order to remain in power. In either situation, strategies and tactics will be employed to achieve a common perspective. It seems likely however that these may vary according to whether the elite is wishing to raise recruitment to its cause (a top down model of ideological operation and control) or whether it is seeking to consolidate its position in the eyes of the people (a bottom up model of ideological operation and control). The Robbins Report is considered to be more an example of the latter than of the former, and it remains to look more closely at the manoeuvres undertaken by the government in this situation. How did the centre achieve the high degree of ideological saturation in initial training which was apparent following the Robbins Report?

Difficult though it is to do so retrospectively, it is important to distinguish between events and decisions which were likely to have been consciously strategic or tactical on the part of the government and those which seemed to have strategic or tactical significance from an objective point of view, but to which such intent cannot be attributed. It has been argued that both the setting up of the enquiry and the choice of members to serve on the Committee were measures which were intentionally ideological. In the first case, it can reasonably be assumed that there was an expectation that the outcome of the enquiry would be an extension of higher education provision and hence be social democratic in tenor. At a time when the general climate of opinion still strongly favoured the wider distribution of opportunity, and when it was necessary also to raise the level of educational attainment if the UK were to compete economically with countries that had been regenerated in the post-war period, it was almost inconceivable that the Committee would do anything other than propose an expansion of university and college courses. Secondly it was crucial that whatever the recommendations of the Committee for the future of HE which were likely to reflect social democracy in some way, there was the highest possible chance that these would be accepted and implemented by the educational and wider communities. Careful choice of the Committee members was a means of carrying forward into the educational institutions of society as uncontroversially as possible, measures that were likely to reflect the prevailing ideology. Given the electorate's rather low opinion of the government at the time, both the setting up of the Committee and the selection of its members can be regarded not only as ideological therefore but also as politically tactical, for if all went well and the extension of higher education were to go ahead without difficulty, the popularity of the government would surely be raised.

But once the Committee had been chosen, matters were no longer influenced directly by the government, and the further one progresses along the chain of events, the greater becomes the distance from direct control by the centre. Probably there was no need for it. Even had the Committee not been independent and even if direct intervention in the curriculum had not been opposed by convention, there would have been no need for the government to attempt to influence the deliberations of the Committee and of the members of the Hull Conference. The country as a whole remained strongly committed to the principles of social justice and there was no reason to believe that the members of the Committee and the academics at the Conference were likely to be exceptions to this. Thus although the curriculum proposals that emerged from the Robbins Report were to structure the intellectual environment for the student of teacher training in a way that comprehensively represented the declared priorities of the state, this must be attributed to the social democratic convictions, whether overtly recognized or not, of these two groups. It can be concluded therefore that although the teacher training programme that finally emerged from the Robbins Report was indeed representative of current government philosophies, this was only partially a consequence of specific ideological tactics by the government. However, the chain of events discussed above can also be viewed from the perspective of ideological *strategy* and it is suggested that the enquiry can be interpreted as an example of the strategy of 'naturalization' (see chapter 1). The aim of this strategy is to 'create as tight a fit as possible "between ideology and social reality" and thus to deny or close up contradictions which might provide opportunities for the development of alternative ideologies'; and this will be the case whether ideology is led centrally or from the mass. Where there is a potential weakening of ideological consensus, the strategy becomes one of ideological confirmation. The Robbins enquiry provided opportunities for those of influence outside government circles to publicly confirm and so strengthen the prevailing ideology. The enquiry also demonstrated that the government continued to espouse social democracy and therefore fundamentally and despite the scandals that threatened it, had the interests of the people at heart; and the quite remarkable speed with which its main recommendations were accepted surely indicated to the electorate that here was a government which was as good as its word and which sincerely wished to support such an altogether admirable scheme. There could hardly be a better demonstration of the inseparability of the ideological and the political. The Robbins Report succeeded in enhancing the status of the government in both dimensions. Moreover, the Labour party when it came to power in 1964, supported many of the populist proposals of the report. Those recommendations which it rejected, such as the end of the binary policy, were on the whole, those items which were of much less interest to the individual voter.

In initial teacher training the curriculum which was to emerge from the report realized the ideology of the government to a remarkably high degree. The outcome of this infusion of the social institution of training with the principles and the priorities advocated by the centre appeared to be the possibility of strengthening the hegemonic grip of the state. The next task is to examine this assumption more closely and in so doing respond to the third question posed at the beginning of this chapter: was the report hegemonically successful?

Summary

The conclusions reached in this section on the Robbins Report as an Ideological Strategy are as follows:

- the setting up of the Robbins Committee was both a political and an ideological act, it being recognized that its anticipated recommendations would bring benefits of both kinds to the government;
- the selection of the Committee members was tactical, it being designed to ensure that the recommendations of the Report were authoritative and were therefore likely to be implemented;

- in its aims and its substantive proposals, the report reflected the principles of social democracy. This was also true of its recommendations for the development of initial teacher training;
- the professional community was given the task of selecting the substantive content of the new course. The government could be confident that their choice would also be social democratic in tenor because this was the prevailing social climate at that time, and these principles were deeply embedded in the common sense of the people.

Implications for Ideological Theory

Further:

- The setting up of the Robbins enquiry clearly indicates the inseparability of politics and ideology.
- Given a sufficient degree of ideological consensus, a governing elite is enabled to operate ideologically through the offices of non-political figures — a strategy which is implied but not developed in Gramsci's discussion on the role of intellectuals in the defence and extension of ideologies, and which is rarely noted or considered in ideological theory.
- The importance for successful ideological intervention of receptive cultural practices is supported.
- It was the intellectuals who strengthened the current ideology by ensuring its installation in the important social institution of initial training.

Ideological Achievement: The Hegemonic Failure of the Post-Robbins Curriculum

The implication of the strong post-Robbins commitment to theory in the form of the disciplines of education was that for a high proportion of the training period, student teachers were exposed to a hidden curriculum of values which echoed the priorities of the government(s) of the day. The issue to be reviewed below is whether this revised curriculum that developed in response to the report, socialized tutors and students into the principles of social democracy and therefore acted as a vehicle for ideological recruitment. Definitions of hegemony focus upon the total outlook of the values, perceptions, attitudes, beliefs of the group or individual, and the extent to which this outlook coincides with the values of the state. A claim of hegemonic success therefore entails demonstrating not just that ideology bearing structures have become established in the social environment, but that the values that they embody have become internalized as a consequence. Or if these values already exist in latent common sense form as was the case at the time of the report, that they become strengthened. Since no surveys on the political attitudes of tutors and students in the colleges of education in the middle or late 1960s could be found, an alternative approach had to be taken. The ideological efficacy of the training curriculum in this case has been assessed (and it can only be an assessment) by the degree of commitment shown towards it by those who would have transmitted the principles it embodied to the next generation, that is tutors and students. If the new curriculum were accepted, there was the possibility that it may have acted as a channel of socialization for the political perspective. On the other hand, if it were to be rejected, then clearly it could not have performed this function. The extent to which the new theoretical curriculum was either accepted or rejected by the various parties in training will therefore be considered in this section.

The introduction of the more academic post-Robbins programme of training which included the disciplines of education — and hence the values they embodied — was attractive to the leadership in the colleges for it offered the possibility of status enhancement. Although at the time of the report about 90 per cent [2] of new recruits to teaching received their initial training in the colleges, the universities dominated the world of teacher training. They offered intellectual leadership and also controlled the content and validation of college courses through the Area Training Organizations. The report had explicitly acknowledged that it was no longer justifiable to hold the colleges in such inferior regard since they were capable of administering their own affairs and many of their students were deemed to be as able as their university counterparts. It is not surprising that the colleges were quick to take up the opportunity to 'academize' the curriculum, and so demonstrate their worth and independence. Even so, Eason and Croll (1970) in their study of college principals identified a tension between the need to introduce and maintain higher academic standards and the need to keep alive the tradition of the commitment to a vocational training.

In time this tension was to permeate the staff rooms of the colleges, but meanwhile the lack of qualified staff to teach the new disciplinary courses, particularly at degree level, was a serious problem. The best possible solution to this shortfall would have been to recruit new staff who were not only well qualified in the disciplines of education, but were also trained and experienced teachers. Such people were not easy to find and so a compromise was necessary. Since the education theory component was the degree qualifying element of the course, and, one may assume, the colleges were well staffed by those with an expertise in teaching, the most logical course was to recruit well qualified social scientists. This point has often been made (for example, Alexander, 1984) but the full implications for the future course of teacher education have not been acknowledged so readily. The dominance of the disciplines in the curriculum of initial training came about because they represented institutional progress to the colleges but also because their presentation became the responsibility of university educated tutors many of them with masters degrees. The disciplines had cachet. Their inclusion in the curriculum was justified epistemologically (see below) as well as professionally and they were delivered in the style of university lectures. The assignments associated with them were essays or the preparation of seminar papers not lesson plans or the making of materials for teaching practice. They disdained the practicalities of the classroom. They were the passport to achievement both for the colleges and for the individual student.

This curricular dominance of the disciplines of education was no guarantee of hegemonic dominance however. If it is accepted that the psychology, sociology, history and philosophy of education did encapsulate the values of the state, then by definition they can only qualify as hegemonic transmitters of those values if students voluntarily internalized and hence legitimated the particular perspectives, both substantive and methodological, that the disciplines promoted. There is some indication that this became the avowed aim of many of those teaching the disciplines of education in the colleges. If achievement here were to be the measure of degree level ability and attainment, then it was recognized that, as Musgrave (1965) puts it: it became 'essential . . . to equip the future teacher with a broad theoretical framework of sociology so that he learns the concepts and the main models that are used in this discipline . . . The stress is not on the learning of social facts, but on thinking sociologically' (p. 44). Although it cannot be either confirmed or disconfirmed (since students may have learned to demonstrate the appropriate academic skills in order to meet course requirements) it is suggested that the commitment to the substance of the disciplines of those students who took them at fourth year level was sincere, even if their handling of the methodology may have been weak. It is not unreasonable to assume that this group of potential graduate students evaluated the disciplines favourably. Since the take up of the BEd degree was slow (less than 5 per cent at the time of the report by Willey and Maddison in 1971) they were a minority group and their choice was likely to have been a positive one. Nor is it unreasonable to assume that having gained degrees in their respective subjects, the tutors who taught these students according to the university model at fourth year level were committed to the psychology, philosophy, history or sociology of education and probably would have conveyed this commitment to their students. There are therefore sound enough reasons for accepting that in the aftermath of the Robbins Report the curriculum of initial teacher training did indeed function hegemonically to sediment the ideology of the state but for only a limited number of students.

But it cannot be assumed that despite their popularity in some quarters, the disciplines of education with their power of ideological influence went unopposed elsewhere. Thus it is necessary to estimate the general degree of support that they attracted. It will be suggested in the following discussion that within the college and school community as a whole, commitment to the disciplines was less than whole hearted and that therefore the ideologically inspired Robbins Report achieved its hegemonic potential in the area of initial teacher training to only a limited degree. If the disciplines and the rigorous intellectual approach to learning that they embodied were welcomed by the more able students who stayed on for a fourth year and who had serious intellectual intentions, they were rejected by many other students as irrelevant for what went on in the classroom. In his detailed study of a college of education, Shipman (1967) found that students, the real target in the hegemonic process, 'gave a pragmatic school-oriented emphasis to their work and devalued professional theory' (p. 426). Apparently this was the response of many teachers in schools also. In an extensive survey of teachers and students which he undertook before the implementation of the Robbins revolution, Williams (1963) found that theory was ranked low on its value for teacher training in comparison with other aspects of the training course by both students and teachers. Even when theory alone was being considered, 'academic psychology was rejected in favour of psychology applied to the classroom' (p. 33). As might have been expected, students were found to be 'preoccupied with their ability to teach in the classroom and therefore welcomed plenty of opportunity to practice' (p. 32). That teachers exhibited little interest in theory was confirmed in another study by Griffiths and Moore (1967). When interviewed, nineteen out of twenty headteachers of schools taking students on teaching practice, appeared to have no detailed knowledge of the theoretical content of college courses, and none of them suggested that it might be useful to have this information. Given

Shipman's finding that the 'staffs of schools used for teaching practice were found to be an important influence on professional values' (1967, p. 426), it is concluded that the greater proportion of the student body were unlikely to have had much interest in the disciplines of education.

What of the rest of the tutors in the colleges who had had this unfamiliar form of theory[3] thrust upon them? Not only was it a form of theory which was alien to cultural norms, but the college staff were ill equipped to cope with it. What Bernbaum (1972) describes as the 'action orientation' of teacher training in the colleges, meant that there was little time or inclination to absorb these new perspectives. The tradition of intensive visiting of students on teaching practice, the small scale of many of the institutions which precluded subject specialization and encouraged tutors to be actively involved across a number of curricular fronts, in addition to the appointment of staff for their experience as teachers rather than for their academic attainment and the historical and cultural tradition which emphasized the importance of training in the practical skills of the classroom over the ability to engage in intellectual debate — all these factors were to ensure that in general the new form of theory fell if not on rock, at least on somewhat stony ground. If the disciplines were welcomed by some members of staff and particularly by the principals and other leading personnel within the colleges, they were also disparaged by others for they were perceived as contravening the college tradition of pragmatic professionalism. As one tutor put it, writing on *The Idea of the College of Education*: 'The tradition of the colleges, their concept of their duty as institutions of higher education, and the professional expertise, interest and concern of their staffs alike require the devotion of a substantial proportion of their energies and efforts towards the promotion of teaching skills. The colleges have no intention of being boxed and coxed out of this duty . . .' (*Education for Teaching*, 1967, p. 11). 'The student rightly demands from his higher education the achievement of some vocational objective . . .' (p. 12).

There seems to be quite substantial evidence that the introduction of the disciplines was accompanied by divisive tensions between staff. In 1969 Wadd constructed a model of the inclinations and attitudes of two ideal typical tutor types: the 'academic' and the 'personality oriented'. S(he) suggests that 'potential conflict between the two approaches is likely to be endemic in all Colleges of Education' (p. 30) and that this occurs particularly over the organization of the course, over teaching methods and in the education departments where some of the teaching was still done by personality oriented rather than academic staff. Evans (1969) confirms that the new measures were generating conflict:

> The colleges have to concern themselves with both the academic and the professional aspects of training, but the earlier emphasis on the professional has been replaced by a new found bias on the academic . . . Individual members of college Education departments have differing interpretations as to where they stand on the professional/academic continuum. Some see their manifest roles as 'pedagogics', with practical teaching as their prime concern, and the school as their reference group. Others see their manifest role as 'academics' emphasizing educational theory with the university as their reference group. These differing role perceptions reflect the different backgrounds, qualifications now to be found in education departments . . . (p. 51)

That these distinctions and divisions became institutionalized or structurally differentiated is acknowledged by Bartholomew (1975) who agrees that '. . . theory has grown as a study in separation from curricular and professional courses. It must also be noted that this separation is not just a knowledge separation, but that the knowledge separation is manifested in colleges and departments of education as a human separation' (p. 71). The new form of knowledge, theory, had generated its own kingdom which was not only conceptually and attitudinally but also structurally and socially distinct.

These events seem to support Gramsci's view that not only the content but the presentation of an ideology must be acceptable for its legitimation, and that this means matching it to the views, ideals and preferences of its target population. The same ideological principles underpinned both the pre- and post-Robbins forms of education studies but the university model received only variable endorsement from members of staff in the colleges for reasons which had little to do with its function in elevating the status of courses, but which reflected what might be termed its normative distance from the college culture with its emphasis on teaching as a practical activity.

To the reasons that have already been mentioned why theory was rejected can be added confusion over the nature of the theory–practice relationship. The location of education studies principally at the end of the training period where they remained divorced from work in schools, the influx of staff with disciplinary expertise but no necessary experience of, and perhaps little interest in, teaching in school, and the subsequent division within the staff according to teaching interests and commitments, all contributed to a separation of the overtly theoretical elements of the curriculum and the practical elements. Yet throughout this period, the importance of uniting theory and practice was stressed.

Discussing this relationship at the time of the Robbins Report, Hirst (1963) makes it clear that theory and practice should be closely integrated:

> Educational theory is primarily concerned with making practical judgments in answer to practical questions and it looks to philosophy and other studies for the particular forms of help they can provide. (p. 64)

There is no doubt that Peters (1967) also supports this view on this relationship: 'Selection from the content of the basic disciplines must in the main be determined by what is relevant to the practical problems and interests of teachers in training' (p. 156). These sentiments with respect to all four of the disciplines of education are reiterated throughout the 1960s. 'Theory . . . deals with the way educational thought is put into practice' (*Education for Teaching*, 1965, 67, p. 19). 'Theoretical studies should be designed to suggest practical lines of investigation or should arise and be developed out of real situations' (*ibid*, p. 26). 'There is a potential danger . . . that (the disciplines) could become more and more divorced from the central study of education and operate autonomously at a theoretical level. In an initial course of teacher training, the study of education should be based on what takes place in schools' (*Education for Teaching*, 1968, 77, p. 37). There was therefore agreement that theory of whatever kind — whether the impressionistic diffuse theory found in the colleges, or the more rigorous analytic theory of the universities — should have immediate practical value for the student's professional training.

Thus in addition to the distance between theory and practice in training (theory is seen as irrelevant), rhetoric and practice were also at odds. Moreover, the epistomological quality of the relationship between theory and practice was not clear. That there was confusion here is exemplified in the first quotation above (*Education for Teacher*, 67). What does 'deal with' mean here? Does theory guide practice or practice generate theory as the next quotation suggests? There was considerable disagreement and confusion about the nature of this relationship as the following quotations will show:

- —the theory of education 'forms a meeting point of different disciplines out of which a coherent basis for action can be created' (Grieff, 1967, p. 43);
- —'One of the values of theory is that it should construct "if . . . then" arrangements, thus providing a guide to action' (Evans, 1969, p. 54);

— 'Much theory will emerge through practice, many of the principles on which (students) future teaching will be based may be arrived at inductively' (Nias, 1974, p. 51);
— 'The function of theory is to determine precisely what shall and what shall not be done, say in education . . . yet . . . educational theory is in the first place to be understood as the essential background to rational educational practice' (Hirst, 1966, p. 40);
— 'there is no lack of agreement that educational theories are meant to guide and advise teachers in their educational activities' (Best, 1965, p. 40);
— 'suppose . . . a student is working under the supervision of a tutor; after the lesson, perhaps he will discuss it with the tutor and they will have a conversation about what was right or wrong with the teaching. They are theorising at a very practical level . . . This might easily lead to some development of social or psychological ideas . . . such discussions inevitably open up the way for more detached general and systematic study of various theoretical aspects of education' . . . (Reid, 1965, p. 19–20);
— '. . . in attempting to deal with all problems of education through a cluster of broad principles loosely organized, the theoretical statements, although apparently consistent, are in fact vacuous, for they permit no clear application to practice or even to the broadest policy making'. (Archambault, 1965, p. 3)

Education theory is then, a guide to practice or it determines it; it is the background to practice or the product of practice. Or it is so thin that it is really of very little use at all. It is suggested that this confusion about the way in which theory might be related to practice contributed to the discrediting of theory by both staff and students and hence to the rejection of the high status, centrally legitimated ideological element of the curriculum.

Thus the initial training system with all its apparent potential for the enhancement of hegemonic control in the post-Robbins era, seems to have had only limited success in this regard. It has been hypothesized that although the disciplines of education became well established as a consequence of a government intervention which was highly ideological in tone, and although they embodied the ideology of the state, they attracted only limited active consent from the tutorial staff and the students in the colleges and therefore did not fulfil their ideological promise. That the disciplines failed to a large extent to gain the type of support that would have made them fully effective instruments of hegemonic domination was due to factors which were quite beyond the influence of central government and the complexity of which it would have been difficult to anticipate. They were not challenged on ideological but on cultural grounds: the traditions of professional preparation as they existed in the colleges at the time. The ambivalent response to them which emerged in many colleges was born on the one hand of a recognition that this was where the future of teacher education lay and on the other of feelings of anxiety and resentment at the way in which they had usurped the curriculum and undermined what teacher training was all about. Some staff and fewer students were normatively committed to their presence and most probably their content also and therefore could be said to have become hegemonic subjects. But many staff particularly those engaged in teaching professional or curriculum courses, and possibly the majority of students who did not intend to take a degree and so only sampled the disciplines at a lower level, found them an irksome intrusion on the real business of training as they perceived it. That the new training curriculum was hegemonically weak should not be taken to imply that members of the college community did not support the values which the government espoused however. On the contrary, they are quite likely to have done so since these values were held by a high proportion of the electorate, but the curriculum of training was not the source of the strengthening of these values.

Summary

The conclusions reached in this section on the Hegemonic Failure of the Post-Robbins Curriculum are as follows:

- the reception afforded the theoretical curriculum which embodied the principles of social democracy varied within groups. Many tutors in the colleges of education rejected it because it contravened the traditions of teacher education in the non-university sector; and most students rejected it because it was deemed irrelevant for their immediate concerns as practitioners. However, it is likely that a minority of tutors and students were committed to the disciplines and the academic structure of the new curriculum;
- theory was also discredited because its relationship to practice remained controversial;
- in the colleges, divisions emerged between those teaching the disciplines of education and those teaching curriculum/

professional courses. This division became institutionalized in departments and faculties.

Implications for Ideological Theory

Further:

- Even where there seems to be every likelihood (in terms of the strength of its ideological representation) that a social structure will become hegemonically functional, this may not happen. The events described above confirm the importance that Gramsci attributes to the 'receptivity' of the target culture.
- There is no direct association between individual adherence to an ideologically infused institution and the personal ideological commitment of that individual. It is possible to subscribe to central values yet not support institutions which embody them, just as it is possible to entertain the alternative tension. The ease with which Althusser's subject is interpellated is therefore called into question, and a distinction must be made between ideological and hegemonic control. That individuals work in and are controlled by an environment which represents the ideology of the governing elite (ideological control) does not imply that they are necessarily hegemonic subjects.

Notes

1 *Education for Teaching*, the journal of the ATCDE and later of NATFHE, has been used as the source of much of the data on the developments in teacher education during the 1960s. The events and opinions recorded in a journal article are likely to be exceptional and therefore may not be representative of routine events in the training institutions. However, cumulatively the papers in *Education for Teaching* are considered to indicate current trends. For example, articles on the nature of the sociology of education at about the time of the Robbins Report suggest a confusion of direction and status.

2 The Robbins Report gives the number of students receiving teacher training in colleges of education in 1962/63 as 49,000 (p. 110) and those receiving postgraduate training in UDEs in 1961/62 as only 4450 (p. 26). For this reason the discussion of this chapter focuses on events in the colleges of education.

3 A reminder: the term 'theory' in this study, except where otherwise

indicated, refers to the disciplines of education and those curricular forms into which they evolved over time; and the term 'practice' to the practical elements of the curriculum: school experience and professional/curriculum/teaching methods courses.

3 The 1970s: Loss of Ideological Contact

Introduction

This chapter on the developments in the ITT curriculum which took place during the 1970s is divided into the same three sections as the previous chapters: ideological belief, ideological implementation and ideological achievement. The ways in which events during this period are reflected in these titles needs explanation however. In the section on ideological belief, the discussion focuses on the *lack* of a stable ideological message emanating from the centre during this period. It will be suggested that the political scene was confused and unsettled, the consensus which had been maintained in public by both parties, but which for some time had not been subscribed to quite so readily in private, having finally came to an end. There was no clear ideological presence. The parties were preoccupied with redefining their respective philosophies and the implications that these had for their political commitments. Neither Conservative nor Labour managed to stabilize its ideology either in terms of content or in terms of electoral support, and both were thrown off course by international events beyond their control.

With regard to initial training the response of successive governments to the economic dilemmas of the decade, and more particularly to the falling birth-rate, was to rationalize the public sector training institutions and then to rationalize them again through a prolonged programme of closures, diversification or amalgamations. It was the training system itself rather than the curriculum which was the major and urgent target of central intervention therefore. Only at the time of the James Report (1972) was there the possibility that the government might directly influence the initial training curriculum and this was not borne out to any significant degree. This was a period when the state and the teacher training system drew apart. It was a time when the professional society reached a 'plateau of attainment' (Perkin, 1989). Perkin defines a professional society as one which 'accepted in principle that ability and expertise were the only respectable justification for recruitment to positions of authority and responsibility . . .' (p. 405).

The mid-1970s were the fading years of an era when the intellectuals enjoyed considerable freedom from political control and when 'university teaching became the key profession which educated for, controlled access to and did much of the research for the other professions' (p. 395). The universities were powerful, therefore, and it is suggested that in the 1970s, when government was perceived as weak, the professionals as authoritative laymen, filled the vacuum created by the lack of political leadership. Perkins suggests that 'the professional ideal was the organizing principle of post-war society' (p. 406). Yet by the end of the decade the influence of intellectuals on national policy was beginning to diminish and during the 1980s, they were largely ignored (Paxman, 1990). If the centre neither displayed ideological leadership nor intervened in the teacher training curriculum in the 1970s then two questions arise. First, how did the curriculum evolve in this ideological vacuum and second, who was responsible for steering the curriculum in the direction that it took. These questions are dealt with in the second section of this chapter which is therefore also concerned with an absence — that of ideological implementation.

The first question is investigated by analyzing three samples of proposals for training courses, submitted for validation to the Council for National Academic Awards during the period 1972–1982, (data from the university departments not being available for this period), and six research reports published at the end of the decade. The major dimensions used for this analysis are those of curriculum structure and personnel involvement (Furlong *et al*, 1988). Although developments in the curriculum of training during this period have been fully described by several writers (for example, Alexander, 1984; Lynch, 1979), this investigation of course curricula was deemed to be necessary nevertheless, for the following reasons:

- in studies of teacher training, curricular developments tend to lack political contextualization and in order to fully explore the evolving relationship between ideology and the culture of training it was felt necessary to study curriculum change in detail;
- teacher training is rarely presented as a sub-culture and to portray it from this perspective requires the identification of areas of stability and continuity as well as areas of change. Studies of the training curriculum tend to explore the latter much more fully than the former;
- ideology is reflected in the distribution of power, and accounts of curricular development rarely include information which will make possible an assessment of the power relations between

> the various groups in teacher training, particularly between the schools and the training institutions, the term 'partnership' being a catch-all description which tells us little.

The analysis of course submissions to CNAA shows that at the beginning of the decade, the disciplines of education dominated training. Within ten years, in the public sector institutions at least, emphasis within the curriculum was shifting away from the disciplines of education (theory) towards curriculum courses and school experience (practice) and a closer association with schools. These changes, which were of a slow evolutionary nature, are also found in a number of studies of initial training in the colleges and polytechnics which were published at the end of the decade. However, a comprehensive survey of UDEs published at that time indicates that in the universities, training courses had changed little. The revaluation of courses which had taken place in the public sector institutions did not herald a return to the pre-Robbins form of training however. The theory which had been introduced in the aftermath of the report was in time to become practical theory. Thus teacher training retained a theoretical element, but could be said to have domesticated the ideologically infused input from the government. These events suggest that the institution of teacher training actively engages with ideological intervention. The Robbins Report had been a far reaching, highly intrusive government measure, which had significantly influenced the course of training programmes. But during the 1960s and 1970s, the curricular reforms introduced by the report underwent a process of gradual change, and ironically prepared the training system to receive a further ideological onslaught in the 1980s. The second question above concerns the locus of responsibility for these curricular changes. Having reviewed the developments that took place, the discussion continues with an assessment of the influence of six potential agents of change: central government, the participants in training, those participating in academic debate, CNAA, the professional associations, and HM Inspectorate. It is concluded that the modification of the theoretical curriculum can be attributed principally to dissatisfaction with the *status quo* within the teacher training community itself, and that therefore the evolution of training came about largely as a consequence of reflection and critique within the professional discourse.

There can be no question of hegemonic gain on the part of the government if there has been no ideological intervention. Therefore the opportunity is taken in the third section of this chapter to elaborate the dynamic relationship between the curriculum as a cultural tradition and ideology from the perspective of the former rather than the latter. It is concluded that culture must intrinsically oppose ideology, but that it may also facilitate its penetration. To illustrate these points, reference is made to the college curriculum in the 1960s and to parallels to the ideology of Thatcherism in the college curriculum of the late 1970s. It is hypothesized that the relationship between ideology and culture at the site of the curriculum of initial training is therefore interactive.

The aims of the following chapter which considers the events of the 1970s are as follows therefore:

(i) **Ideological belief**
to demonstrate the loss of consensus between the two political parties and the subsequent lack of a firm central ideological message;

(ii) **Ideological implementation**
to demonstrate (a) the way in which in the absence of an ideological input, the curriculum evolved towards a more practical form of training, and in the absence of government intervention to assess (b) the respective contributions to this development of a number of agencies;

(iii) **Ideological achievement**
in the absence of any possibility of ideological achievement, to explore further the culture-ideology relationship from the cultural perspective, and to suggest that culture can both oppose and facilitate the penetration of ideology.

Ideological Belief: The Loss of Ideological Consensus

The events of the 1970s strongly support Althusser's emphasis on the strength of the relationship between ideology and the economy. The ideological saturation of economic policy and hence the impossibility of considering the economy apart from ideology except for analytic purposes is exemplified in Keynesianism. With its goals of full employment, price stability and economic growth, and the interventionist role allocated to the state in maintaining these through demand management, this approach to macroeconomic policy did indeed reflect the principles of the consensus. Throughout the 1960s Keynesianism had been supported by both Labour and Conservative governments in turn and its success as an economic strategy had seemed possible, for despite all the difficulties of expansion followed by retrenchment that characterized that decade, there was sufficient economic growth to fund the public sector. Successive governments had managed to maintain the balance necessary in a mixed economy between social spending and growth in the private sector (Plant, 1983). But as the 1970s advanced, it became increasingly difficult to fund the social justice programme from the profitability of private industry without the inflationary pressure of increased public borrowing. From 1974–76, total public expenditure was over 50 per cent of GDP (Gould and Roweth, 1978) and of this, the 'transfer payment' element (i.e. unemployment benefits, social security payments etc) was a very substantial element. As the levels of government expenditure required to meet the aims and ideals of the founders of the Welfare State continued to rise, the economy, particularly after the oil crisis of 1973/74, became progressively less able to support these demands. Following the increase in the price of oil the balance of payments went into deficit, taxes and interest rates were raised and stock building and capital formation both declined. Hughes (1986) summarizes the developments which characterized the deindustrialization of the UK during the 1970s in a series of dimensions of decline. These include the fall in manufacturing employment, the weakening of net exports, the decline in manufacturing's share of GDP and the decline in manufacturing investment. The outcome of such developments could only be that revenue fell as state expenditure increased, generating a 'fiscal crisis of the state' (O'Connor, 1973). A more detailed account of the reasons for our relative economic decline is neither relevant nor possible here. Our concern is with the effect of that decline on the ideological climate of the times. There is in any case no agreement between economists themselves concerning the root causes of the UK's loss of economic status during this period. For example Donaldson and Farquhar (1988) point to the inherent weaknesses of Keynesianism: the incompatibility of its objectives, and in particular whether it is possible to maintain full employment without generating inflation. Gamble (1985) prefers to emphasize the influence of developments overseas: 'British decline can only be understood and in some sense only perceived when it is related to the world economy which Britain once dominated and to which it has remained chained long after its dominance has passed away' (p. 10).

The explanations of Donaldson and Gamble are but two of many as the range of papers edited by Coates and Hillard in the *Economic Decline of Modern Britain* (1986) demonstrates. These papers are arranged according to political perspective: The View from the Right, The View from the Centre, Marxist Views of Industrial Decline etc. It thus becomes clear that the economic crises of the 1970s released the political Left and Right from the bondage of a united ideological commitment, since the parties had to find their respective explanations of, and solutions to, these crises. It was no longer necessary to subscribe to social democracy. Rather it became legitimate to comment on its decline from the perspective of alternative political traditions. It is worth quoting at length Coates' own summary of the views to demonstrate this point:

> There is of course no shortage of answers to that question (why British capitalism has proved so vulnerable to the world recession). The excessive power of trade unions . . . is a favourite of many commentators on the Right and Centre of British politics. So too is the thesis of excessive government activity. . . . Monetarists too tend to blame governments for protecting and subsidizing firms and for making credit too easily available, all of which lessens in their view, the impact of those important market pressures which alone can spur essential innovation and rationalization . . . There is also the argument, often seized upon by those with right-wing political leanings, that it is the excessive expansion of state employment that holds the key to Britain's relative economic decline . . .
>
> Explanations from the Centre of British politics tend to be gentler, emphasizing a whole range of relatively disparate factors as causes of economic decline: the low level of demand in the home market, poor quality management, inadequate provision for industrial retraining, deficiencies in our education system, the damaging impact of perpetually changing government policies, the excessive centralisation of decision making . . .
>
> The parliamentary Left . . . tends to emphasise low levels of industrial investment, the absence of economic planning and the persistence of social inequalities as causes of industrial decay. The Labour Left criticize the Thatcher government for failing to reflate the economy . . . They are also highly critical of the financial institutions of the City. . . . and point to the problems of controlling and harnessing industrial activity behind nationally specified goals without an extension of public ownership . . .
>
> *From these arguments . . . very clear political programmes directly emerge* . . . (Coates, 1986, pp. 267–8, *emphasis added*)

Gamble (1985) also notes that economic decline has had 'a major impact on the party system and the authority of the state' . . . 'The failure of either party despite intentions, to reverse or even halt decline, and the steady worsening of Britain's economic problems seriously undermined the stability of the two party system . . . led to a marked polarization between the parties in ideological terms . . . At the heart of the new ideological ferment lies the plight of the economy. Left and Right attacks on the consensus long preceded the recession, but they have been greatly amplified by it' (pp. 40–2). Other authors (for example, Holmes, 1985a; Mosley, 1986) make the same point, though perhaps less forcefully. Thus although there is little agreement on the reasons for the collapse of the consensus, there is considerable support for the view that it was undermined by incompatible economic developments. Whether writers stress political or economic factors as the dynamic of the fiscal crisis (Cochrane, 1989), it is clear that support for the Welfare State was no longer unquestioning and also that doubts about its effectiveness in social terms were being raised (Hill and Bramley, 1986).

By the middle of the 1970s then there was no consistent ideological message emanating from central government, which consequently was considered to be weak. Not only were the parties pursuing their respective and widely divergent ideological tracks, but within each party, further divisions of opinion had become apparent. While many on the Left believed that the Labour party had lost its commitment to socialism, it was the Labour party and not the Conservatives which shattered the consensus, abandoned Keynesianism and had introduced monetarism by the end of 1976 (Holmes, 1985a). The Conservatives were now free to revert to a *laissez-faire* approach, but they also were divided amongst themselves according to the degree with which they supported free market policies.

According to Ecceshall (1990) 'there had always been some Conservatives who disapproved of the party's postwar conversion to "humanized" capitalism' (p. 203). Now the collapse of the consensus enabled them to show their true political colours once again. The recent past quickly became something to excuse, an aberration. As Bogdanor (1976) puts it: 'the role of the Conservative party during (the 1960s) was a passive one: it found itself unable to combat the new consensus, some Conservatives, dazzled by contemporary fashions were happy to accept it, but most Conservatives remained obstinately attached to the *status quo*' (p. 118). Conservatism had not died with the advent of the consensus, but its opposition to it had become covert. The party was biding its time behind closed doors, recognizing that the electorate might not be ready for any substantial change in policy. Ramsden's (1980) account of the work of the Conservative Research Department during the middle decades of this century is a good example of Gramsci's insight concerning the need for those in power to temper their policies with an assessment of the public mood. One of the themes running through this text is the tension between the would-be radicalism of the Research Department and other policy influencing groups and the pragmatism of the government which was cautious of the degree of change that the electorate might tolerate. In summarizing the debates on denationalization in his chapter on the 1950s, headed 'Setting Britain Free', Ramsden comments: 'The problem was balancing practicality (both industrial and political) against the demands of ideology . . .' (p. 154). In 1962, the Research Department 'came round to a more interventionist line' on how to encourage the unions to collaborate on government policy, although its recommendations were 'not a recipe that was likely to appeal to a government in a trough of unpopularity . . .' (p. 221). Believing that the government could afford to be more assertive in meeting its critics, the Department urged that it 'put more passion and enthusiasm into their public approach to our affairs. The public cannot be soothed by kindly moderation' (p. 224). The loss of the 1964 election was to convince many in the party that 'it was now necessary to adopt more radical approaches and in this, many of the subordinated themes of 1959–64 were now to become dominant' (p. 230).

By 1965 as leader of the party, Heath had taken control of policy matters and the Research Department came directly under his chairmanship and was engaged in a programme of consultation with academics, as Gramsci might have foreseen. Heath was well aware of the difficulties of presenting a political case in such a way that it would be understood by the electorate and also appear attractive to them. 'I do believe that we have to find new practical ways in which to apply our principles to current problems. Abstract conceptions are extremely difficult to put across to a mass electorate. If one speaks of preserving market forces or the need to diversify the centres of power in society, one is understood by only a small minority of the electorate (quoted in Ramsden, 1980, p. 241). Even if the sentiments of practicality and assertiveness contributed to Heath's undoing, they were now to become the established approach of the Conservatives. The failure of Heath's government to sustain its free market strategy followed by two defeats at the polls in 1974, forced and also permitted the party to reassess and articulate its policies and to consider taking a more active stance. This change of direction is very apparent in the papers in *The Conservative Opportunity* (1976) edited by Blake and Patten, a text which shows how distant from social democracy Conservatism had become. Blake suggests that a change of climate is occurring. In 1970, the opinion formers were anti-Conservative. There was no serious challenge in intellectual circles to the accepted shibboleths of high public expenditure, high taxation and a rising role for the state (p. 2). Now (1976) there are signs of a revolt against Keynesianism. There are misgivings not only about the economics of welfare, but also about its principles. This being so, 'the Conservatives have an excellent chance of recovering power and doing so on the basis of a new orthodoxy' (p. 7).

The break-up of the consensus should be viewed not only from the perspective of the political parties, but also from the perspective of the hegemonic subject, the member of the electorate. During the post-war period through to the 1960s, successive British governments enjoyed relative ideological dominance, there being public support for their (common) policies. However, Harrop (1986) suggests that 'British elections are more often about competence than policies. They are about the parties' abilities to achieve shared objectives . . . not the objectives themselves. They are about the parties' capacity to govern — their coherence, their direction, their implementation skills' (p. 52). Thus declining support for the government may be attributed either to lack of hegemonic power or the loss of ideological grip; or it may be attributed not to a rejection of the ideology *per se* so much as to the government's lack of success at managing the relationship between ideology and policy. This distinction is an important one since it allows for at least a degree of continuity of support for the ideology of welfare, yet also accommodates the fall in support for the government which took place during the 1970s.

Leys (1989) notes the decline in public support for both parties at this time. The Labour and Conservative combined vote as a percentage of the electorate fell from 64.3 to 54. 9 between 1970 and 1974, with the Conservatives losing rather more support than the Labour party. At the October 1974 election, the Conservatives polled their lowest percentage vote since 1935 (35.8 per cent) and Labour, suffering from splits and defections was returned with a majority of only three over all the other parties. Such a loss of public confidence is hardly surprising. There had been the *volte face* of the Heath government which swung from the withdrawal of state support for ailing industries back to subsidizing them rather than see them collapse. Inflation had increased, so had unemployment. Whole sectors of manufacturing industry were disappearing and there was persistent and damaging industrial unrest. And government policy towards the unions swung between control through legislation (Conservative) and cooperative involvement in decision-making (Labour). The decline in public esteem for a political leadership which appeared weak, indecisive and incompetent was indeed considerable, and this has important consequences for our argument. It is suggested that the lack of political leadership from the centre left a power vacuum which came to be filled by the professionals. Also that in the absence of a strong circumscribing ideological climate, the professionals were free to propose and develop their ideas and practices. The state of political upheaval in the 1970s is deemed not only to have left social institutions bereft of ideological leadership but also to have enhanced the authority of professionals and provided them with the opportunity to promote new intellectual movements.

Summary

The conclusions reached in this section on The Loss of Ideological Contact are as follows:

- during the 1970s the ideological consensus came to an end and the major political parties began to redefine their respective doctrinal positions;
- the factors contributing to this were many and various but principal among them was the inability of the economy to meet the demands of the Welfare State;
- an ideological vacuum developed: no coherent presentation of principles and priorities emerged from the centre;
- this enabled the professions to dominate social life: they offered leadership in an era when central government was inconsistent in both word and deed;
- the government's association with teacher training was limited to severely cutting provision, this decision being dictated by demographic forecasts and the need for economic stringency: it did not intervene directly in the curriculum.

Implications for Ideological Theory

Further:

- The events of the 1970s strongly support Althusser's emphasis on the strength of the relationship between ideology and the economy, and the dominance by the latter of the former. Although as Gramsci maintains, this relationship is not always predictable or unilateral — here both political parties continued to advocate social democratic principles long after in retrospect, the economy was able to meet the demands of the welfare programme (Clarke, 1973) — it was economic crises which finally brought about the disintegration of the consensus.

Ideological Implementation

Curricular Developments in the Absence of Government Intervention

In the 1970s, when a major concern of sociologists of education was the politics of the curriculum, it was recognized that both the substance of the curriculum in its many forms and also the range of teacher behaviours associated with that curriculum could be the means of conveying a particular political perspective. Therefore for the purposes of detecting the continuity or breakdown of ideological influence within initial training, both the content of the curriculum and the tasks, the status and the influence of those who teach that curriculum should be analyzed with respect to the relationship between theory (the disciplines of education) and practice (school experience and courses in subject pedagogy), this relationship having been identified as the site of ideological struggle. A detailed analysis of the curriculum of the kind implied here was not possible for the decade of the 1960s since the necessary data on the courses validated by the Area Training Organizations (ATOs) is not readily available. The arguments of the previous chapter were constructed principally by reference to papers in journals. But in order to demonstrate the ways in which this curriculum subsequently developed and was transformed within the professional community itself, more detailed continuous information is required. What were the processes of cultural elaboration in Archer's terms?

As the 1970s advanced, the availability of information on the training curriculum increased, since after the James Report (1972) many of the public sector institutions turned to the Council for National Academic Awards (CNAA) for validation of their courses and their submission documents remain stored in the CNAA archives and are available on request to the institutions concerned. It was considered that reference to this data should yield a relatively representative portrait of initial training in the colleges and during the 1970s since the numbers of students registered for BEd training:

> developed dramatically from some 400 registrations in 1970/71 to some 15,000 by 1980/81. The institutions involved in this very substantial movement towards CNAA validation included polytechnic departments, monotechnic colleges seeking greater autonomy, diversifying and amalgamating colleges forced into new validation arrangements by the revisions to the system through the mid to late 1970s. They . . . provide . . . a widely representative

> range of views on teacher education . . . Whilst other validating bodies have considerable local significance and national reputation, none comes close to the Council in sheer size, or in national significance, and most have experienced a decline in validation involvement during the period of growth in CNAA . . . (Sharples, 1984, pp. 71–2)

Consequently an investigation was undertaken of three randomly selected samples of course submissions to CNAA taken from the years 1973–74, 1977–78 and 1981–82. These documents were analyzed according to a schedule devised both deductively and inductively, details of which can be found in the Appendix. The outcome of this investigation is summarized below according to the dimensions featuring in the schedule.[1]

- **Analysis of Course Aims**
  Initially (sample 1) aims were expressed more frequently in terms of aims for the student than for the course, and the personal intellectual development of the student in one form or another was the most commonly cited, reflecting the concerns of the Robbins Report. By sample 3 the aims or objectives of all courses indicated the importance attached to the training of students to demonstrate competence in the classroom.
- **Analysis of Course Structure and Content**
  Although there was wide variation between institutions in this category, in general:
  — the time spent by students in school increased considerably during the investigation period;
  — serial visits became commonplace;
  — school placements in year 4 became usual rather than exceptional;
  — initially the disciplines were taught as discrete curricular subjects in most institutions but declined in prominence during the period of the enquiry and by sample 3 were found most frequently as options in the fourth year of the Honours courses but even then relatively rarely;
  — commonly the disciplines became integrated either thematically when they focused on school-related issues, and in time with professional or curriculum courses; or there were attempts to use the disciplines to illuminate classroom practice;
  — time spent in school was increasingly structured, students

being required to undertake defined practical tasks such as observation or a school-based project;
- —units or modules in the general skills of classroom management and organization began to appear: by sample 2, this aspect of training had greatly expanded;
- —on a few courses it was apparent that students would be encouraged to generate grounded theory;
- —in a few cases, education studies was placed within the professional studies division or equivalent.

- **Analysis of Partnership (Personnel Involvement)**
  There was considerable variation between institutions in this respect also:
  - —it remained usual for submissions to refer only to organisational arrangements when discussing school experience; teachers were rarely mentioned.
  - —the term 'teaching practice' was largely replaced by alternative terms such as 'school experience', a change which seems to herald an emerging recognition that training should encompass all aspects of the teachers' role and not merely classroom practice.
  - —increasingly teachers were expected to assess students but relatively rarely were they expected to supervise the student, thereby implying an absence of active authorized involvement in students' training in school.
  - —the domination of schools by the institutions continued though disguised by a cloak of 'partnership': tutors visited schools regularly and tended to define the student's work.
  - —in a very few submissions considerable power, relatively speaking, was to be ceded to the schools; one of these explicitly states the need to bring relationships into line with the integration of theory and practice in the curriculum, another that students would teach within the framework laid down by the school.
  - —teachers were appointed to higher education institution (HEI) committees, but usually in token numbers.
  - —it was now proposed, though infrequently that teachers should lecture in the HEIs.

According to this analysis of initial training submissions to the CNAA, the period between the early 1970s and the early 1980s saw the return to a more equitable balance between the theoretical and the practical aspects of the curriculum. Courses were hugely diverse, yet the general trend over time was one of a reduction in the many ways indicated above, of the status and purity of the disciplines and a more positive valuation of practical work. As has been indicated, these developments were supported with sufficient confidence and faith to become institutionalized in changes in social structures, as education studies tutors lost power relative to those working in the professional/curriculum areas. However, the investigation also suggests that despite a more frequent mention of 'partnership' with schools during those years, the increasing commitment to a more practical form of training in the HEIs had failed to generate a comparable redistribution of power and responsibility from tutors to teachers.

These developments did not mean that 'the Robbins effect' had been eliminated. The report had bequeathed degree standards in training, and training in general had become more demanding. But the other legacy of Robbins — education studies — had been less welcome. Once training to teach had become established as a degree qualification however, it became less necessary to retain the unwanted theory, and the way was clear for re-establishing a more comfortable distribution of theory and practice. In summary: if teacher training in the public sector institutions, and in the colleges particularly, had incorporated certain aspects of the Robbins reforms (academic standards and methods), it had modified others (theory gradually became theorizing) and rejected still others (the dominance of substantive theory). These developments had taken place over time and may be construed as the profession both reaping the benefits of an ideological intervention and in time making that intervention its own through the selective use of what it had to offer.

Research Investigations Published 1979–82

Towards the end of the 1970s, six accounts of research investigations into initial teacher training were published. These included a survey of all the university departments of education (UDEs). Differing in their aims as well as in their methodologies, these studies are difficult to compare. Nevertheless, to a greater or lesser degree, they can be used to confirm (or challenge), illustrate and in some cases elaborate and extend the conclusions reached in the analysis of course submissions above. Second, since these studies record not only intentions for practice but also perceptions of practice, they offer the opportunity to obtain information on how developments in the the substance and processes of training were regarded by the various personnel involved. In general these studies confirm that by the late 1970s there continued to be considerable variation across initial teacher training courses in both of the dimensions used for the analysis of the CNAA samples: the structure of the curriculum and the respective contributions to training of tutor and teacher. It is only now with the availability of data on the university departments of education that the extent of this variation becomes evident, for although there is variety across courses run by the colleges and polytechnics whether these courses are validated by CNAA or by the universities, on the whole these distinctions are not so great as the distinction between these courses and the courses run by the UDEs for their own student teachers. These research studies confirm the conclusions reached in the analysis of the CNAA submissions: that by the end of the 1970s and the beginning of the 1980s, the curriculum of training had become more practical in the various structural and substantive ways already mentioned, but that this shift in emphasis had not been matched by a corresponding increase in the responsibility given to teachers for the training of the students who now spent longer periods in their schools. That the CNAA was uneasy about the lack of collaboration between the institutions and their schools was apparent in its wish that in funding the first research study listed below, 'the further development of a more closely defined framework of co-operation for the benefit of staff in schools and colleges and students in training' (p. 7) might emerge.

The six studies included two edited collections of case studies, three reviews of BEd courses and the investigation of university departments of education. Five of the projects were undertaken by academics, and one by HM Inspectorate. They are reviewed in chronological order and only the major points of interest in each will be listed here:

(i) McCulloch, M. (1979) *School Experience in Initial BEd/BEd Honours Degrees Validated by CNAA*, CNAA
ten teachers, ten tutors and ten students from each of a representative sample of six colleges were questioned for this survey. In addition, reference was made to all BEd submissions already lodged with the CNAA and data (including a questionnaire on assessment) was obtained from all institutions with CNAA-validated BEd degrees.
This study found:

- on course structure and content:
  - — confirmation of the details of the curriculum given in the previous section concerning the time spent in school and the integration of theory and practice;

— that 'the provision of sustained school experience finds great favour amongst all participants in initial teacher education' (p. 29) though with teachers and students to a greater degree than with tutors;

- on personnel involvement (partnership):
  — a serious lack of communication between the two partners;
  — that as a consequence, the role of the teacher in training the student was too often left implicit (p. 31), and since the less well informed partner is disadvantaged, the balance of power favoured the training institution. The college feels the relationship (with the school) to be 'guest/host rather than as equal partners participating in a shared professional venture' (p. 29);
  — reason to believe that in reality, and as might be expected, many teacher supervisors undertook some training of their students, but they neither fully articulated their input to training nor was it acknowledged by the institutions. McCulloch recognizes 'the political significance' of this situation.

(ii) HM Inspectorate (1979) *Developments in the BEd Degree Course: A Study Based on Fifteen Institutions*, HMSO
A survey of BEd courses in three polytechnics, nine colleges and three monotechnics. The BEd degrees at nine of the institutions were validated by universities and the remaining six by the CNAA.
This study found:

- on course structure and content:
  — that the time spent by students in school was rather lower than the CNAA samples, thus seeming to confirm that there was considerable variation between institutions;
  — separate professional studies departments which were usually a recent creation (p. 4) in over a third of institutions;
  — an increased importance attributed to the practical elements of training indicated by the following: professional studies were weighted 'at least as heavily as any others in deciding the award and classification of the degree' (p. 18); 'colleges were developing practical exercises which were college-based' (p. 12); 'the

honours year programme very often included a special study which was to incorporate school-based enquiry'; and in some cases Education Studies could add to expertise in a very practical way (p. 23);

— that 'expression of dissatisfaction by students and in some cases staff were more commonly concerned with (Education Studies) than with any other part of the BEd course . . . The lack of obvious relevance in education studies was the source of most student complaint' (p. 13);

— confirmation of the introduction of theorizing noted in the CNAA samples;

— confirmation that the institutions frequently ran units on general classroom skills.

(iii) Alexander, R. and Wormald, E. (Eds) (1979) *Professional Studies for Teaching*, Society for Research into Higher Education Five essays on issues and trends in professional studies are followed by twelve case studies of BEd courses in public sector institutions, nine of which were validated by the CNAA and the remaining three by universities.

The essays:

- celebrate the new found status of professional studies which is exemplified in the title of the book;
- place professional studies at the heart of training, giving them primacy over disciplinary theory which progressively refines them (Hirst);
- wish to see the status of professional studies raised (McNamara and Desforges).

The case studies:

Most of the courses described in this publication were developed as critiques of the post-Robbins BEd. This text provides an opportunity for the institutions to publicize their respective courses in the best possible light, and it is possible that some claims made here might not be borne out in practice. But a few quotations from these accounts[2] will illustrate the way in, and extent to, which professional preparation has been redirected in favour of school-focused training during the fifteen years since Robbins. Although they have lost their authority the disciplines remain and professional studies are in the ascendant. Theory is being transformed into theorizing. Teachers have little power.

- On course structure and content (the nature and place of professional studies):
  - — '. . . the whole of the final year is "professionally" oriented; it includes curriculum studies, teaching practice and education studies' (p. 101);
  - — 'the professional studies module occupies half the contact time of year 2, three-quarters of the contact time in year 3 and half the contact time of the Honours year' (p. 114);
  - — 'many tutors . . . feel that the course would have benefited if it had provided the students with . . . more substantial periods of school experience' (p. 133);
  - — 'the rationale (of the professional studies course) is firmly rooted on a belief in the uniqueness of the teacher taking decisions according to his own theories of action within particular contexts' (p. 86);
  - — 'a major change occurred . . . All professional work was put under the heading of professional studies . . . the Course Director of the BEd was also the Dean of Education . . . (When he left the Directorship) the Head of Professional Studies assumed this role' (p. 123);
  - — '. . . the structure of the degree . . . defines each major element in relation to the professional context in which the student's knowledge is to be applied . . .' (p. 84).
- On partnership:
  - — 'regular conferences have been held between teachers and tutors, to discuss and agree expectations and procedure, but the nature of the difference between school contexts makes the identification of more than a common core of expectations improbable' (p. 90);
  - — 'close links exist between the college and (the) schools, within each of which there is a designated teacher who gives special support to the (students) there . . .' (p. 108);
  - — 'there are inherent and unstated power conflicts in evidence . . . There is the hierarchy of power between the college which trains and the teachers who do' (p. 71).

(iv) Alexander, R. and Whittaker, J. (Eds) (1980) *Developments in PGCE Courses*, Society for Research into Higher Education
Four introductory papers on background and research projects

are followed by sixteen accounts by tutors of different aspects of PGCE courses. Six of the courses are validated by the CNAA, two by universities and eight are courses run by university departments of education. One advantage of the PGCE course is that it can be more readily revised than a four-year BEd and in the 1970s many institutions took advantage of the opportunities offered by a change to CNAA as the validating body to devise some new highly innovative PGCE courses. The themes in this collection are the same as before: the relationship between theory and practice, school experience and the relationship between tutor and teacher. As before, some quotations of interest have been selected.

- On aims:
  - 'in developing the PGCE course, we have been very much concerned to produce in our students the maximum operational efficiency for a first teaching appointment' (p. 56);
  - 'to equip students with the knowledge, skills and confidence necessary for their first teaching posts . . .' (p. 78).
- On course structure and content:
  - 'we decided to reverse the usual process and we planned the nature and extent of school experience first and then fitted the college course round it' (p. 99);
  - 'even in 1969, we were designing a course against a background of growing dissatisfaction with the traditional form of the PGCE. . . . Our response was to abandon the traditional disciplines of education in favour of curriculum theory as an appropriate field of study: curriculum theory draws from the traditional disciplines of education' (p. 62);
  - 'courses in separate disciplines were ended — in most cases with the relieved concurrence of those teaching them' (p. 67);
  - '. . . the adoption of microteaching techniques and the introduction of a thematic approach to education studies . . . were mainly ad hoc measures in response to the most frequently repeated student criticisms. Transfer to the CNAA as the validating authority for the PGCE encouraged a fundamental re-examination of the rationale and structure of the course' (p. 83);

— 'the focus of theoretical work is limited to issues that will affect the student's practice. The bulk of college time is devoted to identifying and practising classroom skills . . .' (p. 141)

- On partnership
  — 'the teachers are also given details of the education assignments and we request their cooperation not in tutoring the students in any way, but in providing opportunities for the students to carry out the necessary investigations and teaching in order to write their assignments. . . . We also visit the students in school to tutor them at least once a week during teaching practice and we talk to the teachers at the same time' (p. 81);
  — 'the professional course with school attachment as a central part has been planned by teachers in the schools concerned, education tutors and methods tutors' (p. 84);
  — 'teachers are not teacher trainers and, if they are to play such a role in a major way, professional preparation seems essential' . . . 'College tutors have become more a part of the school' (pp. 100–1).

(v) McNamara, D. and Ross, A.M. (1982) *The BEd Degree and Its Future*, University of Lancaster
In contrast to the previous two studies, this survey gives us a broad picture of the current patterns of training. Seventeen institutions of different types (colleges, polytechnics and universities) were studied, nine having their BEd degrees validated by the CNAA and eight by UDEs. Questionnaires were sent to all members of staff teaching on the BEd course and to a stratified sample of 100 students in each institution. This study, better than any other, expresses tutors' difficulty in trying to reconcile academic values ('standards must be seen to be maintained') with an awareness of the importance of professional preparation.
The following points are made:

- that the reorganization of the college network resulted in an increase in the diversity of training programmes;
- that there was general agreement that there had been an extension of bureaucracy as the demand to submit new course proposals had risen. But nevertheless '*the teacher training tradition has clearly been strong enough, so far,*

to persist, whatever the present administrative organisation might be' (p. 17, emphasis added);

- that members of the professional community are struggling to steer training in a more school-focused direction: 'It could be said that the teacher education institutions in the 1970s, particularly those validated by the CNAA , but also those validated by the universities which decided to continue their relationship with the colleges, made important advances towards defining what is meant by a professional degree' (p. 40);
- that a successful response to the challenge of change and development depends particularly on the quality of the leadership within the institution.

(vi) Patrick, H., Bernbaum, G. and Reid, K. (1982) *The Structure and Process of Initial Teacher Education within Universities in England and Wales* (the SPITE study), University of Leicester. In this survey of all staff and students at all university departments of education a further investigation of sub-samples of each group was undertaken. Very little reference has been made to developments in the university sector during the two decades of the 1960s and 1970s, there being a lack of the kind of detailed information that is available on CNAA-validated institutions. However, at the end of the 1970s, Patrick and her colleagues carried out an extensive survey of training in all UDEs. It can reasonably be assumed that whatever this survey revealed in terms of the relationship between theory and practice, that stage of development will have been preceded by a less advanced stage given the general trend towards a more school-based form of training. It is unlikely, for example, that over this period, courses at UDEs had become even more theoretical. Thus given the comprehensiveness of the survey the lack of previous information on university departments is not such a handicap to a discussion on the development of training in the universities as might at first appear. Nor is it considered of great significance that this was a survey of PGCE courses only. Since the structure and substance of a course reflect certain attitudes and priorities within the institution, it is quite probable that all courses in an institution will be based on similar principles. Some comparison with BEd courses is deemed possible therefore.

This study found:

- on aims:
  - when tutors were asked about their personal aims, '... it was clear that the aims most frequently mentioned were essentially practical ...' (p. 203) ... and when asked about the aims of their department, nearly 60 per cent 'thought that enabling the students to develop the skills necessary for the exercise of classroom discipline and control was a highly important aim ...' (p. 202). The aim which fewest staff thought highly important in their department was that of 'inducting the student into the disciplines of education' (p. 202).
- on course structure and content:
  - there was sufficient variation between courses to make sampling difficult;
  - students spent less time in school than their public sector counterparts, more than a third of the UDEs placing their students in school for one long block teaching practice;
  - 'it is worth noting that there are large numbers of students who appeared to do no (school) visiting at all' (p. 49); and 'over 40 per cent of the students never experienced a second teaching practice' (p. 53);
  - opinions on the best way to organize teaching practice strongly favoured existing patterns (p. 196);
  - most students felt that the amount of theory on their courses was about right, but more than three times as many felt that there was too much than felt that there was too little;
  - staff seemed reasonably happy with existing theory courses, particularly where they were thematically integrated; non-integrated courses tended to attract few students;
  - 'most staff who were interviewed believed that the balance between the various components of the PGCE was about right' (p. 205).
- on partnership:
  - 'teachers contributed to and attended courses run in the education department' (p. 196);
  - some tutors were in favour in principle of students spending more time in school, but doubted if the right school conditions could be found (p. 196);

— tutors were clearly unwilling to give up their teaching practice responsibilities whatever the logistical problems. 'They disagreed strongly with the proposition that time spent supervising students could be put to better use and with the suggestion that school staff should take the main responsibility for supervision' (p. 197);

— tutors felt a strong obligation to monitor students' progress in the school. It was felt that students expected to be visited and tutors ought to keep in touch with what was happening on teaching practice.

These studies are revealing in a number of respects. First, they confirm that a general trend towards school-focused training was taking place in the colleges and polytechnics. There are difficulties but there is also excitement at the freedom to be innovative in course construction now that the constraints of the old ATO system no longer apply. The prospect of the classroom competence of the student becoming the organizing principle of training is welcomed in many of the public sector institutions. Second, the SPITE study of university departments reveals how different was training in the universities from that provided elsewhere and how stable it had been over time. This is sharply focused in the Alexander and Whittaker text (1980) in which there are several accounts of university courses. At the University of Reading the disciplines of education are still taught separately; the course is a 'traditional sandwich course . . . rather than one based on integrated themes' (p. 134); and 'school cooperation may not have been explored to the full . . . and short of government directives lengthening the course and allowing for greater school participation in the preparation of teachers . . .' (sic!). There is also the chapter on the course at the University of Bristol in which the author urges that 'teacher training must not be taken over completely by teachers' (p. 122): and even at the University of Cambridge where Hirst, in his role as a member of the academic debate, was so strongly advocating that training should prioritize the learning of the practical skills of the classroom (see below p. 106), the course itself featured simulation of classroom events and activities rather than allowing students to experience the realities of schools for longer periods. An exception to the slow pace of development in the universities was the course at the University of Sussex which had become school-based as early as 1965 (Lacey and Lamont, 1976). This partnership scheme entrusted to practising teachers the responsibility for the practical supervision and training of the students who each week throughout the year spent three days in school and two days in the HEI.

Third, these studies hint at the emergence of two different forms of tension within the system. There are structural disjunctures or contradictions of the kind that Althusser might have identified as conducive to ideological revolution. Despite the rise and rise of professional studies, the power differential between teachers and tutors remained. By the end of the 1970s, many institutions considered that they were engaged in partnership with their schools, but partnership was a vague term which was reflected only very rarely, as on the Sussex course, in an equivalence of status and reciprocity of tasks. This power differential was so much part of the cultural discourse of initial training that it appears to have remained unremarked by even the most enthusiastic supporters and exponents of the new school-focused courses. On the other hand, tutors in the universities seem to have been quick to rationalize their failure to engage teachers more fully in training, providing a number of reasons why this might be an inappropriate step to take. This suggests that they were aware of the trends in the colleges and even to a degree supported them as their aims for training would imply, but that they were constrained by the context in which they operated, thus generating the form of tension identified by Geertz (chapter 1). This is not structural but personal tension and is best exemplified by the tutors in Research Study 5 who were experiencing dissonance in the face of an increase in bureaucratic demands. Geertz suggests that this kind of tension leads individuals to search for a new ideology which might give relief from personal anxiety. Tutors resented the challenge to their commitment to training that the restructuring of the system had introduced, and in the face of it are recorded as striving to maintain the traditions of teacher education . . . and are succeeding in so doing.

The above section has outlined the developments that took place in the curriculum of training during the 1970s. There remained great diversity across institutions but the training that most students received was remarkably changed from that of the mid-1960s when it was dominated by the disciplines. Classroom competence had become a priority. Students were placed in schools for a higher proportion of the training period and there was closer association between schools and colleges, although there was little formal recognition of the schools place in training. A review of the potential agents of these changes will now be undertaken in order to suggest that in the absence of ideological intervention from the centre, it was the teacher training community in the HEIs which had assumed control of the training process and brought about these modifications to the aims and structure of training.

Determinants of Curricular Change in the 1970s

The following section will consider the several influences ((i)–(vii) below) which might be considered to have had potential to contribute to the curricular changes already noted, and will conclude that those changes came about principally as a consequence of the aims, actions, motivations, commitments, interests, prejudices, biases and so on of groups within the training profession, rather than through intervention by the government, the Inspectorate, unions or teachers or students. Reasons will also be suggested why the development of the more practical school-focused curriculum did not take place more rapidly and more comprehensively than was the case.

The potential agents of change to be considered are:

(i) central government;
(ii) the 'participants': by participants is meant tutors, teachers and students engaged in the process of training;
(iii) those engaged in what is referred to as the 'academic debate': this is the ongoing debate amongst academics as it appears in books and journals, on what constitutes the desirable state of affairs in the curriculum of training;
(iv) the CNAA: the membership of the CNAA boards or working parties which were appointed to assess the quality of courses submitted for validation, consisted principally of representatives of other institutions which had already been successful in their bids;
(v) the professional associations: reference will be made principally to the National Union of Teachers (NUT), this being the union which represents the largest number of teachers in the school system, but also that which has been central in the dynamics of teacher-state relations (Grace, 1987); and to UCET which given the former influence of the universities in training may have been expected to have been influential;
(vi) HM Inspectorate: the Inspectorate has served both the profession and the government and at different times in its history has been nearer to one than to the other.

1. The Influence of the Government on Curriculum Change in the 1970s:

That at the beginning of the 1970s, teacher training was a Pandora's box of problems, was acknowledged in a Select Committee (1969/70) the evidence to which was subsequently written up and made publicly available (Willey and Maddison, 1971). The authors of this account concluded that there was 'widespread discontent about the BEd' and 'a growing tide of dissatisfaction with the content and nature of training courses' (p. 98). There was a 'groundswell of protest from the teaching profession that the teachers are not as involved in the training of entrants to their profession as they ought to be, and a general recognition that there is too great a gulf between the colleges and the schools'. There was also evidence of 'wide variation in the qualities of teachers, some of whose standard is unacceptably low' (p. 99) and that the 'Area Training Organizations, on the whole, have not lived up to expectation: the complaint is not that they have exercised too much control but that they have failed to provide the coordination and leadership that has been required' (p. 105). There was much else besides to which the Department of Education and Science had displayed 'monumental indifference' (p. 99) although that the Department's role was 'purely administrative' and had no control over the curriculum was explicitly acknowledged to the Committee by the Permanent Secretary (Willey and Maddison, 1971, p. 11). The disclosures to the Select Committee indicated the need for a comprehensive and thorough investigation of the teacher training system and the Secretary of State proposed that the James Committee be set up for this purpose. The Committee reported in 1972 and concluded that teacher training should consist of three 'cycles'. The first was to be two years of personal education. There then followed a year's initial training and induction (the 'professional' cycle). The third cycle was to be in-service education and training.

The extent to which the James Report was a response to the climate of criticism is apparent. It is difficult to interpret as an ideological initiative, however. Its recommendations did not reflect the ideology of the time which it will be recalled was still that of social democracy. They represented a rather neat solution to the prominent problems of the teacher training system. However, that there was opposition in the colleges (Hewett, 1972) to reducing what was regarded as a professional training from three years to two, seems to confirm the preference within this section of the training profession for a more skills-based curriculum. Though its major curricular recommendations were not implemented, nevertheless, the report may have contributed to a shift in the climate of opinion. By recommending that the Area Training Organizations be disbanded and that the CNAA was to be of equivalent status to the universities in validating courses, the report withdrew power from the universities and enhanced the status of the CNAA. Since the mode of operation of CNAA was to respond to the initiatives of the institutions rather than to direct them, the way was now open for the colleges and polytechnics if they wished to introduce changes in their courses which would remedy the gulf between theory and practice which had come to typify training since the Robbins Report. The irksome obligation on the colleges to negotiate with the universities every change in course structure or content had been exchanged for academic autonomy. No sooner had the James Report been published, than its place in the headlines was taken by the White Paper *Education, a Framework for Expansion* (1972). The White Paper rejected the restructuring of training that the report had proposed, but supported the BEd as a qualification either as an ordinary or an honours degree which could be validated by a university or by the CNAA. The entry requirements and the academic level of these degrees was to be similar to those at university. Thus, the promise of the James Report for an alternative style of curriculum which had an in-built commitment to the practical dimension of training had failed to come to fruition. The White Paper contained two specific curricular requirements: that courses should contain education studies and that students should spend a minimum of fifteen weeks in school, proposals which clarified and confirmed current practice. Thus, in terms of curricular structure, it was to be 'business as usual'. Regarding its effect on curricular development, the James Report is judged to have had a facilitating but not direct influence. It freed up the system, and subsequently a large number of public sector institutions took advantage of the chance to change their validating bodies in the expectation that they would have greater freedom to mount the courses of their choice. This usually meant giving, if not precedence, at least increased attention to the practical aspects of training, although institutions were not immediately as innovative in this respect as might have been imagined (see CNAA below). Following the report, and until the late mid-1970s, the increase in institutions which applied to the CNAA for validation was dramatic (Sharples, 1984).

There were no other interventions in the training curriculum by the government during the 1970s. But successive governments of both parties undertook the reorganization of higher education in the non-university sector. The consequences for the initial training system were dire. In response to a predicted fall in the birthrate, a need for increased economic stringency and the desire of the government to locate teacher training within the general framework of higher education as part of a policy to restructure opportunities for post-school education, eighty-five training institutions were lost.

> The 1970s were punctuated by announcements from the Secretary of State of new figures for teacher training places. The White Paper figure of 75,000 to 85,000 places in 1981 was refined by January 1976 to 60,000 and by November 1976 to 45,000 . . . Each time new target figures for teacher training were announced, they were translated into entry figures for individual colleges by the Secretary of State. This usually meant further reorganisation. (Locke *et al*, 1985, p. 16)

If they were to survive in the face of this continuous and massive reduction in the number of places required, training institutions were unlikely to remain monotechnics. The 1972 White Paper had suggested that some colleges either alone or having amalgamated with other institutions, could diversify and become broadly-based institutions of HE. Others might become integrated into universities; still others might have to be turned over to in-service work or to close. Most were to merge and/or to diversify. Yet the experience of staff members lay within the different areas of teacher training and staff could not be replaced immediately. Modularization emerged as the answer to these challenges. If the curriculum were to be reorganized in terms of individual units or modules which could be combined in a variety of ways to make up any of several qualifications, this would enable institutions to make the best use of the expertise of existing staff, and to offer degrees and diplomas designed to attract students with no interest in teacher training. Students from different courses, including students of teacher training, could now share modules.

It is difficult to argue one way or the other, that modularization effected the balance between theory and practice. It may well have weakened the links between theory and practice and so impeded the trend towards integration. The breaking up of courses into discrete units creates boundaries between areas of knowledge rather than facilitates association. This may have encouraged the isolation of the disciplines of education from professional practice. On the other hand, modularization may have reduced the power of colleagues in education studies departments vis-a-vis their counterparts in professional studies. If modules or units in the disciplines were to be made available to students on other courses, they may have lost their singular educational focus and become decontextualised. Then education tutors would have had a commitment to students from other courses and their colleagues in professional studies would have been left as the true guardians of training. Raggett and Clarkson (1976) conclude that the insistence that 'new advanced courses can be squeezed from existing staff and resources may be good resource management, but is hardly likely to lead to the creation of inspired and imaginative courses' (p. 163). Thus while modularization offered a means of survival by the introduction of curriculum flexibility, it was also intrinsically inhibiting of innovative course construction since the pool of skills which could be made available for this purpose was limited to what existing staff had to offer. And once established as the format for CNAA-validated courses, its very convenience for validation purposes helped to ensure that it remained in place. The presentation of courses in discrete elements enabled validation boards not only to check on the coherence of the course, but also to isolate any modules that required revision while agreeing that the rest of the proposed course was satisfactory.

In conclusion: modularization which developed as a consequence of government action, probably both acted as a constraint against the trend towards a more integrated curriculum and simultaneously promoted the rise in the status of professional studies relative to the status of the disciplines of education. It has also been suggested that it inhibited course innovation. It cannot therefore be convincingly argued that even vicariously through the modularization process, the government had any real effect on the curriculum of training during the 1970s, although government effect on the training system itself was substantial.

2. The Influence of 'the Participants' on Curriculum Change in the 1970s

The term 'participants' in the following discussion refers to all those directly engaged in the training task: tutors, teachers and students.

One of the themes running through the analysis of the course samples above has been the antipathy to theory of students and teachers in particular but also of some tutors. But the expression of this in an interview does not guarantee the ability to remedy events. The tutors in the UDEs in the SPITE study, for example, declared their support in principle for a more practical course, yet apparently either could not or would not change the situation. Instead they declared that after all, they were satisfied with things as they were, perhaps because in the university-based PGCE courses, the tradition of tutor autonomy makes it difficult to achieve sufficient consensus to introduce system wide change. In their study of the BEd degree McNamara and Ross (1982) found that the quality of the leadership of the institutions was of fundamental importance in steering the colleges through the difficult years of the 1970s. Many of those institutions which were the first to apply for CNAA validation in the early 1970s had forward-looking charismatic senior staff who were able to recognize opportunities and take initiatives while remaining sensitive to the needs of their colleagues. An interesting account of the way leadership operated in the colleges and of how some colleges moved ahead while others failed to do so, is given by Raggett and Clarkson (1976, pp. 161–3). They suggest that the pressures on the colleges upset their ability to cope with tactical and strategic decision-making. Many of those in positions of power — principals and members of academic boards — too readily became immersed in the minutiae of change. They lacked the skills of curriculum development which would have enabled them to make decisions which matched the events and constraints of the external rationalization process. However, some institutions had on their staff, tutors who through an ability to take a wider view, by attending conferences, engaging in publication and in the reading of papers and so on became experts in their understanding and knowledge of those events and personnel which were external to the college but were most likely to influence its future development. Thus these tutors — who were not always in positions of high authority in the hierarchy — became powerful leaders of curriculum reform within their institutions. If institutions had on their staff tutors of this type, then they were able to take advantage of the flexibility arising from the revisions to the training system which had been introduced by the White Paper, for example. However, according to Raggett and Clarkson, such people were in the minority and responses to opportunities for creative thinking, with a few notable exceptions, tended to be mundane and unimaginative.

MacNamara and Ross (1982) found that more than half of the tutors interviewed (55 per cent) for their study thought that students were now better prepared academically than previously; but less than a quarter (21 per cent) agreed that students were better prepared practically despite the opportunities provided by the more school oriented courses. Nevertheless, the majority of tutors (64 per cent) believed that students were able to cope with a wider range of teaching situations. These perceptions of the outcomes of training suggest that the extension of the practical component of the course may not have been perceived by tutors as being of significant professional benefit to the student. A possible explanation for these results has less to do with the content of training courses than with the development and goals of the institutions. As has already been pointed out, the emergence of the diversified institution and of the modular course may well have led to course fragmentation. By these means, the traditional teacher training course was destabilized and while tutors remained confident of the academic quality of their courses, they may well have perceived modularization to be detrimental to the provision of a coherent professional training. As McNamara and Ross put it '. . . there is considerable concern among staff in some institutions that the ways in which their institutions have developed during recent years have been influenced as much by the need to ensure institutional survival as by considerations stemming from concern with improving the training of prospective teachers' (*ibid*, p. 69). Colleges had taken a hammering and morale was low. 'The ever present possibility of further reductions in the system, lack of opportunities for professional advancement and the lack of movement of staff into and between institutions is likely to be stultifying rather than enhancing' (*ibid*, p. 73). All of this seems to suggest that most members of staff would have been kept busy following and adapting to changes in the system, although as participants in committees and meetings they could influence new course development.

Several other writers also attribute the reluctance of some institutions to take advantage of opportunities for curriculum innovation to the wider context of system rationalization. Locke *et al* (1985) suggest that the loss of senior staff through early retirement, and hence of leadership, affected college development detrimentally. Of those that remained, many were simply demoralized by the repeated cuts and changes. Mackenzie (1976) indicates the tension introduced by the rapid and enforced changes to training: the

> mass of college staff (were being asked to) contribute formulae for new degrees, formulae for new structures, without the possibility of adequate discussion amongst themselves, they have had to sit in committees making academic decisions while all the time they have had to look over their shoulders at all sorts of internal power play between departments . . . (This) has been undertaken in a climate of anxiety, indeed in many cases of profound anxiety. And also in a climate in which . . . they have not been able to involve the profession . . . (p. 13)

The pressures on colleges for rapid restructuring were so intense that it was not possible to involve those most likely to support an increase in the practical element of the course: teachers themselves.

Alexander (1979, Research Study 3 above) also isolates institutional factors as constraints on the more rapid development of professionalised training courses. He suggests for example, that lecturers in professional studies lacked a professional identity having no qualification in their area of specialism and having neither academics nor yet teachers as their reference group. They also had relatively little power as an institutional group since professional studies tended to lack coherence, although this was not always the case as the creation of professional studies departments indicated. In addition, education studies lecturers, to whom neither of the above applied, are quite likely to have resisted any challenge to their power by their professional studies colleagues. Alexander concludes that 'although an increasing number of institutions have made determined efforts to put Professional Studies at the heart of the new degree course, . . . (there is) ample demonstration . . . that in some institutions little has changed' (p. 12). It can be concluded therefore that, discounting the exceptional tutor as described above, tutors in the public sector institutions are unlikely to have been initiators of innovative courses to any great degree.

What influence did teachers have on course development? Reading texts on the training of teachers during the 1970s it is apparent that most teachers would have preferred training to have been more school-based, although systematic research on teachers attitudes is difficult to trace. However, the CNAA samples suggest that teachers were likely to have had only a minimal influence on course construction through formal channels, their membership of committees being tokenistic. In addition, Research Study 1 in particular, identified the power differential between tutors and teachers which may have had an inhibiting effect on teachers' readiness to speak their minds. Less formal links with teachers existed in many institutions. The SPITE study reported that tutors and teachers often had long-standing relationships based on mutual respect, and in the public sector institutions tutors and teachers often worked together. It is quite likely, but impossible to tell, that teachers influenced the development of less theoretical courses through these channels to some limited degree. But probably any such influence would have been occasional and unsystematic.

A number of surveys have indicated that students would prefer a more school related form of training. In Research Study 5, 51 per cent of student respondents would have preferred more curricular time to have been available for school-based practical teaching studies. Preference for a more school-based course was also found by McCulloch (Research Study 1). In this study, students overwhelmingly regarded block school experience and professional studies courses as the parts of the course which best prepared them for teaching (see also Crompton, 1977). The Inspectorate (Research Study 2) found that nearly all colleges had machinery for allowing student opinion to be brought quickly to the notice of course leaders. Nevertheless their power to change the design of courses is likely to have been very limited. While their views would no doubt have been listened to and even noted in committee, students are not likely to have had sufficient influence to introduce course amendments when institutions were striving to meet the requirements both of the government and of their own survival.

In the 1970s, the leaders of public sector institutions were faced with a range of imposed dilemmas their responses to which would have far reaching consequences for their own institutions. These dilemmas included: which agency to approach for course validation, whether to introduce modular courses, whether to diversify or to amalgamate with another institution and if so which one, or alternatively how to use and influence these decisions when they were to be made elsewhere. It was the quality of the leadership in an institution, whether formal or informal, which was the most crucial factor in determining whether the best was made of these opportunities. Contributing to this was an understanding of the way in which the wind was blowing in the teacher training community at large. This made it possible to be opportunistic in proposing course developments as the situation evolved. It seems unlikely that the mass of participants in training — teachers, the majority of tutors, and students — had much influence on the development of the more school focused curriculum.

3. The Influence of the Academic Debate on Curriculum Change in the 1970s

The term 'academic debate' here refers to that ceaseless ongoing critically evaluative discussion which is at the heart of being an intellectual. It is the democratic exchange of views expressed either verbally in a range of settings from the conference hall to the private discussion or through publication. It is never ceasing because its fundamental principle is that of critique and ideas are always open to critique. Throughout the 1970s, there was a lively exchange of views on the relationship between theory and practice in training. This was a debate which had been initiated years before, which had been given renewed life in the aftermath of the Robbins Report and which during the 1970s was to see the transformation of theory as product to theory as process. Since members of the academic debate were also members of the training institutions, some degree of coincidence between rhetoric and reality can be expected.

The new post-Robbins graduate training course had incorporated the disciplines of education as evidence that teacher training was intellectually sound. As Peters and Hirst argued respectively they were to provide rigour and to clarify the nature of educational knowledge (see chapter 2). They were to dispense wisdom, to provide the answers to the unknowns of pedagogy, and they were taught by academically inclined tutors who may enter a school only occasionally. At this stage, the theory–practice relationship was in practice a unilateral top down model which although attracting criticism within the academic debate was to remain in place for reasons which had little to do with the nature of the debate itself. If a college wished to apply to the CNAA for validation, then it had to demonstrate that it was an institution of sufficient stature, and a curricular commitment to the disciplines was an indication that this was the case. Secondly as has already been mentioned, the theory–practice distinction generated and sustained a distribution of power within institutions. Curricular structures represent people, their careers, interests and areas of expertise and are therefore resistant to change.

From the restructuring of the curriculum, students and teachers had inveighed against 'theory' for its lack of relevance for the student concerned to establish him/herself in the classroom. In 1967 Peters had responded to these concerns in a lengthy paper in which he argues for the retention of theory on two grounds, those of professional competence and personal education, whilst also acknowledging the need for precedence in professional preparation to be given to training in classroom competence:

> It could well be argued that though the main emphasis at the level of initial training must be on the *training* of teachers, we cannot altogether neglect our duty as educators to educate them as persons. Philosophy, psychology, history and the social sciences play a vital role in what may be called a liberal education . . . (Peters, 1967, pp. 153–4)

Thus, if we wish to have an educated teaching profession, the disciplines should be retained, but they should not be the focus of the curriculum, because initial training is about training to be a classroom teacher. Peters therefore wishes to reweight the curricular balance between the theoretical and practical elements, to reverse priorities and give precedence to training in professional skills. In this same paper he also states that 'selection from the content of the basic disciplines must, in the main, be determined by what is relevant to the practical problems and interests of teachers in training' (*ibid*, p. 156), that is, the disciplines must be 'relevant' for the student. Nevertheless, the disciplines should retain their distinctiveness, and once this has been achieved, they 'need to join together in an orderly and coherent conversation about matters of common concern to teachers . . . In brief we must make an end of the undifferentiated mush that is often perpetrated under the heading of educational theory . . .' (pp. 155 and 156).

In the above paper, Peters does not consider the intrinsic nature of the relationship of theory to practice. Other writers take up this theme however. In the same year, Stenhouse (1967) enlivened the debate by suggesting that the immediate priority of training should be to produce the 'competent conformist'. In other words, students should be trained in teaching methods. As the teacher matured, he/she would become more flexible and independent and would be able to generate 'a working professional philosophy'. As for the relationship of the disciplines to classroom practice, Stenhouse reinterprets the role of theory suggesting that the purpose of the disciplines of education is not to underwrite methods, but rather to systematically critique all practice. Stenhouse's views are remarkable for their common sense, but also for their radicalism. In effect he is suggesting that the disciplines are more suitable for experienced teachers, that is in-service training; that teachers 'produce' theory; and that the function of theory is to evaluate practice. At a stroke, it became necessary to reassess the status and the function of the disciplines of education, and their contribution to professional preparation. Two years later, Entwistle (1969) writes in support of this reformulated relationship: that action generates theory, and that rather than determining practice, theory acts as a referent which facilitates the development of practice.

> In terms of the development of particular teaching skills, or techniques, which are the manifestation of the teacher visibly at work in the classroom, it may be that theory has most meaning when drawn out of practical situations, than when offered ceremoniously in the lecture room prior to the event. (Entwistle, 1969, p. 46)

Teacher training therefore entered the 1970s with some of the earlier assumptions about how students best learn to be teachers, overthrown. What had been subservient knowledge, knowledge of practical skills, had now in terms of the immediate requirements of initial training, become superior to theoretical knowledge — in debate at least. That this reassessment of the priorities of training had fundamental consequences for the organization of the curriculum and for the distribution of power between tutor and teacher was recognised by Tibble (1971b). He acknowledges that students are liable to complain that they do not receive enough help with problems of class control. He then goes on — and it is worth quoting him at length:

> This leads me to the observation that the value of the block practice derives fundamentally from its being the modern form of the apprenticeship relationship . . . It is indeed the only sound basis for the acquisition of practical skills. These can only be acquired by the students attempting to do the job in a work situation. . . . But the prevailing system then proceeds to distort and diminish the value of the apprenticeship principle by officially making the apprentice master not the school teacher . . . but the college tutor . . . (p. 105)
>
> Recognition of this has led in recent years to . . . the appointment by departments and colleges of school-based tutors or teacher-tutors . . . The time is ripe for a much wider application of this practice . . . the question that arises for the colleges and the departments is how would such a development for fuller school responsibility affect the role and work of the tutors. (p. 106)

During the 1970s, numerous papers were published on the topic of the relationship between theory and practice and its application for training (for example, Naish and Hartnett, 1975; Golby, 1976; Hartnett and Naish, 1977; Taylor, 1978). Some contributors to the academic debate supported the retention of the disciplines. For example, Renshaw (1973) would have it that 'the judgments and actions of teachers in the classroom must be informed by (this) theoretical knowledge otherwise their claim to professional status would be severely weakened' (p. 222). On the other hand there were others who wished to see training move towards schools. Lewis (1975) would prefer to see the classroom itself become the central focus for all developments in initial training. He goes on to advocate a system of school-based training such as we have to-day in which tutors work in schools alongside teachers and theory is generated by reflection on practice. Assuming that in-service training would be readily available as the James Report had proposed, Hirst (1975) wishes to see the PGCE course 'directed towards the problems of teaching and nothing else' (p. 1). He regards general courses in the disciplines of education as of very limited value. How they 'bear on particular judgments is what matters' (p. 3). According to Hirst, all foundations work (i.e. the disciplines) should be approached through the practical issues of the classroom.

By 1975, Wilson and Pring (1975) were suggesting that the place and use of educational theory in the curriculum had become 'a disaster area', and the notion of alternative practical theory was reaffirmed. This theory can be found in all forms of practice:

> There exists however, another possibility, namely that theory already exists in practices — any practices — and that it can be found there if one looks for it. The improvement of one's practice . . . would consist in the first instance of becoming aware of the theory which one's practice already embodied, . . . Thereafter, improvement of the practice . . . would go along simultaneously with the progressive explicating, elaborating, diversifying, refining, reconstructing etc of the theory which was 'there' from the first. 'Theory' in this sense would be the set of reflective, critical, thoughtful features of the practice of which it was the theory. (p. 3)

This personal theory or theory as process became a prominent topic for debate (for example, Elliott, 1976) and was also the basis of a research project designed to encourage teachers to articulate the principles underlying their classroom practices (McNamara and Desforges, 1978).

About the middle of the decade, the belief that training should be principally concerned with the acquisition and the improvement of the skills of the classroom practitioner had been extended so far in the academic debate that it developed into an interest in the American system of PBTE (Performance-Based Teacher Education). This method of training teachers was based on the assumption that competences needed by teachers could be clearly identified, and that the criteria for measuring these competences could then be stated (Tuxworth, 1982). Between the years 1975–78, a number of books or articles were published on this theme and that of microteaching, its practical application. However interest subsequently faded and the decade ended with a strong statement by Hirst, in his essay in Research Study 3 (above) in which he rejects the traditional place of the disciplines in training, advocating instead the articulation and rationalisation of professional common sense:

> . . . it is in principle quite impossible for the disciplines as such to provide us with all the knowledge and understanding we need to make rational practical judgments in the teaching context . . . The position is rather that in most practical situations we must act from a basis of common-sense understanding acquired through experience and the use of everyday discourse . . . The knowledge base of professional practice is to be found in a rationalised form of common-sense, acquired in direct experience of the job alongside people practising the job . . . (Hirst, 1979, pp. 19 and 20)

Finally this perspective was confidently declared professional public policy as it were in a Consultative Report by the Universities Council for the Education of Teachers (UCET, 1979).

It seems reasonable to conclude that this continuous debate in which the nature and function of theory and practice in initial training and their interrelationship was thoroughly explored, was instrumental in generating the curricular changes which occurred in the 1970s. The analysis of the survey and research studies above show that there were developments in the system which paralleled these discussions. Several of the institutions which submitted courses for validation to the CNAA quote contributors to the academic debate, particularly Hirst, in support of their proposals for changes to more school-focused practices. And authors in the research studies who were recounting the events in their own institutions also quote Hirst as having stimulated the reassessment of their courses. The relationship of the academic debate to the institutions is not unilateral however. It could not be so because it is located within the institutions. It was the problems generated by trying to use the disciplines to direct practice — problems which would have been experienced by the members of the AD as practitioners themselves — that challenged the post-Robbins model of the theory–practice relationship.

4. The Influence of the Council for National Academic Awards (CNAA) on Curriculum Change in the 1970s

That the CNAA may have been influential in transforming the post-Robbins curriculum in which the disciplines of education were so prominent, to a form of training in which practice of whatever kind was considered a more important component than 'theory', has been hinted at throughout the discussion. The CNAA was cited by institutions as their means of escape from the constraints and frustrations of university validation. Course validation under the CNAA offered freedom to develop a programme of training which was more relevant for the student, which was more integrated, which satisfied teachers and which was perceived as a more appropriate form of professional preparation. That the development away from theory and towards practice may have been attributable to the influence of the CNAA seems to be supported by the comparison of the CNAA and university validated courses featured in Research Studies 3 and 4 (see also Smith, 1980, p. 19 for the 'centrality' of school experience on CNAA courses); and by the lack of development of this kind within courses in the university sector. But it is not enough just to assume this to be the case. The role of the

CNAA in steering the evolution of training needs to be analysed more thoroughly.

The task of the CNAA as clearly proposed in both the Robbins Report and in the White Paper of 1972 was to act as a validating body, not as an initiator of course content. Thus from the start the CNAA operated by responding to course submissions, or as Kerr (1976), a CNAA officer put it, by being 'prepared to accept quite different patterns as solutions to the same problems, provided they have been properly thought through by staff, and that the staff have got the resources and facilities to carry through their own proposals' (p. 86). Any influence that the CNAA had on developments in teacher education during the 1970s will therefore have been by creating a context or climate in which such developments could take place rather than through any form of direct intervention. This may be one reason why the evolution of the more school-focused course was so protracted, given the degree of support for a more practical approach to training that was currently being expressed. In the following comments, consideration will be given first to those aspects of the relationship between the CNAA and the training institutions which facilitated the shift to practice and then to the aspects of that relationship which constrained that development.

One factor contributing to the development of a more practical curriculum may have been the way in which those colleges which were dissatisfied with validation under a university department of education perceived the CNAA. The CNAA had been set up in opposition as it were, but also as equivalent, to the universities; its origins lay in the practicalities of technical education, and its operating principle was that 'colleges should be given the maximum freedom in devising their own courses. (CNAA) leaves colleges free to plan their own syllabuses and curricula for courses in both new and traditional fields of study . . .' (CNAA, 1968, Paper 1a/2, p. 1). These sentiments are both challenging and flattering. They imply that the bidding institution has considerable freedom in the matter of course construction and moreover also has the perspicacity and expertise to submit a well balanced and well justified proposal. Chambers (1975) calls this 'the heady freedom of the CNAA' which he contrasts with the 'old, admittedly friendly relationship with the university (which) was in many cases far too dependent, and (where) the difficult decisions about course control, course structures and patterns of assessment were often taken for the colleges' (p. 3). The greater autonomy that the CNAA offered appealed to both those colleges which remained monotechnic institutions and to the institutions which were forced into new validation arrangements by the revisions to the training system itself. The consequence was that a substantial number of institutions opted for CNAA validation. Over the five-year period prior to 1976, the number of education courses validated by the CNAA increased from one to nearly sixty, and by 1978, this had increased to a total of 122 courses in forty-eight institutions (Lynch, 1979, pp. 62 and 64).

But the CNAA was established to ensure that the standards of courses in the colleges became comparable with those in the university departments, and to a degree this obligation was a source of tension in how the Council operated. This is exemplified in the following comments from the Council document 1a/2 above: 'The Council emphasizes that its subject Boards in looking at courses are anxious to encourage new developments . . . The onus is therefore upon colleges in their written proposals and in discussions during visits to convey clearly . . . that the treatment of the subjects of the course makes intellectual demands comparable with a university degree course at the same level' (para. 6.3). The delegation of responsibility for course construction to the training institutions may also have enhanced indirectly the power of the colleges over the schools. Evans (1976) advocates the closer association of teachers in school with teachers in colleges in a partnership. But he goes on: '. . . tutors are exercising greater control than ever before over the courses they are going to teach . . . It follows that they have substantial power to set the professional partnership firmly within the design of the courses' (p. 127).

A second operational principle of the CNAA was that of peer evaluation. Submissions for new or revised courses were reviewed first of all by the Education Committee and then by a working party or panel nominated for the particular expertise of its members. It was the task of this panel which consisted of CNAA officers and colleagues from other training institutions to carry forward the validation process either by reviewing the proposal with representatives of the submitting institution at the CNAA offices or by visiting the institution and conducting a more broadly-based assessment of the academic and practical viability of the proposed course. For this study it was not possible to review the responses of the various validation panels to the sample course proposals since this data is confidential. But these arrangements for course validation undoubtedly enabled the CNAA to act as a forum for curricular debate (Davis, 1979) and, it is suggested, contributed to the dissemination of a more practical model of training throughout the public sector institutions. In the most general terms, the colleges had deserted the universities for the CNAA as a validating body both because the CNAA offered increased autonomy, but also because it offered opportunities to propose courses that were less dominated by the disciplines of education than hitherto had been the case. The proposals that came before the working parties for validation may therefore have been more innovative than conservative in their approach to course construction. Thus meetings of the validation panels convened to review these submissions provided opportunities for the exchange of ideas, attitudes and information between the members of the several training institutions represented. McCulloch (1979) notes that, as might have been expected, institutions tended to nominate their senior members for CNAA service. These heads of department, deans of faculties or vice principals were well placed on their return to introduce into their own institutions ideas gleaned from their participation in the validation process. Research undertaken by Francis (1986) confirmed the benefits to an institution of having a member on a board. It not only conveyed status on that institution, but also provided access to information on trends and the scope for interpretation of policies and brought close contact with members from other institutions.

What may be regarded as a third operational principle of the CNAA — that members of the committees, boards and working parties should be recruited by invitation and moreover should receive no remuneration for their work from the Council — may also have contributed indirectly to the emergence of a more practical form of training. Davis (1979) discusses the many reasons why members of the profession might wish to offer their services in this way. Whatever these may have been, it is unlikely that anyone from the universities in particular would have agreed to become a member of a CNAA working group had he/she not already been familiar with, and supported in principle, the aims and objectives of the CNAA; and Davis explicitly states that university representatives did not defend their sectional interests but were committed to the success of the CNAA (p. 205). It is suggested in other words that most, though of course not all members of validating panels were likely to have been of a liberal persuasion and sympathetic to innovation in training.

If there were these diverse ways in which the CNAA operated which facilitated the development of a more innovative school-focused form of training, there were also simultaneously operating a number of constraints on course development, some of which were the inverse of the features already discussed. A major constraint was the obligation placed upon the CNAA to ensure that the standards of its awards were equivalent to those of universities. The White Paper of 1972 placed the CNAA on an equal footing with the universities as guarantor of the quality of teacher education, stating that universities and the CNAA were jointly responsible for academic validation — 'here taken to mean determining whether the conditions of entry to and the structure of courses, including school and other practical experience, the content and level of syllabuses and the standard of achievement required, justify the award of a certificate, diploma or degree' (para. 90); and in the following paragraph confirming their equivalence of status and authority as awarding bodies: 'some colleges . . . may seek academic awards from a university, others from the CNAA' (para. 91). As an organization therefore the CNAA was publicly accountable to a high degree. By providing evidence of the quality of its awards it demonstrated its competence and worth. With respect to the speed of course development, the consequence of this concern were twofold: the introduction of explicitly bureaucratic procedures for course construction and submission; and a tendency to be cautious when confronted with the more radical proposals. Both of these characteristics of the Council tended to restrict the freedom of the colleges to be as innovative in their new course proposals as CNAA policy may have implied was possible.

Both McCulloch (in Research Study 1) and Alexander (1979) at greater length, consider the inhibiting effects of the necessarily bureaucratic approach of CNAA from the perspective of its bidding institutions. When undertaking her research, McCulloch found that the 'CNAA emphasis on the need for academic rigour and honours standards was felt by colleges to inhibit the use of school-based work as the central focus for BEd. programmes' (p. 55). Alexander acknowledges that 'any course validating body offers institutions both freedoms and constraints' but suggests that the constraints imposed by the CNAA are considerable. These include regulations governing the validation of courses, guidelines on course components which state desirable practice (which although they are intended to guide, not to direct, have a habit of becoming the basis of policy (p. 32)) and the views of those who validate the courses. With respect to the last of these, Alexander suggests that a degree of conservatism is inevitable. 'Whatever our commitment to open-mindedness on innovation, we are all to some extent imprisoned in existing operational definitions of what counts as a valid course . . .' (p. 33). The outcome for the institutions is that they are invited not to conform to a uniform pattern, but 'this invitation is qualified in the "detailed procedures" which ask colleges to follow a fairly standardised pattern covering aims and objectives and how it is proposed to achieve them . . .' (p. 34). He concludes that 'the CNAA approach to validation, for all its apparent fairness and freedom from preconceptions about what constitutes a "good" course, is firmly embedded in a set of assumptions about curriculum which may tend to shape and constrain courses in action in certain fundamental ways and which can manifest themselves in practices which contradict the Council's stated assumptions' (p. 44). Or as Billing (1979), a CNAA officer puts it: 'the image of the CNAA as reflected in its practice does not always match its claim that it wishes to encourage the growth of new ideas in the Colleges . . .' (p. 55).

Both peer evaluation and the composition of CNAA validating bodies which were presented above as facilitating course development can also be seen to have their constraining aspects McCulloch (1979) found that not infrequently there were disagreements misunderstandings and poor communication between senior college staff and their junior colleagues concerning new initiatives, course arrangements or the relationship of the institution with CNAA. These disclosures of tension between the leaders, who at validation meetings participated in a national network for the exchange of ideas on developments in training — and led in the public sector institutions — demonstrate the difficulty of institutional change and may suggest a reason why the revision of training did not progress more evenly during the 1970s. Furthermore, the generally open attitude towards innovation that it is assumed most members of validation parties displayed was not incompatible with a concern for the maintenance of quality in training. Davis (1979) suggests that the CNAA committee members had 'a fair degree of commitment' to the 'academic disciplines rather than to institutions and dedication to the business of course assessment' (p. 20). So once again we find an aspect of the way in which CNAA operated that appears to have both created conditions that fostered innovation in training and yet was at the same time potentially inhibiting.

Nevertheless the degree to which the CNAA facilitated the movement towards a more school focused training must surely be less equivocal than this assessment of constraints on its influence may imply. As a member of the Council, Kerr (1976) concludes that '. . . in a number of colleges that have come to the Council there is quite a lot (of innovation), demonstrating for example a total professional orientation within some of the courses. Other courses have got a very heavy concentration of professional preparation of the teacher and an analysis of the role that the teacher actually plays in the classroom . . .' (p. 87). As a member of the profession, an outsider, who on occasion was a member of validation panels, Chambers (1975) concludes that there is ample evidence of curriculum innovation in the colleges and that these innovative trends spring in part from '. . . the influence of external validating bodies, notably the Council for National Academic Awards' (p. 3). The analysis of the samples of CNAA courses submissions undertaken for this research would seem to support this view. Davis (1979), who studied the principles and procedures of the CNAA at length, avoids simplistic alternatives. He suggests that the readiness of the CNAA to innovate developed over time as its comparability of status with the universities became confirmed: '(CNAA's) aims were often divergent; consideration of status sometimes eroded the commitment to innovation, whilst new developments could be weakened by pressures to confirm with the landscape of university orthodoxy. As time passed and the Council grew in stature and assurance, so the willingness to embark upon new ventures . . . increased' (pp. 162–3). He does, however, agree that although the CNAA's policies do not suggest 'radical innovation or particular distinctiveness . . . In 1974 the degrees offered by the CNAA and its general academic policies lay within the broad spectrum of British higher education . . . although they had . . . stronger professional orientation and a greater stress on applied studies' (p. 163). It can therefore be concluded that the Council — that is, members of its panels who were drawn from the UDEs and colleges — contributed to the development of the training curriculum during the 1970s quite substantially by providing a generally supportive but critical environment in which the college leadership could introduce innovative courses which gave greater priority to the practical aspects of training. But in addition it can be concluded that there were constraints on extremism in course design, constraints that can be attributed to the principles underlying the CNAA validation procedure and also to the way in which CNAA was perceived by the submitting institutions. It is thus suggested that as well as a promotion effect, CNAA had a stabilizing effect on curriculum change.

5. The Influence of the Unions or Professional Associations on Curriculum Change in the 1970s

Lodge and Blackstone (1985) suggest that there are special tensions peculiar to professional unions. 'On the one hand, they wish to represent the interests of their members with respect to pay, job opportunities and working conditions; on the other, they wish to be a responsible and influential force in the pursuit of wider aims concerning professional standards which they perceive to be in the national interest' (p. 219). It is difficult to fight on two fronts simultaneously, and which of these two aims is given priority at any one time by a union or professional association is likely to be determined by the current economic conditions or context. At a time of economic hardship, when there is pressure from central government to constrain wage or salary claims, it seems probable that union activity designed to maintain or raise members' remuneration will take precedence over other interests. When financial conditions are satisfactory and not under threat, then there is time to debate forms of practice and consider how improvements can be made to the quality of training. If this distinction is a valid one, then it is to be expected that as the 1970s progressed and available resources became less plentiful, the attention of both teachers' and lecturers' unions would progressively have focused on conditions of service rather than upon the nature of initial training. But before this, more attention would have been paid to the provision of professional preparation. In general this seems to have been the case.

In the 1960s, the National Union of Teachers (NUT) was particularly vociferous in its advocacy of a professionally biased education for teachers. In 1969, a report by a sub-committee recommended 'closer, more positive links with schools', and 'wider forms of student experience in schools other than the traditional teaching practice'. The report which did not become policy, but nevertheless was publicly disseminated, also expressed resentment at the degree of control exercised by the universities and suggested that it was 'very probable that the Council for National Academic Awards provides a valuable alternative with respect to establishing more coherent and imaginative schemes of professional education' (para. 2.12). The following year the NUT issued a policy statement which was highly critical of the lack of teacher representation on ATO boards, pointing out that 'if the ATO structure precludes teachers from contributing to discussion or advising on the content and character of courses in teacher education, the gap between theory and practice becomes even wider' (1970a, para. 6). In the same year when giving evidence to the Select Committee on Education and Science, the NUT proposed that teachers 'should have much more to do with the training of the teacher in school'. However, on being asked by the Committee what part the Union had played in the generation of policy it was admitted that its influence had been negligible. Notwithstanding, the Union continued to voice its dissatisfaction with current forms of training. In 1971, the NUT issued a lengthy policy statement: 'The Reform of Teacher Education'. In this it stressed: the need to provide integrated professional courses which will draw on the disciplines and which will enable the student to examine practical problems theoretically . . .' (para. 3.11); the importance of placing teaching practice at the core of the professional education of teachers, in which the serving teacher has a vital contribution to make (para. 316); that there is research which suggests that there are advantages in more short periods of teaching practice where the student is in close contact with the school (para. 3.19); that school/college relationships should be based not merely on teaching practice, but within the whole ambit of college of education activities (para. 3.22); that due to a lack of national co-ordination course content is arbitrary and does not appear to stem from fundamental academic or professional needs (para. 3.36). This document is a comprehensive and forceful presentation of the views of the Union on initial teacher training and as has already been demonstrated many of its recommendations were implemented in the succeeding years.

However, the curriculum was soon to lose its place as the major focus of interest. In its response to the 1972 White Paper the NUT (1973) first upbraids the Government for concentrating on scale, organization and cost rather than educational content, although it 'accepts the traditional view that the Department does not have responsibility for content' (p. 3). Thereafter the paper passes little comment on the curriculum, but as is appropriate considers the outline proposals for changes to the structure of training. This was the beginning of a shift of interest within the union in favour of what were becoming more pressing concerns, concerns such as the pay and conditions of service of its members. By the mid-1970s, when the economy was in deep trouble, the NUT had became an active trade union. The traditional partnership with the DES had lost much of its credibility, and teachers were forced into confrontational politics and union action in order to gain what was regarded as an acceptable settlement (Grace, 1987, p. 212). Given the extent to which the consequences of a declining economy threatened the status and livelihood of those in many of the public sector occupations during these years, the relative lack of concern of the NUT during this period with the curriculum whether in school or in training institutions, comes as no surprise.

A shift away from concern about the curriculum can also be discerned in the history of the Association of Teachers in Colleges and Departments of Education (ATCDE). But unlike the NUT, which responded to government constraints with assertive opposition, the ATCDE retreated when confronted by the plans for college reorganization. Before and during the early 1970s it had run conferences with the DES which had had 'a profound influence on the development of education studies and the interaction between theory and practice' (Porter, 1976, p. 47); and it had published the journal *Education for Teaching*, the contributors to which came from a wide range of institutions on both sides of the binary divide. In his description of the reaction of the ATCDE to *Circular 7/73*, Hencke (1976) indicates how unprepared the Union was for confrontational politics. He tells us that 'the General Secretary of the ATCDE accepted both the economic and academic logic of the DES arguments' (p. 36); also that the ATCDE had minimal resources with which to challenge the proposals and concentrated on getting good redundancy terms for its members. In 1976, the Union amalgamated with the Association of Teachers in Technical Institutions (ATTI) to form the National Association of Teachers in Further and Higher Education (NATFHE) the better to represent and fight for the interests of their members within the reorganized system.

These brief comments suggest that the issue of the curriculum of training became marginal for both the NUT and the ATCDE as the worsening economy obliged the government to intervene in the occupational conditions of both groups. They also suggest that the preoccupation of both bodies with the curriculum during the 1970s progressively diminished, and a short review of three ways in which influence was possible (consultation, representation and issuing policy statements) will confirm that their influence on curriculum development in initial training was likely to have been slight.

In 1974, Locke was able to claim that the NUT was highly influential and an essential part of the process of consultation. Relationships with the DES were friendly and union representatives were included on DES temporary and permanent working parties. The unions were attributed with the power to shape public opinion and to contribute to government policy. At least where schools were concerned. Lawn and Ozga (1986) take a rather less effusive view but confirm that during the 1960s at least, the Department was careful to consult its partners — a style of partnership which they refer to as 'indirect rule' (p. 225). But in evidence to the Select Committee of 1970, Britton of the NUT had admitted that 'the matter of teacher training is an area where the teaching profession has had less opportunity of making itself felt than in most areas of education . . . The only way in which we could do it was by passing resolutions, putting out statements and hoping that these . . . would fall on ears that were not too deaf.' By 1973, the NUT was starting to complain about the lack of consultation by the DES on the reduction of teacher training places (NUT, 1973).

From its inception CNAA had stressed the importance of including teacher representation on both validation panels and on committees in the institutions (Kerr, 1976). For the former task at least, the teachers were usually selected by the NUT. However, it is unlikely that in either context, these teacher representatives dominated or even modified many of the decisions taken. It has been noted that on institutional committees they were heavily outnumbered, and with regard to their effectiveness as members of CNAA panels Davis (1979) suggests that 'whilst professional association members may have acted as effective pressure groups on some subject boards, they did not have a pervasive influence upon the Council. Insofar as it is possible to make a general comment, it would be that the role of the professional associations . . . was less assertive than might have been expected' (p. 209). Thus the NUT at least appears to have had little influence on the training curriculum through CNAA. The influence of the ATCDE by this means is considered to have become weaker over time. The decision to set up the Committee for Education, which was to assume overall responsibility for teacher training, initially 'met only grudging acceptance' from the Union. But the relatively high representation of the Union ('to weaken ATCDE hostility') appointed to the Committee once it was established may have resulted in the ATCDE having some power to steer curricular development. But since in due course decisions on validation became devolved to subject panels (Davis, 1979) and the concerns of the Committee for Education became those of management and administration rather than the curriculum, any influence that the ATCDE could have exerted initially by this means was probably reduced.

Both unions may have been more influential through the printed word, at least during the early years of the decade. The policy statement of the NUT which was quoted above is a powerful document and it is difficult to believe that it did not significantly contribute to current discussion on the nature of training. Similarly, *Education for Teaching* contained articles on many aspects of the relationship between theory and practice, on partnership and on curriculum development. It was distributed widely throughout the public sector institutions and surely must have stimulated ideas and provoked discussion.

All of this suggests that the NUT did not directly or significantly influence the development of the teacher training curriculum during the 1970s, although it may have had an indirect effect through its policy statements where these mentioned the nature of training. The case for the ATCDE before its amalgamation with ATTI is somewhat stronger. Through *Education for Teaching* its members in the training institutions had access to and were able to contribute their views on curriculum development. Their interest was maintained by the journal which provided them with a forum for discussion. To this extent both the ATCDE/NATFHE and the NUT contributed to a general climate of debate. Rather than working through other agencies, the NUT declared its policies on training to the professional public, and the ATCDE gave space for the expression of views, with the hope that as Britton put it, they would fall on ears that were not deaf.

The influence of the Universities Council for Teacher Education (UCET) on curriculum change should also be assessed. To do so, however, is problematic since it is difficult to separate out the influence of

UCET as a body from that of individual members of the UDEs who during the 1970s dominated the world of initial training through a variety of channels such as the ATOs, membership of CNAA boards and panels, as well as through publications. To the reader of the reports and policy statements of UCET, it appears that the major concern of the Council from its inception has been the maintenance of standards in initial training. In its evidence to the 1971 Select Committee, UCET justifies UDEs retaining a central role in training on the grounds that this would help to ensure the highest standards of scholarship, professional competence and research (p. 3). Reflecting this concern it suggests that 'no group of teachers should be excluded from studying the traditional disciplines to at least main course level. It is essential to teacher training . . . that it should involve some study in depth, making real demands on the student's intellect and on his powers of critical thinking' (para. 12.0). Nevertheless, it acknowledges the alleged failure to relate the theory part of the course to the practical (para. 13.1) and refers the reader to some proposals for closer cooperation with schools elsewhere in the document.

This concern for the intellectual quality of training is apparent in the regular UCET bulletins. Bulletin No: 2 (1970) states that it is UCET policy that the BEd degrees should be a degree in which honours might be gained. In No: 8 (1976) UCET supports the phasing out of the Certificate of Education. This emphasis on 'standards' and the traditional nature of training courses in the UDEs which the SPITE study revealed, seem to suggest that UCET as a body may well have had a constraining effect on course change during the 1970s. However, in 1975, UCET ran a conference on initial training which was attended by 200 delegates and as a result of which some courses were apparently altered (Bulletin No: 8, 1976). The collection of papers from this conference is remarkable for its diversity of viewpoint — indicating the unsettled nature of training at that time — though the editor, Hirst, makes it clear that these papers represent personal opinion only. Most of them share a concern with practice. Hirst's paper concludes that 'the PGCE course should aim exclusively at training graduates for the general demands they are likely to meet in their first posts and should concentrate severely on a properly professional approach to the central duties of teaching and discipline' (pp. 1:6–1:7). The paper by Stones is titled 'Teaching teaching skills'. That by Gorbutt and Goulding places school experience at the centre of the curriculum. A paper by Martin, Burgess and Spencer is an account of an experiment to resolve the 'tension between curriculum and foundation courses' by inviting teacher-tutors from schools to become members of the institution for one day a week. The only paper which goes against this trend is that by Simon who argues for not only the maintenance but also the strengthening of the theoretical aspects of the course. This is on the grounds that students demand theoretical clarification and the schools deserve well prepared practitioners.

What is to be made of this? As far as it is possible to make an assessment, it is suggested that the influence of UCET on curricular development may have been variable during the 1970s depending at least in part on the views of its Chair. In the early part of the decade, it probably acted as a brake on change in UDE courses at least, but by the middle of the decade, its wider influence over the system as a whole seems to have been in support of the trend to practice.

6. The Influence of H.M. Inspectorate on Curriculum Change in the 1970s

The decade of the 1970s was one of considerable change in the status of HM Inspectorate. It was the time when it came in from the cold. From the 1960s HMI had adopted a low profile. The 1967–68 Select Committee on Education and Science had agreed that full-scale formal inspections of schools should be discontinued and that in future informal visits would be adequate. The Select Committee of the following year confirmed this change of responsibilities, the DES representative commenting: 'the balance is shifting from full inspections followed by formal reports and will continue to do so'. It seems then that at the beginning of the decade the inspectors were working with educational institutions informally, almost casually. Their involvement was low key, and this was with the knowledge and sanction of the DES. It was not until the mid 1970s that the Inspectorate became centralized and began to play a role in curriculum innovation (see chapter 4). Given this scenario it seems somewhat unlikely that the Inspectorate had any substantial influence on initial training in the 1970s, although it is difficult to say for certain, since their reports of that time are not in the public domain. Then in 1979, the survey of fifteen training institutions (above) was published. This has already been discussed but it is worth noting here that in this document the Inspectorate appear to support the idea of a training that emphasizes the acquisition of practical skills.

This section has attempted to respond to the two questions which were asked at the beginning of this chapter: in the absence of ideological input from the government (a) how did the curriculum of initial training develop? . . . and (b) who were the agents of change which brought these developments about?

Summary

The conclusions reached in this section on the Curricular Development of Initial Training in the 1970s in the absence of ideological intervention are as follows.

An analysis of three samples of course submissions to CNAA and of six research studies suggests the following:

- that throughout the decade there was considerable variation in courses of initial training on almost every dimension: the weighting of theory and practice, integration of the elements, time spent in school, relationships with teachers and so on;
- but that nevertheless, in the public sector institutions, there was a trend towards a curriculum in which the disciplines of education (theory) became less prominent, the status of professional studies rose and students spent more time in school in a variety of patterns of school experience. Thus the curriculum was returning to a more equal balance of theoretical and practical elements;
- this development was expressed in a change in the aims of courses from aims for the personal intellectual development of the student to aims for professional competence;
- that in the university departments courses remaining wedded to the disciplines to a much greater extent than in the public sector institutions and students' time in school continuing to be less flexibly ordered;
- that in the colleges structural changes followed this change from an emphasis on theory to an equal regard for practice, thus institutionalizing it: departments were reordered, professional studies courses subsumed educational studies, and students were offered courses in the practical skills of the classroom;
- the relationship between theory and practice was reversed; theory no longer dictated practice, but serviced it. Attempts were made to generate practical theory from professional practice;
- at the beginning of the decade, teachers were infrequently mentioned in course submissions, although some institutions had moved some way towards 'partnership';
- the control exercised by the training institutions over the schools and teachers continued to be considerable and to go unrecognized throughout the decade; the reality of partnership was

therefore significantly at odds with the rhetoric: there were a few exceptions to this;
- the demands made on the colleges to adjust to the violent reduction of the training system caused some tutors to experience tension between the increased bureaucratic demands of course reorganization and their desire not to see teacher training undermined.

Six agencies which might have contributed to these changes were then reviewed, and it was concluded that:

- it was members of the teacher training profession in the institutions who, acting in a variety of contexts — as members of CNAA panels, as leaders of their institutions and as members of the academic debate — generated the developments summarized above;
- those agencies deemed not to have had any significant influence on curricular developments were: teachers in schools, students, HM Inspectorate, the teachers' unions and the government;
- that all the above developments can be attributed to professional rather than government action.

Implications for Ideological Theory

- The curricular developments of the 1970s are considered to have been an interesting example of the way in which in Gramscian theory, ideology and cultural common sense interact; and also an example of Archer's concept of cultural elaboration.
- Adhering to the cultural traditions of training, the college community largely rejected the imbalance of theory and practice that followed the Robbins Report on the grounds that this was an inappropriate form of professional preparation; it contravened its view of 'what training was about'.
- Elements ('residues') of the Robbins curriculum were retained.
- These residues, which included intellectual standards and theory, were absorbed, transformed and became part of the common sense of initial training; they therefore lost their original function.
- Through a variety of means members of the community of

training turned this ideological intervention back towards a professional cultural norm.
- The pull away from this ideological curriculum may have been strongest in the public sector institutions because there it was more discrepant from the cultural traditions into which it was introduced than was the case in the university departments.
- This presentation of the interaction between ideology and cultural tradition in the particular site of the training curriculum represents members of the cultural community as active opportunistic agents (Archer).
- Structural contradictions and personal tensions had developed which according to Althusser and Geertz might suggest that the system would be receptive to a new ideology.

Ideological Implementation: The Interplay between Culture and Ideology

Discussion so far on the relationship between culture and ideology has in the main been from the perspective of ideology. This section takes the perspective of culture. It will be suggested that culture intrinsically *offers resistance* to ideological penetration, and to illustrate this point reference will be made to the academic cultural tradition of the 1960s. It will also be suggested that culture *can facilitate* ideological penetration, and this will be illustrated by reference to the extent to which the emergent curriculum of the late 1970s prepared the way for the introduction of the ideology of Thatcherism. It is therefore hypothesized that over time, the relationship between the particular sub-culture of initial teacher training and the ideology of the state takes the form of a dynamic dialogue.

The changes in training that were described in the previous section are summarized by McNamara and Ross (1982) in their study of the BEd degree.

> The period may be characterized as one which began with concern to justify the award of a degree by stressing the academic, rather than the professional . . . The period ends with what some might regard as a revival of the philosophy which had inspired the two-year course in the training colleges pre-1960. That revival was made possible because the institutions, having established their academic credibility in the eyes of the

> validating bodies could now begin the task of redefining the degree. (p. 41)

Alexander (1984) also takes up this theme noting that the devaluing of professional skills and practical experience was the high price paid for academic respectability, and that commitment to the professional ideal of skilled practice is at odds with the drive for occupational status. He supports McNamara and Ross's view that once the colleges had achieved academic recognition, they reclaimed ownership of training by giving high priority to practical competence. '. . . It is not surprising that beyond the nominal and structural changes of the 1970s initial teacher education curriculum, the practices, assumptions and epistemologies of the 1960s and earlier should have persisted . . . people do not change that easily' (p. 152).

These quotations celebrate the endurance of cultural practices in the face of ideological imposition, and this has been implicit in the previous discussion. It is a perspective that is well illustrated by reference to the way in which the colleges received the Robbins reforms with which in many respects their academic traditions seemed irreconcilable. This culture was studied intensively by Taylor in the 1960s. In summarizing its characteristics Taylor (1984) indicates both how comprehensive and how integrated it was, and hence how powerful an ideology would have to be if it were to transform it. The whole ethos of the colleges from lifestyle to relationships between the staff and the students, from a serious concern with the teacher's responsibility to society to attitudes towards the curriculum, together signified a somewhat gentile, but caring and morally driven community. Taylor interprets the curriculum at this time as: 'a playing down of the importance of subjects and of disciplinary frontiers in favour of a child-centred, problem-focussed approach; anxiety about the dangers of academicism coupled with fears about the limitations of over-emphasising relevance and the practical' . . . and a stronger commitment to values such as moral seriousness and integrity than to 'training in critical analysis' (p. 18).

McDowell (1971) seems confident that the cultural patterns described by Taylor were not unusual. He supports the emphasis on the college community but chooses to devote more time to the examination of the values underlying the curriculum. He suggests that 'teacher education in the colleges rests on an inherited set of unexamined assumptions about the purpose of education and the nature of teaching . . . *The system and its values are showing remarkable tenacity*, first because they have been left alone so long as they satisfied official criteria for success, . . . and second because the imprecise state of knowledge in education encourages experience and spontaneity at the expense of systematic enquiry' (p. 62, emphasis added). He recalls that elementary education for which the colleges undertook the training of teachers, was as much a means of 'gentling the masses' as of educating them — a context in which the teacher is an agent of social consensus, 'imbued with a deep social and moral purpose which is to equip the unsuccessful majority to lead useful and moral lives within an established social and occupational structure' (p. 63). This means that the focus of the teacher's effort is the child. In espousing child-centred rather than subject-centred education, the colleges provide a training that was 'neither thoroughly professional nor intellectually stimulating' (p. 65). Educational theory is 'taught selectively rather than thoroughly, so as to emphasize those elements which will stress the diffuse aspects of the job . . . Teaching practice assessment will normally stress good personal relationships with both pupils and staff; ability to cooperate and neatness of dress . . . and a "good set of lesson notes"' (p. 67).

McDowell gives the impression that the theoretical post-Robbins curriculum had hardly dented the much more fundamental and long-lasting college culture of training, but as it were, just lay on the surface of it. Given the degree of discrepancy between the new and the old this may be a reasonable hypothesis. Here were cultural structures and practices that were grossly at odds with the university model of learning introduced in the post-Robbins period, with its emphasis on the rigorous study of knowledge, universal standards and independent study. Nevertheless, and despite the presentational mismatch which MacDowell implies, was there a *substantive* basis for engagement between this curriculum and the instrument of ideological confirmation? After all, a sense of social justice and concern for others emerges in the above accounts. But for several reasons it does not seem appropriate to equate these concerns with social democracy as a national movement. The notion of 'gentling the masses' contravenes social democratic principles being about domination rather than creating the conditions for freedom from domination. Nor can the tightly focussed concern with the individual child be regarded as 'social democratic' since social democracy is a broadly based political movement, though both have in common a humanitarian concern for the other. From the perspective of the curricular culture, rather than from that of the ideologically infused intervention, there seemed little prospect of engagement. This culture was powerful, being both ubiquitous and cohesive. It was also diffuse and of long standing. It was thus difficult and hostile terrain for ideological penetration which must be deep and pervasive if it is to bring about hegemonic allegiance.

An alternative way of expressing the continuity of culture is in terms of its autonomy. Alexander (1990) reviews a number of cultural theories and concludes that these 'converge in their emphasis on the autonomy of culture from social structure'. Yet he also suggests that 'powerful groups often succeed in transforming cultural structures into legitimating means' (p. 26). There is a paradox therefore. If, as Alexander suggests, culture is susceptible to the influence of powerful agencies (and this would include ideologically motivated interventions) and if it also demonstrates durability, then it must be characterized by certain qualities. Over time culture adapts and is modified, yet it retains its central unique recognizable form. If ideological structures are introduced, then depending on numerous factors so will their impact on a given culture vary. Cultural elements may be significantly altered or 'contaminated' by ideological intervention, or they may undergo only minor changes. Yet nevertheless the culture itself will continue. The degree of permanent cultural change in its own likeness that an ideological intervention generates will be evidence of its power. On the other hand, the power of culture will be demonstrated by whether over time it can reshape in its own image and to its own ends the ideology that has been introduced into its structures and patterns of thinking and behaving. The ideological input is retained but in time, under cultural influence its form is changed. It becomes part of a slightly different culture to which is has contributed. 'Every philosophical current leaves behind a sedimentation of common sense. This is the documentation of its historical effectiveness. Common sense is not something rigid or immobile, but is continually transforming itself, enriching itself . . .' (Gramsci quoted in Femia, 1981, p. 132. By 'philosophical current' Gramsci means ideological intervention). In Gramscian theory then, common sense may be modified by the introduction of a philosophy or ideology, but it is not taken over by that philosophy. Rather it absorbs it or parts of it. Thus culture *actively* transforms itself. In this way, culture is the site of resistance to ideology although this is not necessarily active or knowing resistance. Culture provides natural or unavoidable resistance to ideology by virtue of its innumerable parameters, huge variety of interlinkages, and vastly diverse patterns of thought and action. If ideology is to succeed in its aim of establishing hegemonic dominance, it has to overcome or contend with this complexity and become embedded in the mores of a culture which it itself has transformed.

Archer's (1988) representation of cultural evolution has already been mentioned (see chapter 1). She suggests that most theorists (including dominant ideology theorists) working in this area ignore the interface between cultural structure and agency. It is the interplay here which is the source of cultural dynamics. Archer suggests that analysis of this relationship should start with consideration of contradictions in the cultural system and that this should be at the level of ideas: 'In short, analysis opens by examining the effects of holding ideas with particular logical relations . . . not with the reasons for these being held. . . . Contradictions mould problem-ridden situations for actors which they must confront if and when they realize, or are made to acknowledge, that the proposition(s) they endorse is enmeshed in some inconsistency'. When this is the case, the consequences depend on whether those concerned choose to ignore the inconsistency or 'if they want to go on holding (the proposition) non-dogmatically, then their only recourse is to repair the inconsistency . . . (p. xx). In other words the focus of analysis is what members of a particular cultural system think and then do (agency) when they find themselves in a situation of cultural 'contradiction'. Their actions which are aimed at 'repairing' the inconsistency lead to 'cultural elaboration'. Archer goes on to recommend that 'the macro unit of structural analysis is properly the institutional, for these are the parts between which contradictions develop . . .' (p. 278). The above discussion provides a framework in which the events so far covered in this study can be located. Perceived in terms of the unavoidable and continuous sparring for dominance between ideology and culture, the developments in training in the 1960s and 1970s can be interpreted as an attempt by the profession (agents) to 'repair' the 'contradictions' generated by the introduction of an academic curriculum (ideology) into an unreceptive (college) culture.

Over time the ideological curriculum of Robbins fared badly. It was reduced at the hands of the profession to a mere shadow of its former self. This 'shadow' or 'residue' took the form of a theory now converted to servicing practice or to theory-as-process and also the raised intellectual standards that the academic curriculum had enforced. This was no mean achievement on the part of the professional culture. However, there are occasions when culture is more receptive than this to the material representations of an ideology and the academic nature of training in the universities at the time of Robbins was just such an occasion. In the universities, the curriculum of initial training was hardly affected by the Robbins Report. Ideological (that is social democratic) intervention was limited to an expansion of the number of places available to university students in general and increased funding. There was to be no significant disjuncture between government ideology and the form of training found in the UDEs. In 1954, Holmes wrote a paper on the teaching of teachers which illustrates the contrast between the respective cultures of college and university as reflected in their curricula. Speaking of the colleges, he refers to the deeply embedded practical nature of their culture: 'The tradition that teachers can best be trained in the schools under practising teachers dies hard . . . Firmly convinced of the efficacy of traditional methods . . . (advocates of this model of training) stand in the path of educational change. The undue emphasis in some training colleges on teaching practice to the neglect of problems of theory, and the difficulties of establishing education as a university discipline are symptomatic of these traditional views' (pp. 4 and 5). Holmes goes on to suggest that on the other hand, 'real scholarship' is a 'prerequisite' in the teacher and he laments that 'the shortness of professional courses, makes a thorough study of the key theoretical studies in education impossible' (p. 11). Tibble (1961) who was also a member of a UDE shared the view that the disciplines of education represented the university ideal of scholarship, claiming that: 'The strength of the University Department of Education lies in its witness for the study of educational theory and practice as a proper subject for enquiry and research at University level' (p. 13). Thus the curricular culture of the university departments of education was if anything confirmed by the Robbins Report. Ideology did not repudiate it as it had the curricular culture within the colleges. For these and other reasons, we should not be surprised at the apparent lack of development in the curricula of UDE courses which the SPITE study reveals. What had been imposed on the public sector institutions had challenged their traditional view of training. Not only had there been no ideological intervention in the curriculum of the UDEs, but what was being introduced into the public sector institutions seemed to support their own (university) views of what should constitute the training of teachers.

How then can the movement towards a more school-focused training in the UDEs, limited though it was (except in the case of the University of Sussex) be accounted for? How did the academic approach to training of the universities come to be redirected towards the college model as was implied in the papers to the UCET conference in 1975? Two influences are suggested. The first of these is the assumption that the contributors to the academic debate who wished to see more emphasis on the practice of teaching were in the main members of the UDEs. They did not operate *in vacuo* but influenced practice where and to the extent that this was possible in their own institutions. It is likely however, that proposals that the participation of schools in initial training should be increased, attracted only limited support given both the strong commitment of the UDEs to theoretical scholarship and the more general problems of introducing change within these organizations.

Second, during the 1970s cooperation between members from opposite sides of the binary divide became increasingly common. Sites of such cooperative activity — and one can surely assume mutual learning — included the working party which produced the UGC/CNAA Guidelines (1973) and the many boards and validation panels of CNAA. By these means the public sector institutions and the universities were able to share perspectives and the isolation of the one from the other was diminished. In these ways, the UDEs became increasingly aware of an alternative perspective on training.

If, as has been suggested here, culture is the potential gadfly of ideology, thwarting its aims and transforming its structures, it has also been suggested that it can facilitate the introduction of an ideology. These two apparently opposing interpretations of the culture — ideology relationship can be alternatively interpreted as different stages during the progression of this relationship. Culture must be the source of ideology, not only in the obvious sense that ideology is itself a cultural form which will develop from a cultural base, but in a more specific and defined sense which makes it possible to trace the interaction of ideology and specific cultural elements over an historical period, following the way in which the relationship develops as a series of stages which may perpetuate an interactive pattern: ideology is introduced into a cultural form ------> the cultural form is transformed ------> it then domesticates these ideological representations in some way ------> this process will prepare the way for another ideology ------> and the cycle repeats itself. To propose this fourth step in the ongoing relationship between ideology and culture is not to argue teleologically from effect to cause but merely to reiterate that an ideology can only be successfully introduced into a culture if they share some elements in common. Thus the state of a culture does not determine the advent of the next ideology. What it can do is to offer a receptive context for the introduction of ideology X rather than ideology Y. The shared culture of training at the end of the 1970s appears to have offered the incoming Conservative government just such a context.

By that time, initial training had developed a number of characteristics which were also characteristics of the ideology which was to become known as 'Thatcherism'; and it is an irony that these had emerged within the world of training principally as a result of professional activity. Teacher training was to attract ideological intervention under the new Conservative government for two principal reasons: because it was so variable that comparability of standards of training could not be guaranteed and because the system as a whole is considered to be a potentially valuable channel of ideological effect. But the training system was made relatively easy to access first by points of similarity between it and the new ideology and second by the existence of the structural contradiction which has already been mentioned. The philosophy of the market place was to become the basic principle of the new ideology and within training, the emergence of CNAA as an alternative to the university departments had created a 'free market' in validation. Public sector institutions now had the power of consumers and were able to seek validation from either body according to their particular needs and demands. The programme of college closures which had taken place during the mid 1970s had also inadvertently prepared the ground for the advent of Thatcherism in two respects. As teacher training places were reduced, so were the remaining colleges, most of them now diversified, obliged to compete with each other for students. The continued existence of many of the establishments which had previously specialized in teacher training now depended upon their ability to attract students to study for other qualifications, and this became an important consideration in the design of new courses. Opportunism had become a useful characteristic in the college principal. The modularization of courses which was a further outcome of the rationalization of the higher education system not only permitted but encouraged students to operate in the spirit of 'individualism'. It was an advertised benefit of many courses in initial teacher training that to some degree at least, students might construct their own courses from the modules available according to their own personal preferences. Alongside competition in the market place, personal responsibility for one's life history was to be a central tenet of the new ideology. In addition, two further principles of the incoming ideology were to be a commitment to practice and the marginalization of theory; and teacher training, as has been demonstrated above, was developing in this direction. Training had become increasingly skills based and in this respect was to chime neatly with Thatcherism. All these characteristics which had emerged as the outcome of the reformulation of the previous ideological intervention, offered a receptive context for reintervention by the exponents of Thatcherism. However, these parallels refer only to the material representations of ideology, yet ideological dominance is also about the distribution of power between social groups and the way in which this represents the principles being advocated. As we have seen, there had been only a minimal redistribution of power from the training institutions to the schools as the trend towards a more school-focused form of training had progressed, despite the frequent mention of partnership in course curricula. At the end of the 1970s, the teacher trainers still dominated relationships with the schools. There was thus a looming discrepancy between rhetoric and superficial social practices on the one hand and the underlying distribution of power on the other, a discrepancy which needed remedying and which therefore offered a site for intervention. Furthermore, the profession had lost control of the training system as a whole. In a comparison of the James Report, the 1972 White Paper and *Circular 7/73*, Hencke (1976) notes the erosion of the influence of the academic voice in favour of those of politicians and civil servants. 'The reorganization of colleges, which was originally suggested in James solely for academic reasons, now becomes purely a question of politics and economics' (p. 27). Given the task facing the government, that of the transformation of higher education, including teacher training, within the context of changing demographic conditions and burgeoning economic constraints, this does not seem a surprising development. Nevertheless a new form and degree of central control had been introduced. Moreover, Hencke identifies a further transfer of power 'from the wider world of economics and politics to detailed planning' (p. 28). In order to carry through successfully the many and rapid changes that were to reshape the structure of higher education, it was necessary to rely on administrators whose control was enhanced as a consequence. If during the 1970s therefore, the teacher training profession dominated events and structures within the system, they lost power to influence the development of the system itself. This was a yet further way in which the developments in the training system during the 1970s, inadvertently helped to promote and cushion the introduction of Thatcherism.

But if, at the end of the 1970s, training appeared likely to be a receptive context to the ideology that lay ahead, there were also potential constraints to intervention. In terms both of its *modus operandi* and its contribution to the independence of the professions, the Council for National Academic Awards was a powerful institution. Although the members of its Council were nominated by the Secretary of State for Education and Science, these appointments had not been notably political. The reviewing and validation of courses, which were its routine business, were undertaken by members of the various occupational groups — engineers, teacher trainers, accountants and so on — which used these facilities, supported by a relatively small administrative staff. The CNAA had devised its own operational rules and without being an interventionist institution, nevertheless managed to exercise a considerable degree of control over the development of a wide range of professional and semi-professional occupations by steering, monitoring and approving their training courses. Thus its membership and its influence permeated social and economic life in this country. To any government bent on introducing and stabilizing a new ideology, the CNAA was therefore both a challenge and a potential prize. There was also the power of the professionals to be confronted. The 1970s was the decade which in general witnessed the culmination of the trend towards the professional society, described by Perkin (1989) as a society based on human capital and specialized trained expertise rather than ownership of land and property, and on the ideal of the good society rather than that of entrepreneurialism.

This then was the scene as we move into the 1980s. The Conservative government came to power in 1979, eager to gain ideological ascendancy and stability after the many years of political indecisiveness. It confronted a teacher training system which was characterized by diversity, but also by a professional confidence which was derived from more than a decade of successful independent management of its own affairs.

Summary

The conclusions reached in this section on the Interplay Between Ideology and Culture are as follows:

- the characteristics of a culture which enable it to combat ideological onslaught include density of knowledge, continuity over time, flexibility, and the ability to absorb foreign elements while retaining its essential identity;
- culture *must* be resistant to ideology; its inherent complexity confronts intervention with a many layered pattern of interwoven aims, practices, principles, beliefs, artifacts, routines and so on, which can never be fully penetrated (made hegemonic). The power of cultural resistance is demonstrated by viewing the post-Robbins curriculum changes from the perspective of the colleges;
- nevertheless if the ideological input is sufficiently strong and pervasive, culture will retain an 'ideological effect', a 'residue';
- culture does not determine ideology, but it constrains it;
- culture can 'assist' or favour the introduction of an ideology by providing a sympathetic context;
- over time the relationship between a sub-culture and a central ideology is dynamic and interactive.

Notes

1 The submission documents to CNAA were sampled by institution rather than by course, it being thought likely that the relationship between theory and practice in a submission, whether BEd or PGCE, primary or secondary, would be governed above all by the philosophy of the institution. In many cases this was found to be the case, some institutions using the same general material (e.g. on aims of training or the principles of teaching practice) across courses. Elsewhere, the accounts of the changing status and function of professional studies collated by Alexander and Wormald (1979) seem to confirm that an institutional approach did exist. Necessarily however, for reasons of space, the detailed findings of this survey have been omitted in this account and only the most general trends across all kinds of courses in initial teacher training are indicated. That these trends may not have been universally accepted or that they may mask dissension and power struggles within institutions is implied elsewhere by comments on the divisions that emerged between staff groups.

2 It is readily acknowledged that this technique is highly selective. Nevertheless, quotations can be selected only if they are there and the aim is to give a flavour of the way in which courses are developing rather than specific details. Cumulatively the quotations are considered to do that satisfactorily.

4 The 1980s: Advent of a New Ideology

Introduction

The previous chapter concluded that it was the profession rather than the government that initiated developments in the curriculum of training during the 1970s. Control of the curriculum by the professionals had been facilitated by three external factors: the occupational climate of the time which allowed professionals in general to enjoy considerable autonomy in the execution and monitoring of their affairs; the tradition of non-interference in curricular matters by the Secretary of State; and the preoccupation of successive governments with the need to respond to crises in the economy by revising their principles and priorities. It is doubtful whether during that period, more than marginal consideration was given to the content of the training curriculum by the Department of Education and Science, priority being given to rationalizing the training system itself in response to demographic changes. The major concern of the teacher unions was the occupational status and remuneration of their members, and as far as it has been possible to judge, the influence of the Inspectorate on training remained slight. Thus there were few external constraints on the teacher training community concerning the development of the curriculum. Both university and public sector institutions enjoyed a high degree of freedom to select and organise the substance of the training that they offered.

This did not mean that individual training institutions exercised an uncontrolled and irresponsible freedom with regard to the curricula of the courses that they mounted. Within the professional community there were numerous checks and balances: the tradition of peer evaluation of existing practice and new knowledge which is so fundamental a principle and procedure within the academic community, the stabilizing influence of the Council for National Academic Awards, the difficulties of introducing organizational change, the different cultural traditions of the universities and the colleges and their respective emphases on either theory or practice . . . these and other factors ensured that change in the training curriculum was steady rather than headlong, considered rather than rash. These were also factors which encouraged diversity across courses and at the end of the decade, it was possible for a student to receive a training in which the disciplines of education still featured prominently or a training in which the school (though not teachers themselves) was regarded as 'central' and in which professional or curriculum courses took precedence over educational theory.

This situation must be viewed from the perspective of the Conservative government which came to power in 1979, ready to transform the political climate with its alternative ideology. Any government, of whatever political persuasion, will seek to impose its own agenda on those social institutions to which it can gain access. Education, including initial teacher education, is a particularly attractive target for government intervention because it appears to provide opportunities to influence the attitudes and beliefs of future generations, and because the education system makes a vital contribution to economic growth and development. Yet at this time, the teacher education system appeared to offer more constraints upon than possibilities for political manoeuvring. The power of the Secretary of State, although apparently all embracing in the terms of Section 1 of the 1944 Education Act, was in fact limited by the structure laid down in the rest of the Act and by the convention that 'successive ministers do not seem to have invoked (Section 1) to justify their actions. The mechanism by which the Secretary of State might exercise control and direction exists only patchily' (Raison, 1976, p. 14). Second, the new government was confronted by a training system in which diversity of provision was thoroughly entrenched. Together with the lack of control over training by the DES, this had been clearly identified as a problem in 1971 in the Willey and Maddison Report; and despite the success of CNAA in raising standards in the public sector institutions, by the beginning of the 1980s it would have been rash to assert that courses across the country provided an equivalent training on a number of dimensions: the coherence of the curriculum, access to schools, partnership with schools, the quality of teaching, standards of assessment and so on. The prospects looked bleak for a government wishing to influence initial teacher training for the twin purposes of ensuring a certain standard across courses and of disseminating its views.

But if there appeared to be constraints which might inhibit the new government from intervening in teacher training, there were also other factors which were enabling. It was suggested in the previous chapter that the way in which courses had developed during the 1970s had predicted as it were, within the structures and practices of the curriculum, several of the elements of the new ideology. Or rather, the entry of this new ideology into teacher training would be facilitated because the context was already receptive to it. In addition, a redistribution of power between the traditional partners in the educational system — the LEAs, the unions and the DES — was taking place. The centre was becoming increasingly dominant at the expense of the periphery, and while this did not directly impinge upon the development of training, a climate of centralized control was emerging.

The post-war period until the mid-1970s is often regarded as a golden age for local government: spending continued to increase, ever greater responsibilities were assumed and services were delivered at local level apolitically and with reasonable efficiency. By the early 1970s local government was sufficiently confident, powerful and solvent to able to offer a range of services which were the practical embodiment of the Welfare State, and in a further indication of the general rise of the professional, many of these services were deemed to require a 'professional' type relationship with the client (Cochrane, 1993). Up to this point, the LEAs had enjoyed considerable autonomy. They had controlled their own capital expenditure and had had the power to achieve their objectives in the face of opposition from central government (Ranson and Tomlinson, 1986). But as the economic crises deepened, and the availability of funding levelled off and then fell during the late 1970s, the power of the LEAs gradually diminished. Furthermore, the influence of the chief officers, including those for education, was reduced when the local authorities were reorganized in 1972 as part of the Labour party's drive for modernization. As corporate management techniques were introduced, the authority of the chief executive increased relative to that of others (Simpson, 1986). Thus by the time the Conservatives were elected to office at the end of the decade, the ability of the LEAs to constrain government initiatives had been substantially reduced.

Similarly the potential of the teachers' unions to influence events had declined. A relative fall in salaries, the William Tyndale affair, internal squabbles between unions, and in the eyes of the public an excessive interest in financial rewards rather than in professional competence, had all weakened the status of teachers (Price, 1986). Seifert (1987) in whose book on teachers' strikes, the chapter on the 1970s is headed 'Fragmentation and factionalism', shows that teachers were heavily involved in local and national disputes throughout this period. As a member of the TUC, the National Union of Teachers was engaged in opposing general government legislation to control the unions, and by 1976 teachers across the country were beginning to confront the LEAs of whose declining budgets they were now the victims. By these means teachers had lost much of their credibility and power as respected negotiating partners.

It might be imagined that as the power of the LEAs and of the teachers' unions was gradually eroded, that of the centre would have increased. But Price (1986) points out that the DES also was subject to financial constraints and in addition suffered a series of weak and minor ministers as Secretary of State. However, there were two significant developments which presaged the dominant position of the DES under the Conservative government of Thatcher. In the mid-1970s, there were two reports on the DES. That of the House of Commons Expenditure Committee (the Fookes Report) recommended that the Secretary of State should take part in shaping the curriculum but not in controlling it, and criticized the DES for equating planning with resource allocation. That of the OECD accused the DES of conservatism and of being rooted in the historical traditions of the civil service. Although both these reports were critical, both legitimated a more interventionist stance on the part of the Department.

The second development was the growth of interest in the curriculum at the centre. Within the DES it was noted that the response to the 1972 White Paper had been unfavourable in some quarters, the criticism being that it had concentrated on logistics rather than on the curriculum itself. At about the same time the DES Report on 'School Education in England' was leaked to the press. This suggested that the Department should give a firmer lead and should take every opportunity to exercise influence over the curriculum and over teaching methods. Lawton and Gordon (1987) consider it likely that the Inspectorate contributed to this survey, and they go on to indicate the ways in which 'since 1977, HMI (were) increasingly active in policy making in curriculum matters' (p. 28), having been progressively drawn into educational planning by the DES. But it was the Labour Prime Minister in his speech at Ruskin College in 1976 who first publicly advocated a return to traditional teaching, a core curriculum and the fostering of links between education and industry, and in so doing voiced the need for the recasting of education policy along more instrumental lines. This event was followed by the Green Paper of 1977 which Lawrence (1992) suggests 'represents the formal arrival of central government intervention in matters which broadly speaking had traditionally been left to the good sense of teachers . . .' (p. 82). The Green Paper was concerned with the management of teachers and with the relationship between school and employment as well as with the curriculum. It criticized child-centred primary methods and the organization of the curriculum at secondary level. In addition, in 1976, the Assessment and Performance Unit was set up. Lawrence regards this as 'a clear sign that central government wished to play its own central role in the development of the curriculum and in the control of teaching' (*ibid*, pp. 85–6).

These events had all taken place under the auspices of a Labour government. Thus by the time the Conservatives were elected to office in 1979, curricular matters had become a priority, power had accrued to the centre, and the old tripartite partnership of the DES, the LEAs and the NUT had been considerably weakened; and the Inspectorate had become actively engaged in monitoring and influencing the curriculum and was working more closely with the DES. This remarkable change in events, which was to be continued and extended by the Conservatives in their turn, was regarded as justified by the widespread conclusion that the failure of the economy could be attributed to weaknesses in the schools which had neglected to provide industry with an appropriately skilled workforce. Both parties accepted that it had become necessary to reappraise the fundamental principle on which the whole of the educational system had been based — that equal educational opportunities for all would create a fairer and more just society — and place a greater emphasis on training, skills and a curriculum which would contribute to economic growth. In summary, concern about the control and content of education now replaced concern about access, and the power of the DES and the Inspectorate had increased while that of the LEAs and the teachers' unions had declined. This was the context that Thatcher and her government inherited when they came to power in 1979.

The following chapter is sub-divided into the same three sections as before, and its aims are are as follows:

(i) **Ideological belief**
to review the characteristics of the ideology of 'Thatcherism';

(ii) **Ideological implementation**
to further consider the ways in which the principles of 'Thatcherism' were reflected in the model of training to which the teacher training community was moving at the end of the 1970s; and to consider the ideological strategies of the Conservative government with respect to teacher education during the 1980s;

(iii) **Ideological achievement**
to assess the ideological success of these strategies, that is to investigate whether the government succeeded in bringing the teacher training community to a hegemonic state.

Ideological Belief: The Nature of 'Thatcherism'

Since the origins of several of the events just mentioned can be traced to developments in the economic system, the comments above raise once again one of the most fundamental issues in ideological theory, that of the relationship between the economy and ideology. It is assumed here that it was the worldwide recession of the 1970s in general and the economic problems of the UK in particular — high inflation, a lack of competitiveness, industrial unrest and above all the need to continue to finance the ever increasing cost of the Welfare State — that contributed to the emergence of Thatcherism. But it had been the Labour party and not the Conservatives which had reduced public expenditure and kept tight control of the money supply, thus finally dispensing with the social democratic consensus and introducing monetarism. 'It was forced to do this by the severity of Britain's economic crisis in 1974–76. These were the subterranean events that broke up the post-war political consensus, not Thatcher's victory at the polls . . . Thatcher and her colleagues simply gained from the work that had already been done and rode down the path that had already been cleared' (Holmes, 1985a, p. 167, quoting Hodgson whose analysis he regards as 'quite correct'). Holmes does not mean by this that the government of Thatcher had followed the lead of the Labour party and suddenly lighted on the principle of monetarism as the solution to the economic crises of the day. The ideology of Thatcherism did not unexpectedly emerge at the end of the 1970s to dominate political life for the next decade. It had become increasingly salient in the political arena in general. Before the 1979 election, two attempts, the first by Heath, a Conservative but the second by Callaghan of the Labour party, had been made to put some of the principles of what was to become Thatcherism into practice. Both had failed. The new ideology had been waiting in the wings as it were until it was perceived as a possible acceptable solution to current economic and political ills.

This moment came in 1979 and was the electorate's response to the Labour party's apparent incompetence and indecisiveness. Rowthorn (1983) describes the scene: the government had 'lost all sense of direction and its economic policy became even less coherent than that of its predecessors. Buffeted by inflation and balance of payment crises, it lurched from one emergency to another, pursuing a highly restrictive combination of deflation and wage restraint, and the result was almost complete industrial stagnation' (p. 69). It was this that won the Conservatives the election. Less than half of those who voted supported the Conservatives but this was sufficient to claim a mandate from the people and to put into practice the radical programme of policies which were a complete break from social democracy.

Throughout the 1970s, the New Right movement had been gathering momentum. It emerged in several countries of the Western world and was as much a general backlash to the social permissiveness of the 1950s and 1960s as an attempt to provide solutions to the economic ills resulting from the world recession. It is generally agreed by writers in the area that 'Thatcherism', its political representation in the UK, consists of two strands: those of neo-liberalism and of neo-conservatism (Gamble, 1983; Jacques, 1983; Levitas, 1986; King, 1987) which are variously emphasized by its different exponents. The central thesis of neo-liberalism is that economic prosperity stems from the unconstrained operation of market forces. Hence, interference with the market in any way, for example by funding either industry or welfare services, will reduce its efficiency. The role of the government is to facilitate the working of the market. It should not intervene through an excess of bureaucratic controls but let competition run its course within a framework of enforceable enabling rules. It also has the task of exercising firm control of the money supply in order to maintain stable prices. The market can operate successfully only if individuals are free to make their own choices and all collective measures of whatever kind, including the operation of the unions, are regarded as constraining individual liberty. They therefore not only generate inefficiency but are also morally inadmissible. It is the right of an individual to be as free of state control as can be made possible, and the more freedom that the individual has, the more productive will he/she be in the economic dimension. The second strand of Thatcherism, that of neo-conservatism, promotes and elevates the nation over the individual. Patriotism, authority, cultural heritage and national unity are all held in high regard, as are the concomitant principles for social living: law and order, the family unit and adherence to traditional standards and moral values.

Some quotations taken from the first few pages of the collected speeches of Thatcher (1989a) to Conservative party conferences will illustrate the above points. Substantively they emphasize the limited role of government, the need for a tight control of the money supply and the moral and economic benefits of individual effort. But they also hint at hegemonic intent. They embody Gramsci's belief that exponents of a new ideology must demonstrate its continuity with the culture of the target group.

- 'I believe that just as each of us has an obligation to make the best of his talents, so governments have an obligation to create a framework within which we can do so' (p. 15).
- 'The policies which are needed are dictated by common sense . . . The only way to safety is to stop borrowing and stop borrowing soon; and moreover to show that we can and will repay our debts in a strong currency and on time . . . the only common sense answer is to reduce government spending . . .' (pp. 23–4).
- 'It was not restraint that brought us the achievements of Elizabethan England . . . that started the Industrial Revolution . . . (or) that inspired us to explore for oil in the North Sea. . . . It was incentive — positive, vital, driving, individual incentive . . .' (p. 25).
- 'We have won minds — but we must now win hearts . . . On matters that concern ordinary men and women it is we who represent the majority view . . . Today we are all working people . . .' (p. 27).

To a considerable extent the forcefulness with which social change was to be introduced by the Conservatives once they came to power can be attributed to the length of time Thatcherism had been waiting its turn. By 1976, the principles that were to become the basis of the new Conservatism were being articulated in the public domain. In his collection of essays jointly edited with Patten and written while the party was in opposition Blake (1976) summarizes what was soon to become the basis of the doctrine of Thatcherism in his critique of recent and current events. He dismisses unequivocally the paternalism and welfare consensus which had dominated British politics since the 1940s. He is in revolt against Keynesian control of the economy, has misgivings about the cost of the Welfare State, a thorough dislike of burgeoning bureaucracy, and he mistrusts the power of the trade unions. In the paper by Peele in this collection, there is less advocacy and a greater appreciation of the need for the party to redefine the principles for which it stands, to re-establish its ideological base. Ideology is recognized as being both intellectual and moral. It is a battle of ideas. Peele displays many of the characteristics of Gouldner's ideologue bent on establishing a new 'historic bloc': disregarding convention ('No government need take any notice of the House of Commons so long as it has an effective majority' (p. 16)); identifying opponents and exaggerating their evil ('There is talk of infiltration by extremists into the landscape of British politics' (p. 17)); indicating that the Conservative party has its own agenda for improving the condition of society; and acknowledging the role of intellectuals in promoting the new doctrine. Peele also reminds us that 'Tories have distrusted the applications of abstract doctrines to politics and have preferred instead to follow the dictates of common sense and experience' (p. 13).

Blake (1976) detected what he referred to as a 'changing intellectual climate' which would carry the Conservatives to victory in the next election — as indeed it did. By the time his paper had been published, Thatcher had already given a speech at a party conference in 1975 in which she urged the case for less government and more freedom for the ordinary person since 'We believe that you become a responsible citizen by making decisions for yourself, not by having them made for you' (Thatcher, 1989a, p. 16). This is a significant remark since it subsumes not only individual responsibility but also the desirability that one should make up one's own mind and not be influenced by the 'theories' of others. By the time the Thatcher government stood for election, many of the natural supporters of the Labour party had finally overcome their reluctance to oppose a government which was usually regarded as safeguarding their interests. Jacques (1983) suggests this was symptomatic of a general shift to the right in the latter years of the Labour party's period in office. Disillusionment with governments of both parties neither of which had been able to deal competently with the continuous round of economic crises in the 1970s led to a realignment of political affiliation and the emergence of a grassroots popular 'rightism' which saw the solution to the country's ills in a reassertion of traditional values and a traditional way of life: within the family,without immigrants, in accordance with a firm morality and dissociated from the progressive movements of the 1960s. Blake (1976) notes that Heath had made the same appeals as did Thatcher in her turn, but 'the difference is that the climate of opinion has changed. What could plausibly . . . be dismissed in 1970 as reactionary, . . . cannot be laughed off today' (p. 7).

To complement this brief account of the rise of Thatcherism, it needs to be confirmed that Thatcherism *was* an ideology. Since it is the intention of the ideologue to capture the hearts and minds of the people, to obtain hegemonic dominance over them, a comment by Thatcher that 'we must reach out not only to the minds, but to the hearts and feelings and to the deepest instincts of our people' (1989a, p. 28) is almost sufficient to confirm this. However, we should also look at the criteria used to define an ideology in ideological theory. According to Gramsci an essential characteristic of an ideology lies in the provision of 'intellectual and moral leadership'. That ideologies should have both an intellectual and a moral dimension seems plausible given that the aim of ideological exposition is to persuade the listener to act in accordance with a particular doctrine, and this aim is more likely to be achieved if that act is perceived as rationally justified and morally desirable. An ideology must indicate both how and why people should behave, and if it is to be effective in redirecting both thought and action, the hows must be consistent and the associated whys convincing. If intellectual leadership is interpreted in terms of clearly articulated recommendations for social behaviour, recommendations which are logically supported by certain chosen principles, then Thatcherism meets this criterion. In her many public addresses made over the years, Thatcher does not waiver from her commitment to the same interlocking themes such as the need to rejuvenate the nation through a return to moral standards and personal endeavour, and the importance of reducing the influence of the state if the market is to flourish. These exhortations simultaneously explain the causes of current economic and social ills and also offer the means of escape from these same dilemmas. There is no doubt either that Thatcherism is moral in both the substantive and presentational senses. Minogue (1985) notes that all ideologies are intrinsically moral since they present the hidden truth about the evils of the world in the form of social analysis and Thatcher herself likens her policies to a 'crusade' (for example, Thatcher, 1989b, p. 205). Jenkins (1987) devotes a whole chapter of his book on Thatcherism as a moral response to the ills which seemed to be engulfing society in the 1970s. Decline had become a moral issue (p. 60). For Thatcher, the Welfare State and moral decay go hand in hand, and moral worth is synonymous with commitment to her perspective: 'A moral being is one who exercises his own judgment in choice on matters great and small . . . In so far as his right and duty to choose is taken away by the State . . . he becomes a moral cripple' (Thatcher, quoted in Jenkins, 1987, p. 66). But the most obvious attempt to convey the moral worth of her doctrine must be her speech to the General Assembly of the Church of Scotland (1988) in which the right to choose as a political act is regarded as reflecting man's endowment by God with the right to choose between good and evil.

However, Thatcherism does not seem to meet the requirement of coherence in Seliger's definition of an ideology (Seliger, 1976). In many respects, the two dimensions of Thatcherism exist in tension. In a number of ways neo-liberalism and neo-conservatism contradict each other: in the role allocated to the state, in the role of the individual and in the nature and scope of freedom (King, 1987; Marquand, 1988). For example, the emphasis on the strong state, on law and order and on authority on the one hand seems to be incompatible with the promotion of individual freedom on the other. Conservatism values tradition whereas Liberalism values progress. But it is possible to reconcile these contradictions in one respect at least: the need for a strong state to ensure that the market operates freely. For Thatcher the state must be powerful in order to enforce the general rules which safeguard the individual liberty which is a necessary condition of this state. What is perceived as intervention by the centre can be justified as facilitating freedom of choice and thus contributing to an efficient self-regulating market. However, as Levitas (1986) points out, ideologies do not need to be objectively logical. The aim of their proponents is to establish as wide a popular base of support as possible and the more flexibility within an ideology, the more likely this is to be achieved.

Summary

The conclusions reached in this section on Ideological Belief are as follows:

- the mid 1970s saw the rise of monetarism as a party–independent response to deep rooted economic and political problems;
- however, in private, the Conservative party had long cherished the principles of the New Right including that of monetarism; Thatcherism represents the political presentation of these principles in the UK;
- the Conservative government led by Thatcher did not win the election of 1979; the Labour party lost it;
- on coming to power, the Conservative government found a centralized educational system already in place, an assertive DES, and an Inspectorate with an interest in curriculum;
- Thatcherism meets the principal criteria for an ideology as expressed in ideological theory; it also meets the three criteria used to define an ideology at the beginning of this study and which have formed the structure of each chapter.

Ideological Implementation: The Ideological Strategies of the Thatcher Government with Respect to Teacher Training in the 1980s

In the previous chapter, it was suggested that some of the features of initial training at the end of the 1970s corresponded to elements of the philosophy of the new Conservative government. There this relationship was reviewed from the perspective of the training institution. In the following paragraphs, it will be discussed from the perspective of the government.

Given the intention of governments to control or at least to influence as many areas of social life as possible, the notion of facilitating conditions is important. But however useful this phrase is to indicate some degree of match between context and doctrine, it should be used warily. It should not be taken to represent any preparation on the part of social institutions, such as the teacher training community, for the advent of the new ideology, nor necessarily any support for it. As was shown in the previous chapter the movement towards a school-focused practical training was the outcome of internal initiatives and was independent of party politics. At that time, the curriculum of training was not politicized except residually. But like any other area of social life, teacher training is not impervious to all external influences, and it is possible to interpret some of the developments in training in these terms. Those elements within teacher training, whether structural or idealistic which were to find echoes in Thatcherism could be perceived as part of the general societal move to the political Right mentioned above from which Thatcherism itself had sprung. For example, the movement towards partnership in validation associated with the CNAA (see below) could be seen as the equivalent of rolling back the state to the extent that it represented a move towards less central control and greater institutional independence. Such deconstruction of the similarities between the two systems seems unnecessarily tortuous however. It is more reasonable just to acknowledge that the climate of the times is crucial in determining whether or not the exponents of a particular ideology come to power and their philosophy is entertained. If, as was the case in the late 1960s and the 1970s, the training community acts upon those curricular representations of the central ideology which have been introduced into the system, and modifies or transforms them in accordance with its own preferences and priorities, then the reverse does not hold. The training system did not shape the ideology of Thatcherism. The effect of the *status quo* must be to constrain to a greater or lesser degree the ease with which an ideology can be introduced as Gramscian theory makes clear.

One obvious point of similarity to Thatcherism within initial training at the start of the 1980s was the value attributed in its many guises to practice, particularly skills, rather than to theory, although it cannot be claimed that this was more than emergent in many of the training institutions. Although ironically the members of the New Right rely on theorists outside the training system (O'Hear, 1988; the Hillgate Group, 1989) to present the case for a form of teacher training in which the role of the theorist is reduced, Thatcher herself often spoke out against theorists. Her mistrust of the theorist was matched by her admiration for the practitioner and for the common sense of the ordinary people — preferences which are directly derived from the philosophy of the market. It is the practitioner, not the theorist dreamer, who gets things done, who exhibits common sense, creates wealth and generates further business. In teacher training, the theorist can be perceived as standing between the teacher who actually 'produces' teaching and the consumer in the learning situation, the student, and thus interrupts their market relationship. For the Thatcher government, theory within training creates inefficiency. In addition, academics are members of the professions and professionals operate according to their own rules and have their own values and standards. This independence contravenes the principles of the neo-liberal economy which for its smooth functioning is dependent upon all participants accepting and adhering to the same set of rules. Furthermore, since the attainment of an historic bloc or hegemony is dependent upon achieving a society in which the relative power of the various groups reflects and corresponds to the principles of the dominant ideology, the promotion of school-based training would redistribute power in the desired direction, in favour of the practitioner. Thus for the new government there were not only sound ideological reasons for reducing theory in training and elevating skills, but also the very possibility of so doing, since courses had already moved in the direction of emphasizing practice.

Then there is the quality of 'individualism', which is so central an element in social market philosophy. It is the personal choice of the unfettered free individual which lies at the heart of liberal economics. In this respect also, the nature of training was leaning towards the new ideology. Or rather individualism was a characteristic that training increasingly demanded from students. Compared with the days when the training college was a *gemeinschaft* community, when tutors and students met in leisure activities and these leisure activities were often an extension of work (Shipman, 1967), training in more recent years had developed a *gesellschaft* quality. To a considerable degree this had been a consequence of the introduction of unit-based courses. Students were required to exercise responsible choice in selecting their unique career patterns. They were, in the words of Lukes (1973) in his essay on political individualism 'independent and rational beings who are the sole generators of their own wants and preferences and the best judges of their own interests' (p. 79). In addition, as students spent a higher percentage of their training period in schools, they became more independent of the training institution and their respective training experiences became increasingly diverse. It was left to the student to make his or her own way, to reconcile the unique experience of time spent in school with the shared time spent in colleges. In these various ways, the courses on offer in the institutions when Thatcher came to power appear to have provided a sympathetic context for the introduction of the new ideology.

The ideological strategies used in the 1960s to install the social democratic curriculum of training at the time of the Robbins Report (see chapter 2) can be compared with those used by the New Right government of the 1980s. Although the setting up of the Committee has been interpreted as a highly ideological move, the total strategic and tactical complement brought to bear at the time of the report was limited. A prolonged 'war of position' was not necessary. There were no protracted confrontations with members of the profession for example, because the proposals were ideologically uncontroversial. The governing principle of the report that all suitably qualified young people should have access to higher education was common-sense in a world which in general still subscribed to social democratic collectivist principles. The proposed changes to teacher education were but a particular case of this. The intervention that was known as the Robbins Report can best be regarded, as was suggested earlier, as an attempt at ideological confirmation when the government was at rather a low political ebb. For Thatcher, the situation was rather different. On coming to power in 1979, she faced the long-term task of converting the electorate to her vision. The Conservatives had not been elected on the grounds that the public wished to see an end to all collectivist policies. There had been some popular annoyance at the power of the unions to disrupt industrial progress and daily living and also at alleged abuses of the benefit system. Agreement with the Conservative view on these matters did not preclude continued support for other social democratic institutions and practices. The possibility of introducing radical new policies was constrained therefore by an awareness of what the public would accept and also by the continued presence in the Cabinet at

Thatcher's own request, of members of the previous administration. If Thatcherism were to fully succeed, that is to become hegemonic, then more than the elimination of opposing voices from the Cabinet and changes in policy would be required. The task of redirecting attitudes lay ahead (Biddis, 1987) and Thatcher's technique for achieving this transformation of public perception was to exercise the power of the Prime Minister as far as its constitutional limits would permit. The difference in the forcefulness of the ideological strategies exercised against the teacher training community by the governments of the 1960s and the 1980s, reflected the tasks facing those governments: ideological confirmation and ideological conversion respectively.

The various ways in which in the 1980s, the power of the government was strategically and tactically exercised in the area of teacher training can be reviewed. These include the use of Circulars, the creation of the Council for the Accreditation of Teacher Education (CATE) to monitor training, the undermining and politicization of the Council for National Academic Awards and the transformation of the Inspectorate.

Circular 3/84 (DES, 1984) was not issued until five years after the election and after the Cabinet reshuffle of 1981 in which Thatcher dismissed most of her opponents. It was the first occasion on which this government had intervened in initial teacher training. By 1984, Joseph the highly committed architect of the New Conservatism who had already established a reputation for doctrinaire monetary policies (Forum, 1986), held the office of Secretary of State for Education and Science in a fully supportive Cabinet. Audacious action within the area of teacher training had become a possibility. The Circular reflects the tension of which the Conservatives had long been aware — that between purpose and realization, or between vision and knowledge of what the electorate or target group might accept. Moderate in terms of its curricular demands but unprecedented in terms of the control that it introduced, it was a watershed in relations between the government and the profession. In its disregard of the traditions associated with the exercise of the Secretary of State's role, it reflects considerable ideological urgency. That a Secretary of State could assume command of the teacher training curriculum had always been possible within the definition of the role in the 1944 Act as Aldrich and Leighton (1985) note. In their paper 'Education: Time for a New Act' which was also published in 1984, they point out that the precise role of the Minister in the 1944 Act is supremely unclear and that in the matter of the balance of power between the centre and the periphery, the Act 'gives an impression of uncertainty over the vital issue of ultimate authority' (p. 24). That it was the intention of the government to extend its political philosophy to the school curriculum had already been established in the Secretary of State's North of England Speech (1984). This begins with a commentary on the need for 'value for money throughout the education service' and continues with statements on the curriculum — that it 'should be relevant to the real world', should contain an adequate practical element and promote practical capability for all pupils' and should introduce all pupils 'to the economic and other foundations of our society'. It then goes on to note the importance of new teachers being 'well fitted to the needs of the schools'. Although none of these comments can be regarded as seriously controversial, they suggest the possibility that the government had a strategy for the ideological penetration of educational institutions through curricular control.

It is difficult to dispute that by the 1980s a more uniform system of training teachers had become desirable on professional grounds. Diversity across training courses remained rife leading to difficulty in establishing standards. In 1981, in a discussion paper: 'Teacher training in the secondary school' the Inspectorate had acknowledged that 'the problem for teacher training is to know what the newly qualified teacher should be equipped with on emerging from his course . . . There is no consensus on this' (p. 17). In this respect, by introducing standard criteria for the training of teachers across institutions, *Circular 3/84* can be regarded as performing a necessary and useful task. But if it were professionally desirable to regulate the content of training rather more, it was also politically important to do so since by this means access is provided to the school curriculum. That it was the intention of Joseph to intervene in the training curriculum was made clear in his speech at the University of Durham in 1982. Referring to a recent report of HMI in which it was disclosed that nearly a quarter of newly-trained teachers were inadequately equipped with the skills needed for teaching (although three-quarters were judged adequately equipped), Joseph declared: 'I am not satisfied with the present contents (of teacher training) . . . and I intend to take action . . .' A particular concern was the 'jargon ridden theorizing' of the disciplines of education which can be 'lamentable substitutes for serious thought and training' (Joseph, 1983, p. 39). The Circular can be interpreted with this in mind. It is a strategy laden document, incorporating two powerful techniques for gaining ideological domination. The first of these is legitimation which Eagleton (1991) defines as 'the process by which a ruling power comes to secure from its subjects an at least tacit consent to its authority . . .' (p. 54). The second is universalization which is the projection of values and interests which are specific to a particular context as of relevance for all (p. 56).

Joseph's action in stating what the content of the curriculum should be, should not just be seen as stretching the boundaries of his constitutional role. It was more than that. It was also a claim to the ownership of a particular area of educational territory, a means of establishing a right to intervene in the curriculum in the future. This was accomplished by what can be called 'transformation', a strategy which Eagleton (1991) identifies but does not name and which is a means of achieving legitimation. It refers to the ability of the dominant group to identify and isolate the particular needs and aspirations of the target group, to translate these into the discourse of its own ideology and then to return them to the group reformulated as legitimated sentiments and practices. This strategy is one of the most effective and reliable routes to hegemony. If the proposals of the dominant group are perceived as reflecting and clarifying the current interests and aims of the subordinate group (yet while simultaneously representing the central ideology) they are more likely to attract agreement and acceptance. The curriculum section in *Circular 3/84* is a good example of this. It reflects the best of current practice which already chimed with Thatcherism in several respects. Education studies is included, also a range of experiences for the student when placed in a school and the student's need for time for reflection. The minimum amount of time that primary courses should devote to training in maths and language is specified but remains flexible, and a relatively uncontroversial minimum number of weeks to be spent in school is indicated. Nor could there be disagreement with the emphasis on partnership with teachers. It is difficult to find much here that is likely to be unacceptable to the teacher training community and in general the proposals in this section of the Circular set reasonable and attainable standards for training. Ensuring that what is promoted is so close to existing practice is sound ideological technique. It demonstrates that the government understands the nature of training and thus it is legitimate for it to speak on behalf of the profession. In this way the right to intervene in the curriculum is established, thereby at least sharing, and so reducing the authority of the profession to determine for itself the nature of curricular content. Even if the proposed curriculum did not exemplify the doctrine of the centre to the extent of the intended curriculum for schools mentioned above, the declaration embodied in the Circular was that the centre could now determine the curriculum of training. Thus a precedent had been set.

Having sought to legitimate its control over curriculum content with all the potential for ideological socialization in the future that that implies, a means of ensuring the universal application of this curriculum became necessary. In this capacity, the Circular announced the creation of a Council for the Accreditation of Teacher Education (CATE) 'to advise the Secretaries of State . . . on the approval of initial teacher training courses in England and Wales' (para. 3). The task of CATE was to 'review all existing approved courses of initial teacher training'. If courses were judged to be inadequate their future was in doubt and since all courses were now to be accredited by CATE or face closure, universities were not exempt. This was a bold move indeed. Traditionally the university departments of education had operated autonomously. Their funding had been administered through their own agency, the Universities Grants Committee (UGC), and their relationship with the Inspectorate which had undertaken amiable irregular visits had been relatively untroubled. In the Circular, an attempt was made to soften the blow of introducing a monitoring agency by the use of two context specific tactics (see chapter 1). The first of these is the the way in which the Circular presents the Council. CATE is portrayed as representing the interests of the profession. The initiative is said to lie with the Council to advise the DES, not *vice versa* and its members are to be drawn from a wide group of educationists. Second, the appointed chair of CATE had for many years worked in teacher training and was well known and respected in the professional community. But such reconciling statements and practices were countermanded by the knowledge that appointments to CATE were to be made 'by the Secretaries of State on a personal basis' and by the realization that the Notes published later to clarify the role of CATE indicated the way in which 'the Circular leached power from the training institutions' (Wilkin, 1992, p. 315). The full criteria for the accreditation of initial training courses (DES, 1985) were issued about six months later and for the purposes of this argument are noteworthy in two respects: for the redistribution of power both overtly and covertly from the institutions to the schools and for the practical nature of the criteria and the non-reflective (i.e. non-theorizing) mode of student training proposed. The first of these is indicated in several ways: staff in training institutions should have recent experience of teaching in schools (para. 2.2), although the reverse is not a requirement. Teachers should be involved in the planning, supervision, support and assessment of students' practical work in schools, and in their training within the institution (para. 3.3). Courses should be developed and run . . . in close working partnership with . . . schools (para. 3.2), and serving teachers are to be involved in the interviewing of students (para. 1.2). These criteria do not seem at all unreasonable in professional terms except perhaps the first of them. However, the perspective taken here is also ideological and the cumulative effect of the tactics embodied in the criteria listed above is to reduce considerably the power of the theorists, the tutors, and enhance that of the practitioners, the teachers. By promoting the school precedence in the ways indicated, the criteria enhance the relevance, value and status of the contribution to training of the school vis-a-vis that of the training institution. And while the institutions are to lose power to the schools, they are also to lose power to the local committee which is to 'meet regularly (to) discuss the planning, operation and review of the courses . . .' (para. 3.1). Secondly, these criteria are strongly practical in tenor and so constitute a further representation of the central ideology. There are only five paragraphs (paras 5.8–5.12) covering subject independent 'theory' (i.e. disciplinary theory) and there is no suggestion here or elsewhere that students should generate their own theory through systematically reflecting on their performance; and although they are to be given opportunities to discuss teaching and learning methods, there is no mention of discussion in the education studies element of the course. Some of the criteria are less controversial and deservedly so. For example, the position of the student whose practical classroom work is unsatisfactory is clarified. This student can no longer be awarded qualified status. But in general *Circular 3/84* and the CATE criteria for training courses deeply penetrated the training institutions at both structural and substantive levels. The strategies and tactics used for this purpose were multiple and comprehensive: compulsory inspection, the loss of power and influence to the schools supported by the shift from theory to practice in the course. And the most powerful incentive of all — the power to close any course which failed to meet the criteria.

In CATE the government had created a new mediating agency to extend or universalize its influence within the teacher training community. The government was also either to transform or to contribute to the demise or transformation of established agencies which had the potential to intervene between the centre and the training process. These agencies include HM Inspectorate and the Council for National Academic Awards both of which were powerful and independent. The growth and development in terms of numbers, power and influence of HM Inspectorate during the 1970s and into the 1980s can be traced in the DES annual reports. In the early 1970s, the Inspectorate does not merit a heading in the contents section of these reports. By 1977, there are four pages. In 1978 there are seven pages giving an account of the range of activities, ventures and associations in which the Inspectorate participated. During the 1980s these reports also give some indication of the nature of the relationship between the Inspectorate and the DES. In 1982, we are told that there was close contact between the Inspectorate and officials in policy branches of the Department (para. 5.27) and in 1984 'in parallel with the Department's work to seek agreement on curricular objectives to which HMI have contributed, HMI began publication of a series of discussion documents under the general title of Curriculum Matters' (para. 6.8). This suggests that the Inspectorate was caught up in the wider centralization process — the focus of which was the curriculum — that was the outcome of the Great Debate, and that it had become a close working partner of a newly assertive and confident DES. However, Thomas (1986), although agreeing that the Inspectorate now had a higher profile and closer links with policy making, considers that it continued to act independently, for it was the Inspectorate who initiated publications on the curriculum rather than the Department.

Reasons for the centralization of the Inspectorate are given in an article headed 'Shake up in the Inspectorate: Focus switches to centre' by Stevens (1977). Here Browne, the Senior Chief Inspector is quoted as having decided that because of the increased number of national exercises, a proportion of the Inspectorate will be made answerable primarily to the centre. Stevens suggests that the aim of this redistribution of responsibility was greater efficiency and to improve the flow of information from the Inspectorate to the schools and teachers; Lawton and Gordon (1987) state that it was a redistribution of interests which was necessary in order to distinguish the national role of HMI from the local concerns of the LEA inspectors. It was a change which strengthened the centre at the expense of the periphery, which contributed to the consolidation of the more prominent position of the DES at this time and which was one element of the propitious distribution of power which had been inherited by the Conservatives on their election. Several years later, the Rayner Report (DES, 1982) approved the balance that it found between central and local interests in the work of the Inspectorate, but alert to the possibility and dangers of further centralization, warned against it. The report did not consider that 'the proportion of (central) programmed time should be further increased at the expense of the time available for general district work' (para. 3.11).

Insight into some of the parallel internal changes — that is changes in ethos, priorities and loyalties — which had taken place within the Inspectorate can be obtained by comparing two publications on its role issued by the DES in 1970 and 1983 respectively. The first of these, *HMI Today and Tomorrow* is a highly moral document in which the work of the Inspectorate is termed a 'duty' and which makes clear the independence of the Inspectorate from the centre with the following warning: 'It has become accepted that whatever instructions (Inspectors) receive, their professional status and advisory function should not be impaired. There are therefore things which the Secretary of State would not wish, in the course of their duties, to instruct them to do' (p. 1). This is one of the few occasions in this text in which the Secretary of State rather than the DES is mentioned. The Inspectors' relationship with the Department is clearly stated: 'In many cases, an inspector is writing or acting as a representative of the Department, but he is recognized as deriving his authority from the expert knowledge he possesses and this gives him the right to exercise a certain independence of judgment' (pp. 19–20). This document is principally about the Inspectorate, its operations, structure, responsibilities, and relationship with the schools. Only secondly is it about its relationship with the centre. The 1983 document: *HM Inspectors Today: Standards in Education* gives priority to the latter over the former, and these relationships with the centre are with the government rather than the Department. There is little mention of duty or advice. 'HMI *have* to tell the Government about the health of education' (1983a, p. 2 emphasis added). Rather the Inspectors have become just that — inspectors — and that there is pressure for their politicization is suggested by comments such as 'To know the targets of HM Inspectorate's work at any time, one looks to the government's policies and initiatives' (p. 12).

The politicization of the Inspectorate begins to seem a real possibility following a policy statement on its work by the Secretary of State, Joseph, in 1983 (DES, 1983). In this statement, which was a response to the Rayner Report, the reliance of the Secretary of State on the informed and independent evidence and judgments of the Inspectorate is stressed. But despite this declaration of support for its traditional independence, the statement incorporates the Inspectorate within the discourse of the market: 'Inspection . . . is the tool by which the Inspectorate audits the system to assess the extent to which . . . it offers an adequate service and secures value for money' (para. 9); '. . . the overall thrust of the Inspectorate's work is towards achieving an education system more actively concerned with the standards of its products and more cost conscious' (para. 1). Can this reformulation of the Inspectorate's role be regarded as an example of the strategy of transformation? Were this to be the case, the Inspectorate would already have been demonstrating these characteristics in its work or subscribing to this philosophy. There is some slight evidence to support this hypothesis in an HMI discussion paper entitled *Teacher Training and Preparation for Working Life* which was issued the previous year (DES, 1982). This paper opens with the declaration that 'It has in recent years become a truth universally acknowledged (sic!) that education should be more closely linked with the world of work . . . and the country's economic performance' (p. 1), and goes onto recommend that initial training should include courses in commerce and industry in order that students should be made fully aware of the curricular implications of this association. Thus although it is considered unlikely that Inspectors, who were appointed for their professional expertise, had entered the arena of central politics with the commitment implied in Joseph's policy statement, it appears to have been a possibility at this stage.

In 1983, an HMI discussion paper: *Teaching in Schools: The Content of Initial Training* (HMI, 1983b) was published. The paper notes that 'there is a widely recognized need for agreed guidelines on the content of training . . .' while not wishing to deny 'the value of institutional freedom in professional matters, and the value of variety and experiment in the curriculum of teacher education . . .' (p. 3). Drawing on a number of its recent reports which had suggested that initial training did not always prepare students adequately for the classroom, the paper proposes that 'successful classroom practice has to determine the shape of all courses' (p. 16). The emphasis in the paper is therefore on the acquisition of the skills required for competent practice. Within this framework, a number of specific recommendations are made concerning the length of courses, the time to be spent in school, the desirability of partnership and so on. These recommendations were to become the basis of the CATE criteria. Thereafter the Inspectorate and CATE were to work closely together since all teacher training institutions had to be visited by HMI before being considered for accreditation by CATE.

With its own vision of quality training now public policy, the Inspectorate had firm criteria on which to base its evaluations of courses. However, in less than two years, doubts were being expressed about their value. Inspectors were having difficulty in applying the CATE criteria in the assessment of courses (*Times Educational Supplement*, 2 February 1986). Some courses which had been praised by HMI had failed to meet the criteria, and courses which did satisfy the criteria were not necessarily judged to be of a high quality. That there was still wide variation between courses and that therefore some institutions might have difficulty in meeting the criteria was revealed in the Inspectorate's survey of thirty training institutions which was carried out during 1983–85 (HMI, 1987). Although many aspects of training were praised in this report, HMI was critical of others: the limited supervision of students in school by training institution staff gave cause for concern (p. 24); teachers should be encouraged to participate more fully in training and themselves trained for this purpose (p. 24); 'scarcely any' BEd courses equipped students to relate their subject study to the needs of primary school children (p. 25); there was insufficient school experience for many fourth year BEd students (p. 17). In general, this report favoured closer and more participative partnership between school and training institution, more integration of theory and practice and more specialized teaching of practical classroom skills. But it also strongly supported the 'reflective practitioner' model of training in which 'students should become accustomed to question, to debate, to analyze, to argue from evidence and to examine their own habitual assumptions' (p. 30). The survey report can be read as reflecting and perhaps promoting the transition through which training was passing. While proposing an extension of what those in the institutions would regard as current good professional practice, it also facilitates the intervention of the government in training in two ways. It recommends those elements of training which reflect the central ideology and it casts doubt on the training institutions' ability to train teachers successfully. There would therefore be every reason for giving more responsibility for training to teachers in schools. By 1988 institutions had had sufficient time to implement the criteria, but an investigation by the Inspectorate of the proficiency of probationers in their first posts (DES, 1988a) highlights the continuation of some of these deficiencies in training. The areas in which new teachers were experiencing difficulties included: 'classroom management and control, identifying and making explicit the aims and objectives of lessons, matching work to the varied abilities of pupils, the skills of questioning . . .' (para. 1.38). A strong recommendation then follows: that 'More attention needs to be given to defining the levels of competence in different professional skills which may reasonably be expected of teachers at the conclusion of their training' (para. 1.39). In the short section on initial training in this document, there is no mention of either theory or of theorizing.

The emphasis on practical skills and the introduction by HMI of competences into the process and assessment of training brought training further within the political orbit of the government. Competences featured briefly in training during the mid 1970s (see chapter 3) but in the 1980s the term developed political overtones due to its association with the series of training initiatives supported by the Manpower Services Commission which were mounted by the government with the intention of regenerating industry. Competences had been a central feature of these initiatives being both an aim of training and a standard of assessment. Their introduction into teacher training has been opposed by the professional community for several reasons, chief amongst which is the difficulty of representing the complexities of the teaching process by a model of training derived from the learning of industrial skills (Calderhead, 1992). However, laying aside the debate about their professional appropriateness and worth, the introduction of competences into training can be regarded as an ideological tactic for several reasons. They are perceived as a-theoretical, being measures of observable behaviour and hence facilitating the assessment of practical skills. They thus represent the anti theoretical stance of Thatcherism and once drawn up they can be administered by anyone and their application is not hindered by self-interest groups, such as the professions, claiming specialist expertise.

'The development of a full range of competence' is listed as an aim of training in the Consultation Document issued by the DES (DES, 1989b) and given equal weight with students' 'ability to analyze and evaluate their own performance' (p. xxiv). However this document is perhaps less noteworthy for this than for its proposal to reconstitute the Council for the Accreditation of Teacher Education. The tasks of the new CATE were listed in *Circular 24/89* (1989c). CATE was to continue to advise the Secretary of State but it was also to be responsible for the monitoring of approved courses 'to ensure that they continue to meet the criteria' (para. 6). CATE's relationship with the local committees in *Circular 3/84* had been limited to ensuring that they met regularly and 'it was not intended that they should act in any way as sub-committees of the Council' (3/84, para. 8). In *Circular 24/89*, the local committees are given a watch-dog function: 'to ensure that (courses) continue to satisfy the new criteria' (para. 7). They are required to report to CATE on these matters. In addition, the local committees now must include in their membership, 'non-teacher-training academic staff, business and other outside interests' (para. 8). With regard to the curriculum of training, *Circular 24/89* retains the disciplines of education in an applied form (para. 6.3), but students are also required to learn about the economic foundations of society and the part played by education in preparing pupils for the world of work (para. 6.1). This comparison of *Circulars 3/84* and *24/89* demonstrates the way in which and extent to which control by the centre over the training of teachers increased during the 1980s. Not only does *Circular 24/89* include in the curriculum the competences which materially represent the central ideology, but it functions to directly control through a network of agencies created by the government. It also controls through bureaucracy (see Alexander, 1979). *Circular 3/84* was ten small pages in length. *Circular 24/89* is twenty-six pages long.

How it was that the views of the Inspectorate and of the government on training came to coincide in so many respects is difficult to disentangle. It would be easy to assume that following the centralization process which took place from the mid-1970s and HMI's movement towards a government model of training during the 1980s, the traditional independence of the Inspectorate had been compromised and it had become an agent of the centre. There could be some hint that this might be the case in Joseph's 1983 policy statement (paras 9 and 25). On the other hand, Perry (1987) in a paper written just before her term of office as Chief Inspector for Teacher Training came to an end, hopes for a more settled era of consolidation and growth after the many changes of the previous few years. It is Bolton however, who became Senior Chief Inspector in 1983, who clarified the relationship between the Inspectorate and the government in a speech at a NATFHE conference in 1985. Addressing the issue of the independence of HMI, Bolton comments: '. . . We are not independent in the sense that we owe allegiance to no-one: we are clearly the servants of the Secretary of State' (para. 17). 'What HMI does have . . . is a professional independence of judgment' (para. 18). He then goes on to describe how this independence is safeguarded, including the agreement that the Secretary of State may not alter any aspect of a report written by the Inspectorate. Bolton's own views were that 'it is necessary for the Inspectorate to state their views clearly and openly . . .' (Lawton and Gordon, 1987, p. 135).

Over the next few years it was to do so, often in a style critical of both government policy and of the teacher training profession. It opposed the government in many areas of education and its views became well known, Joseph, having decreed that HMI's reports should be made public. The Inspectorate's annual reports on the effects of LEA expenditure on the quality of schools and schooling became progressively more critical as the 1980s advanced, and while this state of affairs was principally a matter for the LEAs, the availability and distribution of LEA funding cannot be dissociated from government policy. Throughout the decade, there were numerous specific incidents in which the Inspectorate challenged or opposed the government: its investigation of accusations of racism in Brent schools which found in favour of the council; its generally favourable report on the Inner London Education Authority at the time of its abolition; its hostility to the introduction of the National Curriculum, wishing as it did to retain control over the curriculum (Graham and Tytler, 1993). According to *The Independent* (5 May 1987) when the results of the Brent investigation were made public, they elicited the riposte from 'a senior source': 'We have plans for the HMI. There is increasing concern about the role of HMI in providing ammunition against Government policies and not being as helpful as it should be'. This article also noted that proposals were being made to broaden the base of the Inspectorate and include in it representatives of industry and commerce. There was also pressure from the Right from the Centre for Policy Studies and the Hillgate Group for the reform of the Inspectorate. Despite the support given by HMI to the government's policies on teacher training, it was announced by the Prime Minister in 1991 without consultation, that the Inspectorate was to be privatized. In the future, a reduced Inspectorate was to supervise private companies of inspectors which were to include non-professionals in their teams and which were to bid for employment by the schools. In keeping with the market philosophy of Thatcherism, inspection had become a business rather than a profession. Inspection teams were to become local rather than part of a national network. Their potential to oppose the policies of the centre was therefore weakened. The price that the government paid for bringing to an end the Inspectorate's overt criticisms of its policies — criticisms made by the Inspectorate in its capacity as an independent professional body — was the support of HMI for its teacher training proposals.

If on occasion HM Inspectorate had been a buffer between government policy and its implementation, the Council for National Academic Awards (CNAA) occupied a comparable position, being a powerful institution in terms of the degree of influence that it was able to exercise over post-school education. At the end of the 1970s when the government came to power, the number of students on CNAA validated taught courses had reached almost 140,000; and for the year 1980–81, there were 1703 courses operating (Silver, 1990, p. 140). The outcome of the Council having expanded its operations to this degree was the growth of bureaucratic procedures. This development was anticipated by Ferriman (1973) in the early years of the Council and can be traced through papers available in the CNAA archives. For example, paper 5a/6 (1976) notes the creation of a fifth combined studies board 'in view of the number of interdisciplinary and modular courses that were being submitted . . .'; paper 1a/11 (1978) records that 'the major review of the membership of the Council's committees, boards and panels . . . has proved to be a very complicated exercise, and has taken much longer to complete than was originally planned'. In advising institutions on how to publicize courses awaiting validation, paper 5a/13 (1980) discloses that the validation process is falling behind. By 1982 (paper 6a/10) there are twelve committees and over sixty-five boards or panels. In discussing what he calls 'the growth of CNAA as a bureaucratic machine' Silver (1990, p. 200) records that by 1980, there were over forty senior staff and that in 1978 it had been necessary to appoint a number of Assistant Chief Officers. 'The CNAA was working with what had become an increasingly complex set of procedures as embodied in regulations which had in many cases become more and more cumbersome as they had been revised and re-revised . . . the CNAA had acquired many of the characteristics of a classic bureaucracy' (p. 201).

Perhaps partly as a consequence of this, bureaucracies being so resistant to change, the CNAA had had difficulties in its relationships with the polytechnics under the *Partnership in Validation* scheme. As early as 1971, the Committee of Directors of Polytechnics (CDP) had expressed a wish for their institutions to be granted a greater degree of independence and to be awarded their own charters. Over the next few years, discussions were held on how this might be achieved. The CNAA was unwilling to go so far as to delegate authority for the approval of courses, but in 1975 proposed a scheme for the gradual transfer of responsibility for the validation of their own courses to polytechnics which had demonstrated their maturity in the conduct and standard of their academic affairs. With this in operation, the CNAA would monitor the management of an institution rather than specific courses. Lengthy discussions followed. A working party was set up and reported, and additional amendments were made to the scheme.

Reviewing the *Partnership in Validation* scheme just before it was finally due to be put into operation in 1979, Pratt (1979) in a lengthy editorial in *Higher Education Review*, criticizes the Council for keeping the polytechnics 'under CNAA tutelege'. This was both humiliating and unfair (p. 5). At about the same time, in a collection of comments on the partnership proposals, Bethel (1980) a polytechnic director, evaluated the new scheme: 'The Council's working party on "Partnership in Validation" still has much work to do and Council has yet to decide on its long-term objectives. Until it does this, the over-burdened bureaucratic machinery will continue to struggle to meet its vast day to day work-load and not find time nor develop the will to transform itself into a central monitoring body . . .' (p. 9). Hargreaves, (1982) suggests that 'the concept of validation has been losing out to that of control in CNAA thinking, and control has been increasingly seen in terms of a detailed set of regulations which circumscribe the freedom of boards as well as that of course teams' (p. 86). In his turn Frampton (1981) expresses concern that partnership in validation is diverting the relationship between the CNAA and its constituent institutions into managerialism. He goes on to suggest the implications of this in the future: that the CNAA will become more and more like the DES, adding 'the government is hardly likely to have a use for a quango which spends some of its energy replicating the in-trays of one of its own ministries' (p. 13). Hargreaves (1982) confirms both the increase in bureaucracy and Frampton's views on the trend to managerialism, but further develops the idea, suggesting that 'a key feature of the situation now being developed is centralized hierarchical control with senior officers in CNAA and senior management staff in colleges acting together to frame regulations' (p. 89). Thus, academics were being excluded from the process of validation for which control by the minutiae of ever expanding regulations had been substituted.

The developments outlined above took place over a number of years. By the early 1980s, when the government was beginning to take a proactive stance in education, CNAA showed many of the characteristics of the weaker partner in a take-over bid by the centre. It was highly bureaucratic and hence abhorred by the Conservatives as impeding the market process. As has already been indicated, the polytechnics were beginning to rebel under the yoke of CNAA control. They perceived their development as being constrained and innovation hindered. There was thus a strong case for rolling back the CNAA state. Furthermore in terms of the numbers and variety of institutions with which it had dealings, the CNAA stood between the government and future attempts to control post-school education. Finally, the structures and procedures of the CNAA were now exhibiting the characteristics of industry. It could almost be said that all that the government required to intervene was an excuse. This was to come, and Silver (1990) gives full accounts of the incidents.

In 1978, while the negotiations on partnership in validation were in progress, a visit by the CNAA to Teesside Polytechnic changed the whole tenor of the debate. In its report the CNAA was highly critical of the management of the polytechnic to the extent that withdrawal of validation of the institution became a possibility, and the resignation of the Director was called for. This event elicited a letter to the Secretary of State from the Chairman of the CDP complaining of the way in which the CNAA conducted its institutional reviews, a criticism subsequently supported by the Inspectorate. And, so for the first time the government was drawn into the affairs of the CNAA beyond the limited and routine participation that it had enjoyed: the appointment of members of the Council of the CNAA by the Secretary of State. Its involvement was not substantial, however, until in 1983 the Secretary of State, Joseph, and the Chairman of the CNAA each received a letter alleging political bias in the assessment of the sociology course at the Polytechnic of North London. Ignorant of this letter, a party from the CNAA visited the polytechnic and with reservations reapproved the course. Meanwhile Joseph had arranged for an inspection to take place. The inspectors considered the allegation to have some substance. Thus 'academic rigour, and by implication the validation procedures of the CNAA, were impugned' (Silver, 1990, p. 210).

The HMI report was criticized by the CNAA and its conclusions rejected; and the Secretary of State was informed. In response, Joseph commissioned a committee chaired by Sir Norman Lindop, a former polytechnic director, to look into validation at degree level across institutions. The CNAA was the obvious reason for the investigation and in its report the Committee was critical of the Council, expressing concern 'about the heavy handedness with which the CNAA's approval procedures appear to be operated' (para. 3.21). The report suggested that institutions themselves should be responsible for their own academic standards and that any institution that sought independence should be able to apply to the Secretary of State for the power to award its own qualifications and so become self-validating. If an institution were unwilling to apply or failed in its application, it would continue to be externally validated. With regard to the CNAA, the report concludes with an acknowledgment of the CNAA's contribution to higher education and a recommendation that it 'should shake off its apparent tendency to rigidity if it is to be able to continue to foster rather than stifle the achievement of high standards in institutions' (para. 10.16). It was a year before Joseph responded to the Lindop Report. Anxiety about the fate of the Council was exacerbated by an attack in *The Economist* which drew on a report on the CNAA by a firm of accountants. This had been critical of its financial and economic management and as a result, the CNAA appointed accountants to its staff and Joseph placed industrialists on its Council (O'Connor, 1986). A year on, (Baroness) Cox, a prominent supporter of the policies of the government, held the chair of one of the committees. In a brief statement Joseph finally replied to the report. He welcomed the CNAA's plans to allow institutions to have substantially greater responsibility for validation, and also CNAA's commitment to the simplification of its procedures. He did not agree that certain polytechnics and colleges should be granted full autonomy to award their own degrees (Lindop's option 3), but chose to pursue a variant on option 1 which allowed for a range of validation arrangements under the aegis of CNAA. This response had a condition however. The extent to which CNAA exhibited progress in these matters would influence the government's final decision on option 3. It was assumed that the proposed changes in the pattern for validation would reduce the amount of CNAA's work and also its costs. The DES was to discuss with the Council how savings in staffing, current expenditure and reserves could be introduced. Thus although the Secretary of State retained CNAA, it was to be a considerably less influential CNAA which emerged from the era of the report. A redistribution of power had occurred in favour of the institutions, an event which fully reflected Thatcherism's doctrine of decentralization. From the outside, the DES was monitoring the ability of the CNAA to manage its affairs in accordance with the rubric of, amongst others, members of the business community; and internally it might have been possible to influence its decisions by political associates of the Secretary of State. The power of the CNAA was being whittled away bit by bit. In the latter years of the decade the staff was reduced by a third, the committees by two-thirds. Chairmen came and went. After lengthy negotiations, the CNAA at last agreed to grant accreditation to worthy institutions, and by 1988 twenty-nine institutions, nearly all of them polytechnics, had obtained accreditation for taught courses. The White Paper of 1987 invited the Council to accredit institutions which were ready for this step and to increase delegation to other institutions where possible, a request which in effect asked the Council to devote its efforts to its own demise. Silver (1990, p. 253) notes that 'the CNAA had agreed a strategy for its future relations with institutions, resulting in "virtual self-validation" for many of them'. Having carried out its 'midwife's role' and having been urged to transfer its responsibility for maintaining standards to the institutions, the CNAA closed in 1993.

These events are a reminder of Gramsci's comments on the relationship between the state and bureaucracies (see chapter 1): that bureaucracies with their concern for means rather than ends can seriously impede the introduction of a new ideology. But they do not quite meet Eagleton's (1991) definition of the strategy of 'rationalization': 'ideologies can be seen as more or less systematic attempts to provide plausible explanations and justifications for social behaviour which might otherwise be the object of criticism'. Analogously, however, the actions of Joseph, if interpreted ideologically, can be regarded as rational and hence justifiable. The CNAA was troubled when he came to office and in the forthright manner in which he interpreted his role, Joseph undertook to investigate the Council. His remedies for the ills of the Council were apparently reasonable. It was reasonable to introduce industrialists into an organization which was failing to manage its financial affairs, reasonable to urge the CNAA onwards to grant the polytechnics, now mature institutions, more academic freedom, and again reasonable that savings should be made in the running of the Council, given that the general economic climate required both companies and individuals to husband their resources. In all of these respects, the actions of Joseph extended Thatcherism into a major educational institution.

The Licensed Teacher Scheme (LTS) was introduced by the government in 1988 for the purpose of rationalizing the routes to qualified teacher status. Teachers were to train in schools under the auspices of the local education authorities. This scheme was followed by the Articled Teacher Scheme (ATS) in 1989 (DES, 1989a). In terms of the central ideology, these alternative ways of training extended consumer choice. They may also have accelerated the introduction of school-based training which it has been suggested represents the principles of Thatcherism. But the Licensed Teacher Scheme was representative of the central ideology in an additional alternative way, that of decreasing the influence of the training institutions. The training of the licensed teacher is outlined in a single paragraph (DES, 1988b, para. 27.ii). It is the responsibility of the local education authority or school governors 'as appropriate to determine the requisite amount and nature of training for any particular candidate . . . There could be a variety of patterns of training provision' though HMI were to monitor events. That is all. This is the neo-liberal strand of Thatcherism in action, and it contrasts with the detailed requirements and high degree of control applied to mainstream training. Subsequently, an appendix was issued outlining the knowledge and competence to be demonstrated by the licensee before s/he was granted QTS. The ATS was an experimental scheme in which trainees were to be enrolled in training institutions for two years of which four-fifths was to be spent in school. This scheme was based on market principles for it required institutions to competitively bid for funding, and again, curricular requirements were a minimum though specifying that the training was to be delivered jointly by training institution and school staffs.

The above discussion has indicated the degree of intervention in teacher training by both the Secretary of State and the DES during the 1980s. Cumulatively over the decade this amounted to an ideological onslaught which moved from early attempts to achieve hegemonic control through measures which consolidated current practice to interventions which sought to extend the influence and effects of the policies of Thatcherism with little regard to the *status quo*. A range of strategies and tactics were used, some of them appearing to contradict each other, representing as they did, the complex two-dimensional nature of Thatcherism. Thus for example, the Licensed and Articled Teacher Schemes with their lack of central control can be perceived as expressions of neo-liberalism, and the tight authoritarian control exercised over mainstream training can be regarded as an expression of the neo-conservative dimension. These distinctions lead back to the pure ideology of Thatcherism and raise questions about the translation or implementation process from ideology *per se* to social institution or social act. According to Gramscian theory the presentation of a new ideology and its location and realization within social reality is the task of 'organic intellectuals'. These are intellectuals who are aloof from or outside current practice and can therefore see events with a fresh eye. That one of those recommending school-based training, Hargreaves, is a member of the existing body of practitioners suggests that Gramsci's theory here may be in need of amendment or further development. Nevertheless, the principal intellectual support for placing training in schools has come from academics outside the teacher training profession: O'Hear (1988); the Hillgate Group (1989); and Lawlor (1990). The reasons why these writers, and Warnock (1988) also, support school-based training vary. O'Hear's (1988) wish to place training in school is based principally on a theory of learning. The training of teachers can best take place in the school because only through apprenticeship learning will the spirit of the subject, and values and knowledge unknown consciously either to pupil or teacher, be imparted and absorbed (pp. 12–13). The teacher's knowledge is practical rather than theoretical and 'best acquired through experience and doing rather than through talking and thinking abstractly' (p. 17). He presents the current situation in terms of the market. Teacher training is a 'substantial public industry' (p. 5), the teacher training establishment is the 'monopolistic supplier' and the school, their pupils and their parents are 'the consumers' (p. 9). Warnock (1988) is not of the New Right. Indeed she regards the members of the Hillgate Group as victims of the myth of the born teacher (p. 108) and states clearly her opposition to their recommendations for the abandonment of training. She wishes to see schools undertake more responsibility for training as a means of enhancing the status of the profession. Only if teachers are allowed to speak with the voice of authority on the needs of their pupils and to impose their own professional standards, will they and education regain the respect of the public. The Hillgate Group has five members including (Baroness) Cox whose membership of the Council of the CNAA has already been mentioned. It also includes Scruton whose strong conservative views on the retention of traditional British culture have been expounded in a range of publications. In 1989, a year after the Licensed Teacher Scheme was launched, the Hillgate Group published a pamphlet: *Learning to Teach*. In essence this is a critique of current government policy which is regarded as insufficiently radical. CATE is not achieving its aims because it is being opposed by the teacher training profession. The existing Licensed Teacher Scheme should be extended to an apprenticeship system in which any school should be able to recruit licensed teachers on the basis of demand. Schools should be funded directly to train teachers, these funds being taken from the teacher training budget. Existing training courses are presented as a barrier to the unqualified but suitable applicant but nevertheless they should be retained in the interests of providing competition between different routes to Qualified Teacher Status. In addition, the contents of training courses is inappropriate, being biased and giving insufficient time or attention to classroom practice. Furthermore, the report of the Inspectorate (1988) on newly-qualified teachers suggested that the nation might not be getting good value for money. As with O'Hear, the untrained teacher in the independent school is cited as the example to be emulated. Finally, there should be no need for any form of validation of the training of licensees either by the DES, CATE or the CNAA. Thus the Hillgate Group takes a neo-liberal approach to teacher education, proposing maximum competition and minimum control. Lawlor's (1990) presentation of her case is less market-oriented than those of either O'Hear or the Hillgate Group. She bases her advocacy of total school-based training on a review of the content of a sample of current training courses, criticizing particularly what she regards as the priority given to theory. Finally Hargreaves, who is not a member of the New Right, promotes school based training in a series of short articles written for the *Times Educational Supplement* between 1989 and 1992. His reasons for taking this stance are not clearly articulated although he considers that 'the job can be done at least as well, and probably better by practising teachers' (1989).

O'Hear, Lawlor and the members of the Hillgate Group fulfil their intelligentsia function with some skill. Their task is to reproduce the pure ideology of Thatcherism in the particular context of initial training, to reconstruct and re-present the preparation of teachers in accordance with the ideological principles of the government. To be effective this must done in such a way that their proposals have popular appeal. They present their case in the discourse of the market and their suggestions seem to be based on common sense: that the only way to learn the practical skills of teaching is to be in the company of exponents of those skills. But their critique of teacher trainers also supports their proposals on moral grounds. O'Hear (1988) appeals to public concern about falling standards in teaching, thus introducing a sense of crisis and indicating the need for change but also implying that teacher trainers are failing in their responsibilities. At the same time he describes the 'true teacher' in flattering terms. Many of these are being excluded from the classroom by the monopolistic suppliers, the teacher trainers, who have a vested interest in maintaining the status quo. To the Hillgate Group (1989) teacher trainers are low level intellectuals with Marxist inclinations; famous philosophers are quoted to support the claim that teaching is a craft which is best acquired directly from those with experience; negative evidence of the effectiveness of current courses is cited. Lawlor (1990) approves of recent government initiatives as set out in *Circular 24/89*, but considers that they are being undermined by the profession (p. 12). She quotes at length from the syllabuses of courses to demonstrate her point that there is little of worth undertaken in the standard forms of training. The quality of the arguments of these writers is irrelevant here. What is important is their effect in terms of the aims of their ideological project. The arguments of Lawlor, O'Hear and the members of the Hillgate Group are powerful because they are conveyed with great conviction and good use is made of examples, emotive language and appealing fantasies about the nature of the training process. They exemplify the comments of Manning (see chapter 1) on ideological language: that its purpose is less to convey facts than to convince of the rightness and desirability of a cause.

Summary

The conclusions reached in this section on the ideological strategies of the government with regard to teacher training in the 1980s are as follows:

- the Conservative party had won the 1979 election, the electorate having finally tired of Labour's failure to manage the economy, rather than because there was extensive public support for alternative philosophies; there is no indication that the members of social institutions such as teacher training which structurally reflected Thatcherism in some way were necessarily adherents of the ideology;
- recognizing the task that lay ahead, Thatcher established an assertive approach to the transformation of attitudes and social structures; her Secretary of State for Education and Science, Joseph, interpreted his role in a similar manner;
- when they came to power in 1979, the Conservatives inherited a training curriculum which in a number of aspects reflected their ideology; these similarities were to facilitate the introduction of *Circular 3/84*;
- during the 1980s, the Thatcher government attempted to gain control of the curriculum of teacher training through a variety of means: by issuing circulars; by setting up the monitoring

agency of CATE; and also by reducing the possibility of opposition by facilitating the demise of the CNAA and the transformation of HM Inspectorate;
- its extension of the philosophy of the market was not limited to mainstream training; it also established alternative forms of training which operated in competition;
- by the end of the decade, the government had introduced a system of training which in both structure and content reflected its ideology: its orientation was 'practical', theory was disappearing, increased responsibility had been given to teachers and tutors had been portrayed as inadequate professionals.

Implications for Ideological Theory

Further:

- The above account appears to support the views of Gouldner and others on how a new ideology is introduced: its supporters are in a hurry, it disregards existing institutions, bureaucracies have either to be transformed or removed and alternative codes of morality apply.
- The benefits of recognizing and using a sympathetic context (Gramsci) are illustrated.
- The role of organic intellectuals in promoting a new ideology as described by Gramsci seems to have been taken on by policy makers who remained outside the parliamentary party, but whose publications were likely influences in the 1980s in shaping government policy on initial training; however, when exemplified, this theory is seen to be weak since it is principally a description of the *status quo*.
- The use of strategies and tactics by a government for the ideological transformation of teacher education has again been demonstrated.
- The events outlined above indicate that ideological domination is a process.

Hegemonic Achievement: The Response of the Professional Community to the Ideologizing of Teacher Training in the 1980s.

The same question now has to be asked of this more recent attempt at ideological socialization as was asked following the Robbins initiative: how were these interventions of the government received in the teacher training community? As Thatcherism started to become embedded in the structures and processes of training, was support elicited for the curriculum which embodied the government's principles as Althusser would have us believe, thus confirming the possibility that the curriculum might act as a channel for ideological socialization? Or were these processes found to be alienating, as had been the case following the Robbins intervention, because of their perceived threat to the values of the community at which they were directed? Two types of evidence were used in order to respond to these questions. As before, developments in course curricula were reviewed, and publications scanned.

All those HMI reports (thirteen) on courses of initial training for the years 1986 and 1987 which were publicly available, were examined. These years were chosen because it was considered that by then sufficient time had elapsed since *Circular 3/84* for at least some of the curricular adjustments that it had proposed to have been implemented. Also because it seems possible that reports at this time may have contributed to the proposals of *Circular 24/89*. Since the proposals for the training curriculum in *Circular 3/84* were outlines, the institutions had some freedom of choice in how they responded, and therefore an analysis of these responses is considered to be some indication of the potential hegemonic power of that curriculum. However, when with later circulars the curriculum becomes mandatory, this no longer holds. Then rejection of the curriculum is not possible, and the relationship between central ideology and the curricular tradition of training has to be assessed by alternative means. The conclusions of the Inspectorate in its 1988 report on training (HMI, 1988) will be referred to briefly before the individual documents are analyzed.

The report distinguishes between those courses which had and had not yet been revised. In the latter a tendency to allocate too much time to the unrelated study of educational theory and in general too little time in school, were identified. Although the relationship between tutor and teacher was found to be evolving into that of partners sharing in training in a defined and complementary way, there was variation in the extent to which institutions had thought through the tutor-teacher relationship and introduced changes appropriate to the new more school-based form of training. As might be anticipated, given the apparent reluctance of some tutors to hand over responsibility for training (see the SPITE study) there were still a 'few examples of school based method work where the tutors appeared to view the teachers as providers of facilities rather than as partners in training' (p. 21).

The thirteen reports on higher education institutions engaged in training during 1986/87 which are available for inspection include only one university, universities at that time having the option of placing their reports in the public domain. The reports were analyzed according to the three criteria (aims of training, curriculum structure and personnel involvement) which were used to analyze the CNAA samples during the 1970s. In general, diversity between institutions was again apparent. But nevertheless, there had been a noted shift to closer co-operation with schools and to further integration of theory with practice, both of which were requirements of *Circular 3/84*. There had also been a clear attempt to increase staff development in the way suggested in the Circular, that is tutors gaining experience of teaching in schools. But it is the fine detail of these developments which is interesting, though it needs to be borne in mind that the inclusion of only one university report within the group may raise the general level of school-focusedness given the previous histories of the colleges and the universities in this regard.

The Inspectors interpreted the aims of these courses as almost universally concerned with preparing the student for professional life. Training in most institutions was perceived as professional preparation in the narrowly defined sense of acquiring classroom competence. The institutions recognized that if this were to be achieved, then closer relationships with schools and an integrated timetable were essential. But the extent to which these two aims can be met in any institution depends on the starting point, and given the high level of diversity already within the system, then the outcome of attempts to meet these demands may well be a continuation of that diversity, and this indeed seemed to be the case. Regarding curriculum structure: in one institution students were still being taught the disciplines of education as discrete subject areas, while in others, the curriculum had become so integrated that the reader had difficulty in deciphering its real content.

Terminology reflected this. Educational studies can subsume educational theory and also professional training; or on a course which HMI concluded 'lacked coherence', Teaching studies includes school experience, core studies, required studies, foundation studies and elective studies, but does not include subject studies which are taken in addition. And what can be made of the comment that 'school experience and teaching practice are interwoven'? In these accounts, it seems as if the integration of curricular elements in initial training has become so pronounced that it is possible to envisage a return to the pre-Robbins type curriculum which was so heavily criticized by the philosophers of education for its lack of differentiation between subjects and thence a lack of rigour. Moreover, this tendency could well be enhanced — as may be so here — as a consequence of sharing the responsibility for training more widely between schools and HEIs.

In the area of personnel involvement these thirteen reports suggest that diversity continues to be considerable, although it is clear that there has been a general trend towards closer association with schools, and this is recorded on the schedule (see appendix) as much higher scores in the various categories of this dimension than was achieved for the 1970s. In one case the institution tutors work closely in school with 'teacher-tutors' who assist students to reflect upon their practice. In another institution however, 'college staff were seen as remote figures, and schools only operating in a service capacity'. But even where the relations between school and institution are judged to be good by the inspectors, and where good documentation is also provided as it now frequently is, teachers find it difficult to understand what their role in training should be. This situation is interpreted as the continuation of the same model of 'partnership' that was discussed earlier in chapter 3. Apart from the one example cited, no indication could be found in these reports that partnership was being reformulated in accordance with the redistribution of responsibility for training that was taking place at the level of rhetoric at least. Schools, training institutions and also the Inspectorate, appear to be working within the old model still. Control by the institutions of what goes on in schools is high with frequent visits from tutors, and for the inspectors, a good relationship with schools seems to be defined in terms of regular consultation between the parties, informative documentation, teacher membership of committees and opportunities for each party to teach in the others' institution. The analysis of these reports suggest that in the few years since the last CNAA sample, there has been both considerable development and a lack of it. The training relationship between schools and HEIs has become closer but to a large extent it retains its old form.

How is the government, in a hurry to extend its ideological influence, to interpret these reports? First, some success has been achieved in extending its influence through *Circular 3/84*. Schools and HEIs are working more closely together and teachers are being given increased responsibility for assessment. But at the same time, the contradiction between the ideal of ideological-structural correspondence which is a necessary feature of an historic bloc, and the reality where an ideology which gives power to the practitioner is not reflected in social arrangements, is greater than ever. As theory suggests, contradictions open up access points for further intervention. Presented with the scenario outlined above, the only course open to the government, given its ideological intentions, was to exert greater control than before. Thus within the discourse of the new ideology of Thatcherism, there is a rational and legitimate argument for another Circular (24/89) which does seek to enforce tighter control and which also reflects Thatcherism more intensively. But in increasing control, the centre risks loss of ideological influence (Wilkin, 1992). The transfer from voluntary agreement to enforced compliance, from exercising influence within the Civil State to bringing the forces of the Political State to bear — this is an unfortunate step for a governing elite to take, for it suggests that the target population is eluding its ideological grasp (see chapter 1).

In the first few years of the decade, publications which were overtly critical of the government seem to have been few. But an early editorial in the *Journal of Education for Teaching* (JET, 1983) did appear to acknowledge that the training system was now becoming the object of ideological reform. Or it thought that it did. The text is unfocussed and even slightly jokey in tone, and the author(s) seems almost apologetic at being so obdurate in print. Another writer who is attuned to the political context and its consequences for training, but who takes a bolder line is Bocock (1983), who records the way in which Joseph interpreted his legal authority. Then in a surprisingly outspoken paper — surprising because CNAA officers are not given to strong public expressions of opinion—Billings (1986) writes with some concern about the way in which he feels CNAA was represented in the Lindop Report, implying that the CNAA had become vulnerable to external bodies. In this he gets support from Price (1985) who suggests that though the Lindop Report 'appears to free some of the polytechnics and colleges from the bureaucratic grip of the CNAA, it leaves them as vulnerable as ever to the personal curricular control of the Secretary of State through HMI' (p. 444). Papers such as these suggest an awareness of the development of a climate of politicisation. Then following *Circular 3/84*, the degree of control that the government sought to exert becomes a major preoccupation of the training community. Given the nature of the Circular — that it required little curricular change, but transferred control of the curriculum to the Secretary of State — this reaction is to be expected. Whitty, Barton and Pollard (1987) have no doubt that it is ideological intent which lies behind government interventions in teacher training. Nor about what this means: the transformation of our perceptions and our way of interpreting the world. For Quicke too (1988) 'The intervention of the New Right in education can be seen as part of a broader hegemonic project to construct a political discourse through which the authority of the state and traditional social values can be restored' (p. 5). In 1989 Rudduck wrote a detailed and hardhitting commentary on the establishment of CATE. This covers not only a review of the criteria themselves which are found to be lacking in coherence and educational integrity ('a pretty crude assortment') but also the power and control that CATE exercises through them. The language here is forceful (the Secretary of State has a 'cavalier attitude') and the tone uncompromising.

There were defenders of the government's perspective however. Lawlor and the Hillgate Group have been mentioned. O'Keeffe (1990), who was a member of the education department in a polytechnic, was another supporter of the direction in which training seemed to be moving. He is against the 'progressive ideology' of the training institution with its 'Blue Peter curriculum . . . equal opportunities mongers . . . staff who teach this incantatory stuff'. He also concludes that 'a shocking and dishonest role is played by the inspectors and advisors' (p. 60). Freeing teaching from the institutions will solve all of this: 'Students could learn as well or better in the classroom under the guidance of good teachers without going to college at all' (p. 130). O'Keeffe's defence is on the grounds of curricular content, and if parallels are to be discerned between the reaction of the profession to the Robbins reforms in the 1960s and those of the 1980s, then it is here that critiques of the Thatcher government's initiatives must be sought. Critical reaction to political control is insufficient evidence that ideological intervention offends traditional cultural norms. It seems that it was after *Circular 24/89* which further tightened the political hold on the substance of training that the profession becomes fully aware of the implications of the government's interventions for curricular content. Responses in this mode will be considered in the coda on the 1990s which follows.

Meanwhile the (educational) academic debate continued to address the themes that had been the preoccupation of the profession in the previous few years: Proctor (1984) elaborates the concept of partnership; Dearden (1984) expresses concern that any extension of the developments of the previous decade may mark a shift from education to training and he examines what this would mean; Eraut and West (1984) debate the different meanings now being attributed to theory. And the 'reflective practitioner' had become a growth industry which was to continue on into the 1990s when a survey of all training institutions would disclose that this is the preferred aim of training across

HEIs (Barrett *et al*, 1992). These papers and others like them ignore the political scenario, and in so doing reflect, it can be assumed, the writers' continued commitment to their professional concerns. The debate on the relationship between theory and practice continues to be the ever evolving theme at the heart of teacher training.

Summary

The conclusions reached in the above section on the response of the professional community to the ideological curriculum of the 1980s are as follows:

- after *Circular 3/84* and the introduction of CATE to monitor training, there was strong opposition in publications to the intervention by the centre in the curriculum;
- however, evidence from the HMI reports suggests that training had been influenced by the Circular: in general schools and HEIs were working more closely together and theory and practice were more integrated;
- but across courses considerable diversity continued to exist;
- the degree of integration in the curriculum suggests a return to the pre-Robbins model of training which was so heavily criticized by the philosophers of education and of which the post-Robbins curriculum was a critique;
- control by the institutions remained high although in rhetoric the form of training was that of 'partnership';
- the lack of ideological representation in the distribution of power within the social structures of training, was a 'contradiction' which offered an opportunity to the government to introduce greater control through a further Circular.

Coda: The Early 1990s

The early years of the 1990s have been characterized by an extension and exaggeration of previous attitudes and practices on all sides. The government has engaged in deeper political and ideological penetration of training through the agency of CATE and latterly has issued proposals to control training directly through the Teacher Training Agency (TTA). Members of the HEIs have become increasingly outspoken in their condemnation of the encroaching politicization of training and the threat to the quality of professional preparation that this is considered to generate. Their commitment to a form of training which contains a balance of practice and theory remains. Members of the New Right continue to support fully school produced training.

At the beginning of 1992, in his annual North of England Conference speech, the Secretary of State outlined and justified the government's new proposals for training (Clarke, 1992). Many of the recommendations in the speech echo current good practice. Schools and HEIs are to be partners in training. Schools should receive the support they need to undertake this work and their role should be clarified (para. 17). The appointment of mentors is recommended. They are to receive training and the assistance of the whole school in their work (para. 25). Students are to have time 'away from the hurly burly of the school to think and read about what happens in the classroom and discuss it with tutors and other students' (para. 18). But in addition, this speech contains elements which deny or marginalize the contribution of the training institutions: schools are now to take the lead in the whole training process (para. 22). They are to be reimbursed for the costs of training from the institutions. The time spent by the student in school is to be increased because 'student teachers need more time in classrooms guided by serving teachers and less time in the teacher training colleges' (para. 19). HEIs now have to devise new courses and criteria for the selection of schools and hence bureaucracy is increased. The reason for establishing CATE is clarified: that of 'monitoring compliance' (para. 14).

The accompanying Consultation Document (DES, 1992a) develops these themes and elaborates the role of competences in training. Competences are now to govern training for 'institutions, schools and students themselves should focus on these competences throughout the whole period of initial training' (para. 9). CATE and HMI are to play a greater role in the accreditation process, and this will permit the abolition of the local committees. It is confirmed that the schools are the dominant partner in training, and the permanence of the new arrangements is indicated by a requirement that participating schools incorporate student training into their development plans. Schools and HEIs are to negotiate their respective responsibilities for each area of course content. The culmination of this initiative was *Circular 9/92* which was issued five months later and which includes an additional requirement that schools apply to the HEIs for partnership status. If the Secretary of State has evidence that schools are being treated arbitrarily, then course approval may be withheld from the institution concerned. The competences are set out in detail. They omit any suggestion that students theorise about their practice.

This series of documents and a further Consultation Document which followed in September 1993 tighten the political grip to a quite remarkable degree on a curriculum which more closely than ever reflects the central ideology. Control is achieved through a variety of means. One strategy which appears in a variety of guises in these documents is that of the transfer of power between social groups to satisfy ideological principles: the withdrawal of power from the HEIs and the enhancement of the power of the schools. Some of these means are overt and obvious, some of them quite subtle. Together they reinforce each other. HEIs are to lose funds to schools, schools are to 'lead', to be the more powerful partners. Schools can undertake training independently of HEIs, but the reverse is not possible. Schools may if they wish purchase training and support from outside, but they are not obliged to apply to the HEIs for this. They will be financially supported if they come into the ideological fold. This enhancement of the status and power of the schools is accompanied by a diffuse attack on the culture and authority of the training institutions. It is implied that they have been failing in their responsibility to ensure that the college based part of the course is fully relevant to classroom practice (Clarke, 1992, para. 21). Their 'dogmas about teaching method' are now to be challenged (para. 21). That some of these measures may be commendable for professional reasons or reasons of justice is not questioned here. Our interest is the nature of the change in the teacher training establishment. In this, teacher training is not unique, as Moore (1994) points out. 'Policies since 1979 have systematically attempted to disestablish professional cultures and institutions across the whole range of social and economic life . . .' (p. 7). For Moore, the attitude of the government to the professions is based on three arguments, all of which are derived from the central tenet of Thatcherism: that social life should be ordered according to the principles of the market, and that when this is the case, our economic ills will be remedied. What Moore calls the 'market argument' regards professional groups as representing producer capture against the interests of consumers. The 'values argument' opposes professionals because they espouse an anti-commercial ethic of service and universal rights; also because they value authoritative expertise rather than the enterprise culture. The 'political argument' sees professional communities as making a special contribution to the maintenance of liberal democracy by balancing the power of the state.

Another major strategy was to shed the actual or potential opposition. The local committees, set up by the government to widen the accountability of the training institutions at the local level, but perhaps now considered to be too independent in their political views, were no longer mandatory (*Circular 9/92*, DES, 1992b). Their demise left CATE and the Inspectorate responsible for monitoring training, both directly responsible to the Department for Education (DfE). Within a few months of *Circular 9/92* being issued, it was announced that the Inspectorate was to be replaced by local inspection teams, whom the Inspectorate would train. Any challenge and threat that HMI represented is thus dissipated. Then the later Consultation Document (DfE, 1993) announced that CATE too would go, to be discharged within a year. The aims for CATE were to implement and monitor government policy, and its members were government appointees, but the extent to which it had demonstrated autonomy in carrying out its tasks over the years remains unknown. The proposal to set up a Teacher Training Agency which has direct control over training suggests that even CATE is now regarded as an unreliable mediator of government policy. The potential opposition having been eliminated, the Secretary of State is left directly in control of training through the proposed Teacher Training Agency (TTA). All the members of the TTA, including the chair, are to be appointed by the Secretary of State, who will also determine the funds allocated to the Agency. When it comes to the administration of these funds, the Agency 'will be advised of general government priorities and will be subject . . . to a reserve power of direction by the Secretary of State' (para. 3.6). If the proposals for the TTA come to fruition, it appears that initial training will be under the personal jurisdiction of the Secretary of State.

The comments here and in the previous section indicate the Conservative government's aims for training and the ways in, and extent to, which these aims have been achieved in recent years. In nearly every respect, this reconstructed map of training exemplifies the ideology of Thatcherism. There is a market in training with a variety of courses from which to choose and it is the responsibility of the strong State to ensure that this market operates efficiently. It will do this through the distribution of funding and initially it may be necessary to provide extra resources for the weaker suppliers in order to ensure a sufficient degree of choice, but the outcome will be a cheaper system which can deliver its products more efficiently. As is to be expected in a market system, external monitoring is regarded as a form of unnecessary and unjustifiable control and is to be reduced as far as possible. Institutional accreditation rather than course approval is to be introduced to help lighten control and will now take place only at five-yearly intervals. No (theoretical) nonsense do-it-yourself training is to be encouraged in keeping with the promise so prominent in Thatcher's speeches to return power to the people.

What has been the response of the profession to this? During the first half of the 1990s, publications by members of the profession and critical of government policy have become frequent. The shock and apprehension generated by the Secretary of State's North of England speech in 1992 was profound. Those in teacher training had not been consulted about the new initiatives and in order to allow members of of the profession to express their views, the editors of the *Journal of Education for Teaching* (JET, 1992) surveyed opinion across institutions. Responses were collated and published in an article which showed general support for school-based training, but strong opposition for both logistical and professional reasons to placing training wholly in schools or for what was judged to be too great a proportion of the training period. Opposition to government policies for training has been widely and directly expressed in newspaper editorials (for example, *Times Higher Educational Supplement*, 10 January 1992 and 28 May 1993) and in commentary by senior figures such as the Chair of the Universities Council for the Education of Teachers (Edwards, 29 October 1993), Maclure (1992) and the former Chair of CATE who expressed his opposition to the new Teacher Training Agency as soon as it was announced (Taylor, 1993). There has also been a growth in academic papers which have opposed government initiatives on the grounds that they detract from the professional worth of the current form of training, and once again the focus is the relationship between theory and practice. Elliott (1991) makes out a case for retaining HEIs as a base for initial training although working in close collaboration with schools. Teachers, like other professionals need access to alternative sources of knowledge if reflection on their practice is to be a productive and developmental activity. 'There is still a case for arguing that the disciplines of education can make a significant contribution to teacher education. Within the reflective practitioner model, they could find a new role . . . as sources of ideas which can be eclectically utilised in situational problem solving' (p. 316). Similarly Edwards (1992) and Rudduck (1991) argue that teacher educators in HEIs have a unique and necessary perspective to offer students in training. For Rudduck (1991) this means:

> a perspective that shapes consciousness in schools and classroom and provides students with a variety of frameworks for making sense of what is happening. The development of a capacity for critical reflection should be supported by the development of competent and confident practice: these are complementary concerns which, in the present climate, are set in tension, in a way that threatens the quality of experience that student teachers should expect in their period of preparation for a career in teaching. (p. 319)

Barber (1993), writing as a senior officer of the National Union of Teachers, strongly opposes the way in which the government is gradually severing the links between the schools and the training institutions, because the institutions are the site of knowledge and understanding of principles of teaching and learning, the breadth of which cannot be replicated in schools.

Before it was transformed, the Inspectorate took the same view. At the beginning of the decade, HM Inspectorate issued a report on school-based training in the UK (HMI, 1991). Courses were still found to vary 'considerably' in the amount of time spent in school although in general they were 'responding successfully to present expectations' (para. 5.i) and HMI were able to conclude that 'the principle (of school based training) is sound' (para. 5.vii). Collaboration between schools and HEIs was found to have improved over the decade and where teachers are given time and training for their role, their contribution to training is effective. HMI concludes that 'students benefit greatly from skillful, well organized and integrated school-based experience. A measured increase in the school-based element in initial training would pay important dividends' (para. 5.viii). But the Inspectorate also stress the importance of the contribution of the HEIs to training, since HEIs have 'an academic and professional expertise which is crucial in the support both of individual students and schools' (para. 5.vi). Thus the Inspectorate supported the practice of school-based training where there is an input from the training institution, having evidence that it is an effective mode of training students if the roles of both school and HEI are clearly defined and adhered to. The particular theoretical perspective of the HEI is considered a necessary complement to the student's school-based experience. Arguments against the transformation of the curriculum into an instrument of ideological socialization are therefore both political and professional and where professional reiterate the need for a balance between theory and practice, although that 'balance' may be weighted towards practice.

Apart from the obvious conclusion that this degree of opposition to both the political and professional implications of government measures indicates how distant is the possibility of hegemonic (i.e. willing) control by the centre through the curriculum, how should these responses be viewed in ideological terms? Here we need to return to the discussions of chapter 1 on the nature of ideology itself and of ideological language. Ideologies are belief systems and so are immune to reason. Hence ideological decisions and actions do not require justifying, and the ideologue can use claims which are not supported by evidence as a basis of his/her case. The simple statement that 'students should spend more time in the classroom' (Clarke, 1992) is one such example. Neither does the true ideologue need to heed criticism. The critic is not 'one of us' and therefore is not only to be disregarded, but is perceived, if noted at all, as 'ideological' in thought and practice and therefore likely to be biased. But by definition, the true believer who is one of us, who is inside an ideology and who therefore is a hegemonic subject will fail to recognize his/her personal bias, but will regard the views of those in disagreement as distortions of the truth. This point can be illustrated by a short quote from *The Independent* (29 November 1993). Commenting on the extremist pronouncements of a member of the current government, an aide remarked: 'He said what he did because he believes it — and will not have done a lot to burden himself with research to verify it'.

For academics to confront unwavering commitment to any ideology including that of Thatcherism is therefore liable to fail if success is defined in terms of achieving a change in the direction of government policy through persuasion. In their professional work, academics are committed to the discovery of their 'truth' which is to be attained through rational argument. This truth is an alternative truth to that of governments and arrived at by alternative means. The two notions of what constitutes truth do not coincide. Rational argument is ineffectual against ideological conviction because the two opposing parties do not share the same discourse and so are not bound by the same rules of participation. Although numerous, clearly articulated assessments and critiques of the government's educational policies have been published within the last few years, which have disclosed their ideological bent and rejected their values the government continues to move towards the full conversion of training to a market model as the introduction of the School Centred Initial Teacher Training Scheme (SCITT) indicates. It remains indifferent to the views of those whom it knows do not share its perceptions of how the social world should be ordered and for this reason sees no need for consultation. In ideological terms this is entirely appropriate. Challenging the policies and principles of any highly ideological government from the perspective of any alternative discourse is therefore like pitting a pebble against a rock. Since their respective arguments do not meet, there is very little chance of either side convincing the other of the worth of its assumptions. This would seem to bode ill for the future of teacher training since it implies that the profession is at the mercy of central domination. Yet such an assumption would be unsupported in Gramscian theory which portrays ideology as gaining only partial admittance when it knocks on the door of culture. Nor would it be supported by the developments described in this study which suggest that the relationship between ideology and culture in teacher training may take the form of a dialogue which can benefit both sides. This relationship is discussed further in the conclusion which follows.

Conclusion

This study set out to examine the extent to which during the last three decades the curriculum of initial teacher training has been used by the government for ideological purposes. This has entailed exploring whether the curriculum has reflected the central ideology, where this was found to be the case, identifying how this was achieved, and then finally investigating how it was received within the teacher training community. A number of interesting parallels between the events of the 1960s and the 1980s has emerged.

(i) It has been suggested that UK governments of very different political perspectives have tried in their turn to recast the initial training curriculum in their image — and have succeeded in so doing. The Conservative social democratic government of the early 1960s is deemed to have used the recommendations of the Robbins Report to this end, and since it came to power in 1979, the Conservative Government also has tried to harness the curriculum to its ideology. That both of these governments have been Conservative is not considered to be of any real consequence. All governing elites of whatever political persuasion will attempt to intervene in a whole range of social institutions in the hope that if social structures can be reconstructed to reflect their beliefs and principles then this will encourage people to witness how those principles are successfully implemented in reality and thence willingly lend them their support. In this respect, no distinction is made between the events of the 1960s and of the 1980s as described. On both occasions ideological intervention resulted in a curriculum which mirrored the political principles of the centre.

(ii) A second similarity has been the strategic skill exhibited by both governments. In both cases the mood of the target group was well judged. It was suggested that in the 1960s it was recognized that it would be quite safe to leave the professionals to decide the content of the curriculum. They were likely to be ideologically reliable, and in an era when professionals were held in some regard, it would have been both unnecessary and unwise to intervene too openly or directly. *Circular 3/84* was well considered also. Its proposals for curricular reform were recognized as relatively uncontroversial good practice and this being so, they softened the blow of central control that the Circular introduced.

(iii) In both cases, the training system itself played an enabling role. The curriculum was at least partially receptive to the form that the initiative took. Moreover it was the profession itself which had developed the system to this state. In the 1960s when ideological intervention resulted in a more rigorous and academic curriculum, this met the concerns of those in the university departments who were critical of the intellectual worth of the courses being run by the colleges. And it was the views of those in the UDEs which prevailed although the universities took relatively few students. The status of the UDEs was higher and members played a leadership role within training through the ATOs, membership of national bodies and publication. By the 1980s, it was the curriculum in the public sector institutions rather than the universities which was the more receptive to the new ideology. But by then the status differential between the two types of institution was considerably diminished.

(iv) Both of these interventions have brought professional benefits. In the 1960s, the status and quality of initial training was raised as a direct consequence of the reconstruction of the curriculum in the wake of the Robbins Report. Equally in the the 1980s, ideological intervention has forced recognition of the valuable role that teachers can and should play in training and has confirmed their engagement as real partners in training.

(v) Fifth, on the two occasions studied, ideological penetration has impacted on the relationship between theory and practice, causing this relationship to swing excessively to one end of the continuum or the other. In the 1960s, theory came to dominate the curriculum; in the 1980s it was practice. Despite the fact that in each case the government confirmed the inclinations of the profession (see iii above), the exaggerated lengths to which it took these inclinations was perceived by members of the institutions as disadvantageous to the quality of training rather than beneficial. In each case, the opposition has been based on the same argument. Although the profession appears to be reasonably flexible with regard to the relative emphasis on either theory or practice, there are cultural boundaries beyond which the uneven weighting of the two elements relative to each other is not acceptable. It seems possible that PBTE failed to become established in this country because it was a model of training which was greatly at odds with our professional cultural inheritance (Beyer, 1991).

(vi) For these reasons, the curriculum of training is unlikely to be successful as an instrument of ideological conversion and socialization. Forceful doctrinaire intervention puts at risk the model of the curriculum which seems to be preferred by the profession namely one in which this 'balance' is more moderate. In both the cases under review, the HEIs have opposed government sponsored curriculum change because it has disregarded this central cultural tenet.

But if there is a cultural 'vision' or model of a suitable curriculum of training which is defined in terms of the relative weight given to practical and theoretical elements, and which it is suggested is held by the profession as a whole, then this is to imply not only that this vision has had continuity over time since that is a characteristic of cultures, but also that the training that was provided by the colleges and that which was provided by the universities in the pre-Robbins era can be equated in this way. The first of these criteria has been at the heart of this study, and was deduced from the reaction of staff in the colleges to the Robbins innovations. The notion that training should consist of a not too discrepant distribution of practical and theoretical elements has a long history in teacher training. It was a theme of the McNair Report (1944). In several lengthy paragraphs (paras 215–19) McNair elaborates the nature of principles of education and emphasizes their importance in the training of the teacher. Crucial though they are however, 'effective practice can be obtained only in the schools'. Going further back still in the history of training in this country, the same concern can be found. A recent paper by Gardner (1995, p. 192) provides most interesting insights into these two relationships — that between government and profession and that between theory and practice — during the interwar years. Gardner tells us of 'the construction of a consensus in favour of formal college training as fundamental to the educational needs of the nation in a new century' at this time. There was a political agenda. 'For politicians, the institutionally trained teacher had become a symbol of the elevation of popular education to a central concern of national policy'. This agenda coincided with the concern of the professional educationists which was with 'education as a discipline of theoretical study and not merely as an arena for the development and exercise of practical proficiency'. Regarding the second criterion, that of the curricular equivalence between the colleges and the UDEs, this is not unrelated to the historical example just mentioned. The criticism of the college curriculum at the time when Robbins was appointed was not so much that there was a lack of theory but that the quality of what passed for theory was intellectually unchallenging. Courses in principles of education lacked rigour and in some cases may have been little more than an extension of everyday knowledge. Nevertheless, in the college course this was theory and a balance was sought between the non-practical and the practical curricular dimensions. It is this balance rather than the detailed substantive nature of the two dimensions themselves that constitutes this ideal.

Can we learn anything from the past that will suggest how events may develop in the future? Prediction is risky, but earlier discussion (p. 129) suggests a cyclical process. Once again the teacher training community is being obliged to operate within an ideologically generated curricular structure which offends professional principles. Support for the suggestion that the opposition of the community is professional rather than political comes from our understanding of its reaction to the outcome of the Robbins Report. During the 1960s and 1970s the colleges were required to make significant changes in practice but these conformed to the discourse of social democracy which was widely supported. Yet that the new curriculum was democratic in tenor did not preclude many college tutors and students from opposing it. Had political commitment taken precedence over professional concern, then it seems possible that there would have been more support for the new course structure. Instead from within the ideological discourse the new curriculum was appraised and found wanting and over time was modified in accordance with a professional ideal.

It was suggested earlier that in their reports on training courses at the end of the 1980s, the Inspectorate was continuing to operate within the discourse of training which had evolved from the previous ideological interjection; and this also seemed to be the case for the tutors (and teachers) in these training institutions. Is there any evidence that the profession has moved beyond this stage now and has begun to follow the example of its predecessors who reclaimed ownership of the curriculum from within the new imposed framework? Any indication that the cyclical process might be continuing should first be found in the academic debate, it being easier to propose new courses of action than it is to introduce institutional change. Second, there will be a recognition of the need to work within the new parameters. While the demands made by the ideological intervention may not be welcome, the importance of an initial pragmatic acceptance of them if training is to continue to move forward, will be recognized. Third, the text must reintroduce theory and indicate the importance of establishing once more its value vis-a-vis practice. Two recently published texts might be deemed to meet these requirements in their respective ways. Tomlinson's *Understanding Mentoring* (1995) accepts that students will now be in school for lengthy periods during their training. This is an opportunity and a challenge which teachers support and from which they recognize they and the students will benefit (p. 1). Politics do not feature in this book; its focus is the development of professional practice. Regarding the reintroduction or regeneration of theory, there are theoretical excerpts distributed throughout the text to which mentors can make reference either for the illumination of their own practice or to convey to students. Tomlinson gives the mentor some theoretical responsibility and in so doing, it is suggested, makes an initial move towards re-establishing the theory practice balance; and this is done within the current ideological discourse. Another text which strongly promotes theory is a paper by McNamara (1996) whose views can be said to complement those of Tomlinson. McNamara accepts that in the future the mentor is going to take over more of the responsibility for training students and he believes that the new role of tutors in university departments will be to engage in rigorous independent scholarship. In so doing they may raise the status of education within higher education, and if Tomlinson's proposals come to fruition, they will also be able to provide mentors with research conclusions. Whatever lies ahead, it is unlikely that the ideological flooding of teacher training will disappear without leaving its mark. In this way, ideological interventions are one source of dynamic change in the system. They are, after all seen by one side as reforms. It has been suggested that the professional sub-culture may derive some benefit by being subjected to the sorts of politically induced upheavals that have been described here. In the current example, the government has obliged the profession finally to acknowledge that teachers can and should fully share responsibility for training, and it could be argued with some justification that teachers should have been full participants in training with the necessary power and authority to carry out those responsibilities a long time ago.

The relationship between political ideology and curricular culture in initial training in the UK over the last thirty years has been portrayed as a continuous battle, a Gramscian struggle for dominance. It has been suggested that the proponents of quite diverse political ideologies have tried to convert the institution of teacher training to reflect their own interpretations of the social world. It has also been suggested that their entry into the curricular traditions of the institutions has been facilitated in the first place by the presence of sufficient similarity, both structural and substantive, between the two and also upon the presence of 'contradictions' within the training system which have provided access points or justifications for intervention. When obliged to accept government intervention in the past, the professional community retained and transformed certain elements which were deemed to provide support for or enhance its own aims, and rejected others. Today the government has used the law to support its initiatives and so the situation differs fundamentally from the past. For this reason the culture of the curriculum, as represented by a moderate balance between theory and practice, looks vulnerable although it has been suggested above that there may be some slight indications that the profession is moving once again to reinstate this balance. Little has been said about the role of teachers who are now co-trainers. Will they subscribe to the cultural model that has been proposed in this study? If they do support the view that students need many opportunities for practice in the classroom, but that they also need more general theoretical knowledge that will be of value when they reflect upon that practice, they will be subscribing to the continuation of the cultural commitment proposed here. The relocation of training principally into the schools would reverse the traditional roles of tutor and teacher in that the HEI would service the school and not vice versa. But this would not necessarily destroy the cultural continuity that has been hypothesized. Speculation of this kind is unending. Perhaps one advantage of this study has been to suggest that the current situation is new but not new and that taking the longer view may provide an alternative perspective on today's events.

Appendix

Sampling Procedure for Three CNAA Samples

Three samples were chosen:

(i) 1973–1974: 18 institutions
(ii) 1977–1978: 23 institutions
(iii) 1981–1982: 11 institutions

Each sample, consisting of 50 per cent of institutions submitting course proposals for validation during the two-year period, was randomly selected. If a selected institution submitted course proposals for alternative forms of training (for example, BEd and PGCE) both submissions were included in the samples irrespective of which year of the two-year period they occurred. Where courses were rejected by CNAA and subsequently resubmitted and both initial and resubmission proposals fell within the two-year period, the resubmission document was the one chosen for analysis.

In several cases in samples 2 and 3 institutions updated earlier successful proposals when meeting the requirement to resubmit a course for validation after the initial five-year validation period had passed. The number of incidents of this was not recorded (and not always known) but this may have meant reference to and the inclusion of proposals before the sampling period. This was not considered to be a sampling problem since although such courses represented earlier views on the curriculum, they were also the basis of the new submission and hence also represented current views.

Dimensions of Analysis

In their study of four school-based courses, Furlong, Hirst, Miles and Pocklington (1988) used three indices of integration between the different course elements: course structure, personnel involvement and pedagogical style. Initially these were considered a suitable framework for the analysis of the material in this study, but on their being applied, it became apparent that they would only be useful as a methodological tool to assess the development of integration over the years if they were further broken down into subcategories. This was then undertaken, the subcategories being generated from the submissions themselves. The method used was therefore both deductive and inductive. Since nearly all institutions claimed that they used a wide range of teaching methods (if these were mentioned at all) it was concluded that pedagogical style needed to be revised and interpreted in a particular way (see below). Two further categories — of aims and institutional structure — were included, both of these having been found to distinguish between institutions and to be significant indicators of changes in practice over time. The subcategories according to which course submissions were analyzed and classified were therefore as follows.

Dimension 1: Aims

- Aims for the course:
  that the course is termed 'school focused'
  that the course is termed 'school based'
  that teaching skills or school experience is 'central'
  that it integrates theory and practice
- Aims for the student:
  personal intellectual development
  competence in the classroom
  the ability to reflect on practice

Dimension 2: Structure of the Curriculum

- School experience:
  number of half days spent in school
  whether students undertook serial practice
  whether regular visits were built into course units
- Within the HEI:
  whether the disciplines were taught as discrete subjects
  whether they were thematically integrated
  whether they were integrated with professional courses or with school experience
  whether they were offered as options
  whether units in classroom skills were offered
  whether in year 4 the student undertook a project that required time to be spent in school

Dimension 3: Institutional Structure

Whether there was a Department of Professional Studies
Whether in some way, professional studies could be said to subsume education studies (for example, administratively)

Dimension 4: Personnel Involvement

- Relinquishing power/extending responsibility to the school:
  whether schools receive documentation from the HEI
  whether there were meetings prior to school experience between tutor and teacher
  whether there was a named trainer in the school
  whether the teacher supervised the student
  whether the teacher assessed the student
  whether the school undertook any on-site teaching
  whether there were any claims of 'partnership'
- Relinquishing power/opening up the HEI to the schools:
  whether teachers were involved in selection of students in interviews
  whether they contributed to courses
  whether they were appointed as examiners
  whether they were members of committees
  whether the HEI appointed 'teacher fellows'

Dimension 5: Pedagogy

Whether practical workshops were undertaken either in school or in HEI
Whether students were encouraged to reflect upon their practice

A glance through these categories will indicate that if they are used as a basis for the comparison of samples over time, they will make it possible to record development within courses towards a school focused form of training. Although there were occasional difficulties in interpreting the material, on the whole this schedule adequately served the purpose for which it was designed. However, when the 1986/87 HMI Reports were analyzed, the curriculum categories were beginning to break down, because of the extreme integrated nature of some courses. Despite this it was still possible to use them. On the other hand, the personnel categories came into their own. When analyzing the CNAA course submissions, it was not too unusual to have no score in any column on page 2 of the schedule. By the mid-1980s this situation had changed completely, and one could anticipate a time when these categories also would be redundant and a new schedule would need to be devised.

Assumptions and Interpretations

Social practices do not readily lend themselves to neat classification like this, and this schedule was twice removed from action. Those drawing up the course submissions for the institutions were representing student experiences both as it was already structured in the institution, but in addition as 'favourably' as possible given the purpose of the submission. This material was then broken down and restructured once more by the researcher for a different purpose. Some degree of slippage between result and reality is therefore to be expected.

Although the data yielded in course submissions is frequently (though not always) very full, it was not always as complete as one would have liked. Assumptions sometimes had to be made on the basis of professional common sense and some years' experience as a tutor in a CNAA-validated institution. As a simple example: if reports from school were mentioned, but assessment was not, then nevertheless assessment was scored since it must have taken place in one form or another. Elsewhere if a category was not scored, it does not mean that that event/activity did not take place, but merely that it was not mentioned in the submission. There were also problems of terminology and a general vagueness of phrase. How does one interpret 'tutors visit their students frequently' for example? 'Frequently' here is the sort of term which is included to impress the reader but which does not commit the institution to anything specific. When phrases like this were used, attempts were made to clarify them elsewhere in the text, but this was not always possible.

An entry in the schedule indicates neither quality of experience nor amount. Scores in categories represent gross distinctions only. For example, if in submission X, the disciplines are taught discretely in years 1 and 2 of a course, but are taught in an integrated fashion in year 3, then both of these will be scored, but the nature of that distinction will become lost. Absence or presence of a category is recorded but not weighting or priority. Despite all the above caveats, this schedule, which was both deductively and inductively derived, was found to be a useful instrument for identifying course development.

Institutional: Structure	professional studies subsumes education studies			
	professional studies department			
Structure of Curriculum	professional project			
	applied skills units			
	as options			
	integration with professional studies			
	thematic integration			
	discrete theory			
School Experience	regular visits			
	serial practice			
	number of half days			
Course Aims	integration of theory and practice		reflective practitioner	
	school experience central		competence	
	school focused or based		personal	
	programme			
	institution			

Personnel Involvement	Pedagogy	'reflective practitioner'	
		work shops	
	Transference of Power (within institution)	teacher fellows	
		committees	
		examiners	
		lecture, seminar	
		interviewing	
	Transference of Power (into school)	'partnership'	
		on site teaching	
		assessment	
		supervision	
		named trainers	
		visits, meetings	
		documentation	
		programme	
		institution	

References

ALDRICH, R. and LEIGHTON, P. (1985) 'Time for a New Act', *Bedford Way Papers*, Number 23, University of London Institute of Education.

ALEXANDER, J. (1990) 'Analytic debates: Understanding the relative autonomy of culture' in ALEXANDER, J. and SEIDMAN, S. (Eds) *Culture and Society: Contemporary Debates*, Cambridge, Cambridge University Press.

ALEXANDER, R. (1979) 'What is a course? Curriculum models and CNAA validation', *Journal of Further and Higher Education*, 3, 1.

ALEXANDER, R. (1984) 'Innovation and continuity in the initial teacher education curriculum' in ALEXANDER, R., CRAFT, M. and LYNCH, J. (Eds) *Change in Teacher Education*, Eastbourne, Holt, Reinhart and Winston.

ALEXANDER, R. and WHITTAKER, J. (Eds) (1980) *Developments in PGCE Courses*, Guildford, Society for Research into Higher Education.

ALEXANDER, R. and WORMALD, E. (Eds) (1979) *Professional Studies for Teaching*, Guildford, Society for Research into Higher Education.

ALTHUSSER, L. (1971) *Essays on Ideology*, London, Verso.

APPLE, M. (1982) *Education and Power*, London, Ark.

ARCHAMBAULT, R. (Ed) (1965) *Philosophical Analysis and Education*, London, Routledge and Kegan Paul.

ARCHER, M. (1988) *Culture and Agency*, Cambridge, Cambridge University Press.

ASHFORD, D. (1986) *The Emergence of the Welfare State*, Oxford, Blackwell.

BARBER, M. (1993) 'Till death us do part', *Times Educational Supplement*, 28 May.

BARRETT, E. *et al* (1992) *Initial Teacher Education in England and Wales: A Topography*, Modes of Teacher Education Research Project, London, Goldsmith's College.

BARRETT, M. (1991) *The Politics of Truth*, Cambridge, Polity Press.

BARTHOLOMEW, J. (1975) 'Theory and practice: An as yet unaddressed issue', *Education for Teaching*, 97.

BEER, S. (1965) *Modern British Politics*, London, Faber.

BEETHAM, D. (1991) *The Legitimation of Power*, Basingstoke, Macmillan.

BERNBAUM, G. (1972) 'Sociology of education' in WOODS, R. (Ed) *Education and Its Disciplines*, London, University of London.

BEST, E. (1965) 'Common confusions in educational theory' in ARCHAMBAULT, R. (Ed) *Philosophical Analysis & Education*, London, Routledge and Kegan Paul.

BETHEL, D. (1980) *Evaluation Newsletter*, 4, 1.

BEYER, L. (1991) 'Teacher education, reflective inquiry and moral action' in TABACHNICK, B.R. and ZEICHNER, K. (Eds) *Issues and Practices in Enquiry Oriented Teacher Education*, London, Falmer Press.

BIDDIS, M. (1987) 'Thatcherism: Concepts and interpretations' in MINOGUE, K. and BIDDIS, M. (Eds) *Thatcherism: Personality and Politics*, Basingstoke, Macmillan.

BILLING, D. (1980) 'Maintaining the standards of the CNAA' in BILLING, D. (Ed) *Indications of Performance*, Guildford, Society for Research into Higher Education.

BILLING, D. (1986) 'Judging institutions' in MOODIE, G. (Ed) *Standards and Criteria in Higher Education*, Guildford, Society for Research into Higher Education.

BLAKE, LORD (1976) 'A changed climate' in BLAKE, LORD and PATTEN, J. (Eds) *The Conservative Opportunity*, London, Macmillan.

BLAKE, LORD and PATTEN, J. (Eds) (1976) *The Conservative Opportunity*, London, Macmillan.

BOBBIO, N. (1979) 'Gramsci and the conception of civil society' in MOUFFE, C. (Ed) *Gramsci and Marxist Theory*, London, Routledge and Kegan Paul.

BOCOCK, J. (1983) 'ACSET and initial training courses', *NATFHE Journal*, March/April 1993.

BOGDANOR, V. (1976) 'Education' in BLAKE, LORD, and PATTEN, J. (Eds) *The Conservative Opportunity*, London, Macmillan.

BOLTON, E. (1985) *Education Policy: The Role of HMI*, presentation at NATFHE conference, 10 January.

BUCI-GLUCKSMANN, C. (1980) *Gramsci and the State*, London, Lawrence Wishart.

CALDERHEAD, J. (1992) 'Can the complexities of teaching be accounted for in terms of competencies?', paper presented to the UCET conference.

CALLAGHAN, J. (1989) 'Good-bye to 1945 and all that', *Guardian*, 27 March.

CALLINICOS, A. (1987) *Making History*, Cambridge, Polity Press.

CARNOY, M. (1984) *The State and Political Theory*, Princeton, NJ, Princeton University Press.

CARSWELL, J. (1985) *Government and the Universities in Britain*, Cambridge, Cambridge University Press.

CHAMBERS, P. (1975) 'Course validation and curriculum innovation', *Education for Teaching*, 97.

CHILDS, D. (1986) *Britain Since 1945*, London, Methuen.

CLARKE, K. (1992) *Speech at the North of England Conference*, London, DES.

CLARKE, R. (1973) 'Parliament and public expenditure', *Political Quarterly*, 44, 2.

COATES, D. and HILLARD, J. (Eds) (1986) *The Economic Decline of Modern Britain*, Hemel Hempstead, Harvester/Wheatsheaf.

COCHRANE, A. (1989) 'Britain's political crisis' in COCHRANE, A. and ANDERSON, J. (Eds) *Politics in Transition*, London, Sage.

COCHRANE, A. (1993) *Whatever Happened to Local Government*, Buckingham, Open University Press.

CNAA (1973) Paper 1a/3 *Procedure for Validation of Courses of Study*, London, CNAA.

CNAA (1976) Paper 5a/6 *The Council's Organisation*, London, CNAA.

CNAA (1978) Paper 1a/11 *A Note for Information on Changes in the Structure of the Council's Committees and Subject Boards*, London, CNAA.

CNAA (1978) Paper 2f/9 *Educational Studies in Undergraduate Courses*, London, CNAA.

CNAA (1979) *Developments in Partnership in Validation*, London, CNAA.

CNAA (1980) Paper 5a/13 *Implications of CNAA 1980/81 Budget for the Operation of Committees, Boards and Panels*, London, CNAA.

CNAA (1981) Paper 6a/10 *The Work of the Council: An Introduction*, London, CNAA.

CNAA (1984) *Perspectives on Postgraduate Initial Training*, London, CNAA.

CROMPTON, J. (1977) 'Student expectations and the PGCE', *British Journal of Teacher Education*, 3, 1.

CROSLAND, A. (1956) *The Future of Socialism*, London, Cape.

DALE, R. (1982) 'Education and the capitalist state' in APPLE, M. (Ed) *Cultural and Economic Reproduction in Education*, London, Routledge and Kegan Paul.

DALE, R. (1989) *The State and Education Policy*, Buckingham, Open University Press.

DAVIS, M. (1979) 'The Council for National Academic Awards 1964–74', unpublished doctoral thesis, Loughborough University.

DEAKIN, N. (1989) 'Social policy' in TIVEY, L. and WRIGHT, A. (Eds) *Party Ideology in Britain*, London, Routledge.

Dearden, R. (1971) 'The philosophy of education' in Tibble, J. (Ed) *An Introduction to the Study of Education*, London, Routledge & Kegan Paul.

Dearden, R. (1984) 'Education and training', *Westminster Studies in Education*, 7.

DES (1972) *Education: A Framework for Expansion* (White Paper), London, HMSO.

DES (1982) *Study of the Inspectorate in England and Wales* (*Rayner Report*) London, HMSO.

DES (1983) *A Policy Statement by the Secretary of State for Education on the Work of the HM Inspectorate in England and Wales*, London, DES.

DES (1984) *Initial Teacher Training: Approval of Courses* (Circular 3/84), London, HMSO.

DES (1985) *Criteria for the Accreditation of courses of Initial Teacher Training*, London, DES.

DES (1988a) *The New Teacher in School*, London, DES.

DES (1988b) *Qualified Teacher Status*, (consultation document on the licensed teacher scheme), London, HMSO.

DES (1989a) *Articled Teacher Pilot Scheme* (invitation to bid for funding), London, DES.

DES (1989b) *Future Arrangements for the Accreditation of Courses of Initial Teacher Training*, London, DES.

DES (1989c) *Initial Teacher Training: Approval of Courses* (Circular 24/89), London, DES.

DES (1992a) *Reform of Initial Teacher Training*, London, DES.

DES (1992b) *Initial Teacher Training* (Circular 9/92), London, DES.

DFE (1993) *The Government's Proposals for Reforming Teacher Training*, London, HMSO.

Donaldson, P. and Farquhar, J. (1988) *Understanding the British Economy*, London, Penguin Books.

Douglas, J.W. (1964) *The Home and the School*, London, MacGibbon and Kee.

Eagleton, T. (1991) *Ideology*, London, Verso.

Eason, T. and Croll, E. (1970) *Colleges of Education: Academic or Professional?*, Slough, National Foundation for Educational Research.

Ecceshall, R. (1990) *English Conservatism Since the Reformation*, London, Unwin Hyman

Edwards, A. (1992) 'Issues and challenges in initial teacher education', *Cambridge Journal of Education*, 22, 3.

Edwards, A. (1993) 'Change for the worse', *Times Educational Supplement*, 29 October.

ELLIOTT, J. (1976) 'Preparing teachers for classroom accountability', *Education for Teaching*, 100.

ELLIOTT, J. (Ed) (1993) *Reconstructing Teacher Education*, London, Falmer Press.

ELVIN, H.L. (1963) 'The Robbins Report and the education and training of teachers', *Education for Teaching*, 62.

ENTWISTLE, H. (1969) 'Practical and theoretical learning' in HARTNETT, A. and NAISH, M. (1976) (Eds) *Theory and Practice of Education Vol 1*, London, Heinemann.

ENTWISTLE, H. (1979) *Antonio Gramsci*, London, Routledge and Kegan Paul.

ERAUT, M. and WEST, N. (1984) *The Acquisition and Use of Educational Theory by Beginning Teachers*, Brighton, University of Sussex.

EVANS, L. (1969) 'The role of the education lecturer in the colleges of education', *Education for Teaching*, 80.

EVANS, N. (1976) 'Searching for a new identity' in RAGGETT, M. and CLARKSON, M. (Eds) *Changing Patterns of Teacher Education*, Lewes, Falmer Press.

FEMIA, J. (1981) *Gramsci's Political Thought*, Oxford, Clarendon Press.

FERRIMAN, A. (1973) 'Council will have to choose devolution or expansion', *Times Higher Educational Supplement*, 30 March.

FORUM (1986) 'Editorial: The legacy of Keith Joseph', *Forum*, 29, 1.

FOUCAULT, M. (1972) *The Archaeology of Knowledge*, London, Tavistock.

FRAMPTON, D. (1981) 'CNAA: What price partnership in validation?', *NATFHE Journal*, February.

FRANCIS, D. (1986) 'The board structure of the CNAA', *Journal of Further and Higher Education*, 10, 1.

FURLONG, V.J., HIRST, P.H., POCKLINGTON, K. and MILES, S. (1988) *Initial Teacher Training and the Role of the School*, Buckingham, Open University Press.

GAMBLE, A. (1983) 'Thatcherism and Conservative politics' in HALL, S. and JACQUES, M. (Eds)*The Politics of Thatcherism*, London, Lawrence and Wishart.

GAMBLE, A. (1985) *Britain in Decline*, Basingstoke, Macmillan.

GAMBLE, A. (1988) *The Free Economy and the Strong State: The Politics of Thatcherism*, Basingstoke, Macmillan.

GARDNER, P. (1995) 'Teacher training and changing professional identity in early twentieth century England', *Journal of Education for Teaching*, 21, 2.

GEERTZ, C. (1964) 'Ideology as a cultural system' in APTER, D. (Ed) *Ideology and Discontent*, New York, Free Press.

GENT, B. (1981) *Evaluation Newsletter*, 4, 1.

Giddens, A. (1979) *Central Problems in Social Theory*, London, Macmillan.

Gilroy, D.P. (1992) 'The political rape of initial teacher education in England and Wales: A JET rebuttal', *Journal of Education for Teaching*, 18, 1.

Golby, M. (1976) 'Curriculum studies and education for teaching', *Education for Teaching*, 100.

Goldman, P. (1958) *The Future of the Welfare State*, London, Conservative Political Centre.

Goodwin, B. (1982) *Using Political Ideas*, Chichester, Wiley.

Gould, F. and Roweth, B. (1978) 'Politics and public spending', *Political Quarterly*, 49, 2.

Gouldner, A. (1976) *The Dialectic of Ideology and Technology*, London, Macmillan.

Grace, G. (1987) 'Teachers and the state in Britain: A changing relation' in Lawn, M. and Grace, G. (Eds) *Teachers: The Culture and Politics of Work*, London, Falmer Press.

Graham, D. and Tytler, D. (1993) *A Lesson for Us All: The Making of the National Curriculum*, London, Routledge.

Gramsci, A. (1971) *Selection from Prison Notebooks*, London, Lawrence and Wishart.

Graves, N. (Ed) (1990) *Initial Teacher Education: Politics and Progress*, London, Kogan Page.

Grieff, S. (1967) 'Comments on a postgraduate course in theory of education', *Education for Teaching*, 73.

Griffiths, A. and Moore, A. (1967) 'Schools and teaching practice', *Education for Teaching*, 74.

Hagopian, M.N. (1985) *Ideals and Ideologies in Modern Politics*, London, Longman.

Hall, S. (1981) 'Cultural studies: Two paradigms' in Bennett, T. *et al* (Eds) *Culture, Ideology and Social Process*, Buckingham, Open University Press.

Hargreaves, A. and Reynolds, D. (1989) *Education Policies: Controversies and Critiques*, London, Falmer Press.

Hargreaves, D. (1989) 'Judge radicals by results', *Times Educational Supplement*, 6 October.

Hargreaves, J. (1982) 'A validiction for validation', *Journal of Further and Higher Education*, 6, 2.

Hartnett, A. and Naish, M. (1977) 'Educational theory: Bromide or barmecide?', *Journal of Further and Higher Education*, 1, 3.

Harrison, J. (1962) 'Towards philosophy of education', *Education for Teaching*, 59.

Harrop, M. (1986) 'Voting and the electorate' in Drucker, H. *et al* (Eds) *Developments in British Politics 2*, Basingstoke, Macmillan.
Held, D. (1989) *Political Theory and the Modern State*, Cambridge, Polity Press.
Hencke, D. (1976) 'The reorganisation of colleges of education' in Raggett, M. and Clarkson, M. (Eds) *Changing Patterns of Teacher Education*, Lewes, Falmer Press.
Hewett, S. (1972) 'The future of the colleges of education' in Lawlor, J. (Ed) *Higher Education: Patterns of Change in the 1970s*, London, Routledge and Kegan Paul.
HMI (1970) *HMI To-day and To-morrow*, London, DES.
HMI (1979) *Developments in the BEd Degree Course: A Study Based on Fifteen Institutions*, London, HMSO.
HMI (1981) *Teacher Training and the Secondary School*, London, DES.
HMI (1982) *Teacher Training and Preparation for Working Life* (An HMI discussion Paper), London, HMSO.
HMI (1983a) *HM Inspectors To-day: Standards in Education*, London, DES.
HMI (1983b) *Teaching in Schools: The Content of Initial Training*, London, DES.
HMI (1987) *Quality in Schools: The Initial Training of Teachers*, London HMI.
HMI (1988) *Initial Teacher Training in Universities in England, N. Ireland and Wales*, London, DES.
HMI (1991) *School Based Initial Teacher Training in England and Wales*, London, HMSO.
Hill, M. and Bramley, G. (1986) *Analysing Social Policy*, Oxford, Blackwell.
Hillgate Group (1989) *Learning to Teach*, London, Claridge Press.
Hirst, P.H. (1963) 'Philosophy and educational theory', *British Journal of Educational Studies*, 12, 1.
Hirst, P.H. (1966) 'Educational theory' in Tibble, J. (Ed) *The Study of Education*, London, Routledge and Kegan Paul.
Hirst, P.H. (1975) 'The graduate certificate in education courses: Future developments in content and structure' (paper to UCET).
Hirst, P.H. (1979) 'Professional studies in initial teacher education' in Alexander, R. and Wormald, E. (Eds) *Professional Studies for Teaching*, Guildford, Society for Research into Higher Education.
Holmes, B. (1954) 'The teacher of teachers', *Education for Teaching*, 54.
Holmes, M. (1985a) *The Labour Government 1974–9*, Basingstoke, Macmillan.

HOLMES, M. (1985b) *The First Thatcher Government*, Brighton, Wheatsheaf/Harvester.

HUGHES, J. (1986) 'Deindustrialisation gathers pace: The 1970s' in COATES, D. and HILLARD, J. (Eds) *The Economic Decline of Modern Britain*, Brighton, Wheatsheaf/Harvester.

JACQUES, M. (1983) 'Thatcherism: Breaking out of the impasse' in HALL, S. and JACQUES, M. (Eds) *The Politics of Thatcherism*, London, Lawrence and Wishart.

JAMES REPORT (1972) *Teacher Education and Training*, London, HMSO.

JENKINS, P. (1987) *Mrs Thatcher's Revolution*, London, Jonathan Cape.

JET EDITORIAL (1983) 'Never mind the quality: Feel the ideology', *Journal of Education for Teaching*, 9, 3.

JOSEPH, K. (1983) Speech on teacher training at Durham University, *Durham and Newcastle Research Review*, 10, 50.

JOSEPH, K. (1984) Speech at the North of England Conference, *Oxford Review of Education*, 10, 2.

JOSEPH, K. (1986) *Statement in the House on the Lindop Report*, 17 March.

KATZ, F. (1959) 'Some problems in teacher training', *Education for Teaching*, 48.

KAVANAGH, D. and MORRIS, P. (1989) *Consensus Politics*, Oxford, Blackwell.

KERR, E. (1976) 'Principles and practice of validation' in RAGGETT, M. and CLARKSON, M. (Eds) *Changing Patterns of Teacher Education*, Lewes, Falmer Pess.

KING, D. (1987) *The New Right: Politics, Markets and Citizenship*, Basingstoke, Macmillan.

KLEIN, R. (1976) 'The politics of public expenditure: American theory and British practice', *British Journal of Political Science*, 6, 4.

KOLAKOWSKI, L. (1980) 'Why an ideology is always right' in CRANSTON, M. and MAIR, P. (Eds) *Ideology and Politics*, European University Institute.

LACEY, C. and LAMONT, W. (1976) 'Partnership with schools', *British Journal of Teacher Education*, 2, 1.

LANE, M. (1975) *Design for Degrees*, London, Macmillan.

LAWLOR, S. (1990) *Teachers Mistaught*, London, Centre for Policy Studies.

LAWN, M. and OZGA, J. (1986) 'Unequal partners: Teachers under indirect rule', *British Journal of Sociology of Education*, 7, 2.

LAWRENCE, I. (1992) *Power and Politics at the Department of Education and Science*, London, Cassell.

LAWTON, D. (1986) 'The Department of Education and Science: Policy making at the centre' in HARTNETT, A. and NAISH, M. (Eds) *Education and Society To-day*, Lewes, Falmer Press.

LAWTON, D. (1992) *Education and Politics in the 1990s*, London, Falmer Press.

LAWTON, D. and GORDON, P. (1987) *H.M.I*, London, Routledge and Kegan Paul.

LEVITAS, R. (1986) 'Introduction' in LEVITAS, R. (Ed) *The Ideology of the New Right*, Cambridge, Polity Press.

LEWIS, I. (1975) 'Teacher training: Professional or peripheral', *Education for Teaching*, 96.

LEYS, C. (1989) *Politics in Britain*, London, Verso.

LINDOP REPORT (1985) *Academic Validation in Public Sector Higher Education*, London, HMSO.

LOCKE, M. (1974) *Power Politics in the School System*, London, Routledge and Kegan Paul.

LOCKE, M., PRATT, J. and BURGESS, T. (1985) *The Colleges of Higher Education 1972–1982*, Croydon, Critical Press.

LODGE, P. and BLACKSTONE, T. (1985) 'Pushing for equality: The Influence of the teachers' unions — the NUT' in MCNAY, I. and OZGA, J. (Eds) *Policy Making in Education*, Oxford, Pergamon.

LODZIAK, C. (1988) 'Dull compulsion of the economic', *Radical Philosophy*, 49.

LUKES, S. (1973) *Individualism*, Oxford, Blackwell.

LUKES, S. (1974) *Power: A Radical View*, Baskingstoke, Macmillan.

LYNCH, J. (1979) *The Reform of Teacher Education in the United Kingdom*, Guildford, Society for Research in Higher Education.

MCCULLOCH, M. (1979) *School Experience in Initial BEd/BEd Honours Degrees Validated by the Council for National Academic Awards*, London, CNAA.

MCDOWELL, D. (1971) 'The values of teacher education' in BURGESS, T. (Ed) *Dear Lord James: A Critique of Teacher Education*, Harmondsworth, Penguin Books.

MACINTYRE, A. (1973) 'The end of ideology and the ideology of the end of ideology' in GOULD, J. and TRUITT, W. (Eds) *Political Ideologies*, New York, Macmillan.

MACKENZIE, N. (1976) 'Introduction' in RAGGETT, M. and CLARKSON, M. (Eds) *Changing Patterns of Teacher Education*, Lewes, Falmer Press.

MACLURE, S. (1992) 'A successful disaster', *Times Educational Supplement*, 10 January.

MCNAIR REPORT (1944) *Teachers and Youth Leaders*, London, HMSO.

MCNAMARA, D. (1996) 'The university, the academic tradition and education' in Furlong, J. and Smith, R. (Eds) *The Role of Higher Education in Initial Teacher Training*, London, Kogan Page.

McNamara, D. and Desforges, C. (1978) 'The social sciences, teacher education and the objectification of craft knowledge', *British Journal of Teacher Education*, 4, 1.

McNamara, D. and Ross, A.M. (1982) *The BEd Degree and its Future*, Lancaster, University of Lancaster School of Education.

Manning, D.J. (1980) 'The place of ideology in political life' in Manning, D.J. (Ed) *The Form of Ideology*, London, Allen and Unwin.

Manning, D.J. and Robinson, T. (1985) *The Place of Ideology in Political Life*, London, Croom Helm.

Marquand, D. (1988) 'The paradoxes of Thatcherism' in Skidelsky, R. (Ed) *Thatcherism*, London, Chatto and Windus.

Minogue, K. (1980) 'On identifying ideology' in Cranston, M. and Mair, P. (Eds) *Ideology and Politics*, European University Institute.

Minogue, K. (1985) *Alien Powers: The Theory of Pure Ideology*, London, Weidenfeld and Nicolson.

Moore, R. (1994) 'Professionalism, expertise and control in teacher education' in Wilkin, M. and Sankey, D. (Eds) *Collaboration and Transition in Initial Teacher Training*, London, Kogan Page.

Mosley, P. (1986) 'Economic policy' in Drucker, H. *et al* (Eds) *Developments in British Politics 2*, Basingstoke, Macmillan.

Mouffe, C. (Ed) (1979) *Gramsci and Marxist Theory*, London, Routledge and Kegan Paul.

Musgrave, P.W. (1965) 'Sociology in the training of teachers' in Cluderay, T.M. (Ed) *The Professional Education of Teachers*, Hull, University of Hull Institute of Education.

Naish, M. and Hartnett, A. (1975) 'What theory cannot do for teachers', *Education for Teaching*, 96.

NUT (1969) *The Future of Teacher Education: A Report*, London, NUT.

NUT (1970a) *Teacher Representation: A Policy Statement*, London, NUT.

NUT (1970b) 'Teacher training', oral evidence submitted on behalf of the NUT to the Select Committee on Education and Science, 27 January.

NUT (1971) *The Reform of Teacher Education: A Policy Statement*, London, NUT.

NUT (1973) *The Reform of Teacher Education*, London, NUT.

Nias, J. (1974) 'The postgraduate certificate in education: Some problems and principles of junior school courses', *Education for Teaching*, 94.

O'Connor, J. (1973) *The Fiscal Crisis of the State*, New York, St Martins Press.

O'Connor, M. (1986) 'Will the polytechnics get their freedom?', *Guardian*, 25 January.

O'Hear, A. (1988) *Who Teaches the Teachers?*, London, Social Affairs Unit.

O'Keeffe, D. (1990) *The Wayward Elite*, London, Adam Smith Institute.

Patrick, H., Bernbaum, G. and Reid, K. (1982) *The Structure and Process of Initial Teacher Education within Universities in England and Wales* (SPITE study), Leicester, University of Leicester School of Education.

Paxman, J. (1990) *Friends in High Places*, London, Michael Joseph.

Perkin, H. (1989) *The Rise of Professional Society*, London, Routledge.

Perry, P. (1987) 'The training of teachers for better schools', *European Journal of Teacher Education*, 10, 1.

Peters, R. (1966) *Ethics and Education*, London, Allen and Unwin.

Peters, R. (1967) 'The place of philosophy of education in the training of teachers', *Pedagogica Europea*, 3, 3.

Peters, R. (1977) *Education and the Education of Teachers*, London, Routledge and Kegan Paul.

Plant, R. (1983) 'The resurgence of ideology' in Drucker, H., Dunleavy, P., Gamble, A. and Peele, G. (Eds) *Developments in British Politics 1*, London, Macmillan.

Pope, R., Pratt, A. and Hoyle, B. (1986) *Social Welfare in Britain 1885–1985*, Beckenham, Croom Helm.

Popkewitz, T. (1987) 'Ideology and social formation in teacher education' in Popkewitz, T. (Ed) *Critical Studies in Teacher Education*, Lewes, Falmer Press.

Porter, J. (1976) 'Aspects of institutional change' in Raggett, M. and Clarkson, M. (Eds) *Changing Patterns of Teacher Education*, Lewes, Falmer Press.

Pratt, J. (1979) 'Partnership in validation', *Higher Education Review*, 12, 1.

Price, C. (1985) 'Beware Lindop bearing gifts', *Education*, 17 May.

Price, C. (1986) 'Parliament' in Ranson, S. and Tomlinson, J. (Eds) *The Changing Government of Education*, London, Allen and Unwin.

Proctor, N. (1984) 'Towards a partnership with schools', *Journal of Education for Teaching*, 10, 3.

Quicke, J. (1988) 'The New Right and education', *British Journal of Educational Studies*, 26, 1.

Raggett, M. and Clarkson, M. (Eds) (1976) *Changing Patterns of Teacher Education*, Lewes, Falmer Press.

Raison, T. (1976) *The Act and the Partnership*, London, Centre for Studies in Social Policy.

RAMSDEN, J. (1980) *The Making of Conservative Party Policy: The Conservative Research Department Since 1929*, New York, Longman.

RANSON, S. and TOMLINSON, J. (Eds) (1986) *The Changing Government of Education*, London, Allen & Unwin.

RAYNER, J. (1980) 'The use of ideological language' in MANNING, D. (Ed) *The Form of Ideology*, London, Allen and Unwin.

RAYNER REPORT (1982) *Study of the Inspectorate in England and Wales*, London, HMSO.

REID, L.A. (1965) 'Philosophy and the theory and practice of education' in ARCHAMBAULT, R. (Ed) *Philosophical Analysis & Education*, London, Routledge & Kegan Paul.

RENSHAW, P. (1973) 'A flexible curriculum for teacher education' in LOMAX, D.E (Ed) *The Education of Teachers in Britain*, London, Wiley.

RENTOUL, J. (1989) *Me and Mine*, London, Unwin Hyman.

RICHARDSON, J. (1968) 'The content of 3-year courses in the principles of education', *Education for Teaching*, 76.

RICOEUR, P. (1986) *Lectures on Ideology and Utopia*, Columbia, Columbia University Press.

ROBBINS REPORT (1963) *Higher Education*, London, HMSO.

ROWTHORN, B. (1983) 'The past strikes back' in HALL, S. and JACQUES, M. (Eds) *The Politics of Thatcherism*, London, Lawrence and Wishart.

RUDDUCK, J. (1986) 'Ingredients of a good partnership', *Times Educational Supplement*, 18 July.

RUDDUCK, J. (1989) 'Accrediting teacher education courses: The new criteria' in HARGREAVES, A. and REYNOLDS, D. (Eds) *Educational Policies: Controversies and Critiques*, Lewes, Falmer Press.

RUDDUCK, J. (1991) 'The language of consciousness and the landscape of action: Tensions in teacher education', *British Educational Research Journal*, 17, 4.

RYAN, A. (1990) 'Party ideologies since 1945' in SELDON, A. (Ed) *UK Political Parties Since 1945*, Hemel Hempstead, Philip Allen.

SCRUTON, R. (1980) *The Meaning of Conservatism*, London, Macmillan.

SEABORNE, M. (1971) 'The history of education' in TIBBLE, J. (Ed) *An Introduction to the Study of Education*, London, Routledge and Kegan Paul.

SEIFERT, R.V. (1987) *Teacher Militancy: A History of Teacher Strikes*, Lewes, Falmer Press.

SELIGER, M. (1976) *Ideology and Politics*, London, Allen and Unwin.

SELIGER, M. (1977) *The Marxist Conception of Ideology*, Cambridge, Cambridge University Press.

SHARPLES, D. (1984) 'The growth of CNAA involvement in teacher education' in Alexander, R., Craft, M. and Lynch, J. (Eds) *Change in Teacher Education*, Eastbourne, Holt, Rinehart and Winston.

Shipman, M. (1967) 'Education and college culture', *British Journal of Sociology*, 18, 4.

Silver, H. (1990) *A Higher Education*, London, Falmer Press.

Simon, B. (1976) 'Theoretical aspects of the PGCE course', *British Journal of Teacher Education*, 2, 1.

Simon, B. (1983) 'The study of education as a university subject', *Studies in Higher Education*, 8, 1.

Simpson, E. (1986) 'The Department of Education and Science' in Ranson, S. and Tomlinson, J. (Eds) *The Changing Government of Education*, London, Allen and Unwin.

Sked, A. and Cook, C. (1984) *Post War Britain*, London, Penguin Books.

Smith, R. (1980) 'The participation of CNAA in the development of PGCE courses' in Alexander, R. and Whittaker, J. (Eds) *Developments in PGCE Courses*, Guildford, Society for Research into Higher Education.

Stenhouse, L. (1967) *Culture and Education*, London, Nelson.

Stevens, A. (1977) 'Shake up in the Inspectorate: Focus switches to centre', *Times Educational Supplement*, 4 February.

Tann, S. (1994) 'Supporting the teacher in the classroom' in Wilkin, M. and Sankey, D. (Eds) *Collaboration and Transition in Initial Teacher Training*, London, Kogan Page.

Taylor, W. (1961) 'The sociology of education in the training colleges', *Education for Teaching*, 54.

Taylor, W. (1966) 'The sociology of education' in Tibble, J. (Ed) *The Study of Education*, London, Routledge and Kegan Paul.

Taylor, W. (1969) *Society and the Education of Teachers*, London, Faber and Faber.

Taylor, W. (1978) 'Problems of theory and practice' in Taylor, W. (Ed) *Research and Reform in Teacher Education*, Slough, National Foundation for Educational Research.

Taylor, W. (1984) 'The national context' in Alexander, R., Craft, M. and Lynch, J. (Eds) *Change in Teacher Education*, Eastbourne, Holt, Rinehart and Winston.

Taylor, W. (1993) 'Why government should think again on teacher reform', *Times Higher Education Supplement*, 22 October.

Thatcher, M. (1989a) *Speeches to the Conservative Party Conferences 1975–1988*, London, Conservative Political Centre.

Thatcher, M. (1989b) *The Revival of Britain*, London, Aurum Press.

Therborn, G. (1980) *The Ideology of Power and The Power of Ideology*, London, Verso.

THOMAS, N. (1986) 'The inspectors' in RANSON, S. and TOMLINSON, J. (Eds) *The Changing Government of Education*, London, Allen and Unwin.

THOMPSON, J. (1984) *Studies in the Theory of Ideology*, Cambridge, Polity Press.

THOMPSON, J. (1990) *Ideology and Modern Culture*, Cambridge, Polity Press.

TIBBLE, J. (Ed) (1961) 'The Organization and supervision of school practice', *Education for Teaching*, 54.

TIBBLE, J. (1966) *The Study of Education*, London, Routledge and Kegan Paul.

TIBBLE, J. (1971a) *An Introduction to the Study of Education*, London, Routledge and Kegan Paul.

TIBBLE, J. (1971b) *The Future of Teacher Education*, London, Routledge and Kegan Paul.

TES (1986) 'Inspectors Find Criteria Hard to Apply', 21 February.

THES (1992) 'Back to the Future?', 10 January.

THES (1993) 'The Sacrifice of Professionalism', 28 May.

THES (1984) 'In Defence of the CNAA', 27 January.

TIVEY, L. (1989) 'Left, right and centre' in TIVEY, L. and WRIGHT, A. (Eds) *Party Ideology in Britain*, London, Routledge and Kegan Paul.

TOMLINSON, P. (1995) *Understanding Mentoring*, Buckingham, Open University Press.

TUXWORTH, E. (1982) *Competency in Teaching*, London, Longmans Green.

UCET (1971) *The Education of Teachers: Looking to the Future* (evidence to the Committee of Enquiry into Teacher Education), London, UCET.

UCET (1979) *The PGCE Course and the Training of Specialist Teachers for Secondary Schools: A Consultative Report*, London, UCET.

UNIVERSITY GRANTS COMMITTEE (UGC)/CNAA (1973) *Guidelines: A New BEd Degree*, London, UGC/CNAA.

WADD, K. (1969) 'A source of conflict in colleges of education', *Education for Teaching*, 78.

WARNOCK, M. (1988) *A Common Policy for Education*, Oxford, Oxford University Press.

WEBSTER, H. (1978) 'A new model for BEd degrees: A case study', *British Journal of Teacher Education*, 4, 3.

WEBSTER, R. (1976) 'The future of teacher training' in RAGGETT, M. and CLARKSON, M. (Eds) *Changing Patterns of Teacher Education*, Lewes, Falmer.

WHITTY, G., BARTON, L. and POLLARD, A. (1987) 'Ideology and control in teacher education' in Popkewitz, T. (Ed) *Critical Studies in Teacher Education*, Lewes, Falmer Press.

Wilkin, M. (1990) 'The development of partnership in the United Kingdom' in Booth, M., Furlong, J. and Wilkin, M. (Eds) *Partnership in Initial Teacher Training*, London, Cassell.

Wilkin, M. (1992) 'The challenge of diversity', *Cambridge Journal of Education*, 22, 3.

Willey, F. and Maddison, R. (1971) *An Enquiry into Teacher Training*, London, University of London.

Williams, G. and Blackstone, T. (1983) *Response to Adversity*, Guildford, Society for Research in Higher Education.

Williams, H. (1988) *Concepts of Ideology*, Brighton, Harvester Wheatsheaf.

Williams, R. (1977) *Marxism and Literature*, Oxford, Oxford University Press.

Williams, R.H. (1963) 'Professional studies in teacher training', *Education for Teaching*, 61.

Wilson, P. and Pring, R. (1975) 'Introduction', *London Educational Review*, 4, 2/3.

Index